The Political Calculus

The Political Calculus

ESSAYS ON MACHIAVELLI'S PHILOSOPHY

EDITED BY ANTHONY PAREL

UNIVERSITY OF TORONTO PRESS

© University of Toronto Press 1972
Toronto and Buffalo
Printed in Canada
ISBN 0-8020-1831-9
Microfiche ISBN 0-8020-0156-4
LC 77-185729

Contents

ONE
Introduction: Machiavelli's Method and His Interpreters
ANTHONY PAREL
3

TWO
Machiavelli's Humanism of Action
NEAL WOOD
33

THREE
Machiavelli's Thoughts on the Psyche and Society
DANTE GERMINO
59

FOUR
Success and Knowledge in Machiavelli
ALKIS KONTOS
83

FIVE
Necessity in the Beginnings of Cities
HARVEY MANSFIELD, JR
101

SIX
The Concept of *Fortuna* in Machiavelli
THOMAS FLANAGAN
127

SEVEN
In Search of Machiavellian *Virtù*
JOHN PLAMENATZ
157

EIGHT
Machiavelli *Minore*
ANTHONY PAREL
179

NINE
The Relevance of Machiavelli
to Contemporary World Politics
ANTHONY D'AMATO
209

CONTRIBUTORS
225

ACKNOWLEDGMENTS
226

The Political Calculus

ONE

Introduction: Machiavelli's Method and His Interpreters

ANTHONY PAREL

Neither the passage of time nor the malice of enemies has diminished the relevance of Machiavelli (1469-1527). He is, as Lord Acton observes, not a 'vanishing type, but a constant and contemporary influence';[1] and, as Morley notes, 'a citizen of all countries.'[2] 'It is impossible for any reader of Machiavelli,' writes Allan Gilbert, 'to avoid some sort of application to the affairs of the world of his own age.'[3]

When one examines the reasons for this marvellous contemporaneity of Machiavelli, one is inevitably led to his methodology, his manner of analysing his vision of politics. He brought to the field of political enquiry the scientific spirit of detachment, which like a steel frame holds together his doctrines and gives them durability. Olschki is entirely correct when he remarks that Machiavelli's 'survival and ubiquity depend on the impassible objectivity of his insight into the nature of politics and human affairs.'[4]

Yet, generally speaking, methodology is a relatively neglected tool of Machiavellian studies and interpretation.[5] This is most unfortu-

1 In his 'introduction' to *Il Principe,* ed. L. Arthur Burd (Oxford 1891), xl
2 John Morley, *The Works of Lord Morley,* 15 vols (London 1921), IV, 117
3 Allan H. Gilbert, *The Prince and Other Works: New Translations, Introductions and Notes* (Chicago 1941), 1
4 Leonardo Olschki, *Machiavelli the Scientist* (Berkeley 1945), 54
5 There are important exceptions. See in addition to Olschki cited in n4, H. Butterfield, *The Statecraft of Machiavelli* (London 1940), 1-87; F. Chabod, *Machia-*

4 The Political Calculus

nate, for not only is method at the basis of his 'survival and ubiquity,' it is also the key to the correct interpretation of his thought.

The reason for the relative non-use of method is partly Machiavelli's own fault. He did not give a formal exposition of its features nor explain adequately its importance for a correct understanding of his doctrines. Though fully conscious of being a methodological innovator,[6] he does little more than announce the fact. In taking such a casual attitude towards method, he proves to be his own worst enemy – especially where his unsympathetic critics are concerned. For nothing becomes easier than to quote a rule or a maxim from his writings and to apply it out of context. A more systematic writer, Hobbes or Spinoza for example, would have been less liable to be misused or misunderstood in this way. Indeed anti-Machiavellism is nothing but the consequences of interpreting Machiavelli without doing full justice to his method, or rather, methods.

It should be remembered that Machiavelli used several methods, depending on whether he was writing poems or plays, diplomatic re-

velli and the Renaissance, tr. David More (London 1958), 126-48; L.J. Walker, The Discourses of Niccolo Machiavelli, 2 vols (London & New Haven 1950), I, 80-100. For a new type of misunderstanding and misuse of Machiavellism, see Richard Christie and Florence L. Geis, Studies in Machiavellianism (New York 1970). This book, an empirical study in social psychology based on an elaborate questionnaire drawn largely from The Prince and the Discourses, seeks to find empirical verification for what the authors call the 'Machiavellian personality.' He is one who exploits others for his own benefit. The general conclusion of the book is that 'modern society is becoming increasingly more similar in structure to the kind of laboratory situations in which high Machiavellians win' (p. 358). It is obvious that the authors err in identifying a Machiavellian personality as one who exploits others. The authentic Machiavellian is one who subordinates personal interests for the sake of the common good of the community. If one is to speak of a Machiavellian personality one should mention Moses and Romulus (to use Machiavelli's own examples), or (to use some modern examples), Winston Churchill, and de Gaulle.

6 'I have ... determined to enter upon a path not yet trodden by anyone' Discourses, I, preface. Again: 'And because Dante says it does not produce knowledge (e perche Dante dice che non fa scienza), when we hear but do not remember, I have composed a little work on Princedoms ...' Letter to Vettori, 10 Dec. 1513

ports or scientific works. As a Renaissance man, he was versed in the method appropriate to each. Thus his poems and plays both 'teach and delight'; condemn vice and praise virtue. In them he appears not as a detached observer but as a passionate advocate. On the other hand, he is clinical and objective in his diplomatic writings (which constitute nearly one-third of his works). His superiors in Florence always set the frame of reference of these reports, and with astonishing scrupulosity he remained faithful to their instructions. Consequently from reading his reports one rarely gets any direct hint about his own thought on the matters discussed.

As for his theoretical writings, particularly *The Prince* and the *Discourses,* Machiavelli employed the scientific method. Advocacy and ideology are not absent in them, but they are kept within the bounds of scientific spirit. And because he is the sort of writer he is – a poet and a playwright, a detached observer and an unsystematic political writer who nevertheless cannot be understood correctly except in the light of the system implicit in his theory – the starting point of the study of his thought must be his methodology.

Let me begin by stating two sets of assumptions inherent in Machiavelli's method. First, politics[7] is the pursuit of the political good (not of power, as so often attributed to him). The political good is a necessary good, and (unlike moral or religious good), a material and practical good. Second, so far as possible, the study of the political phenomenon must be scientific. It must find its inner laws, and free itself from methodological dependence on theology, metaphysics, and moral philosophy. Its methodology is analogous to that of medicine and civil law rather than to that of the aforementioned disciplines.

To return to the first set of assumptions. The political good is necessary for the well-being of the individual and is had only in the state or the political community.[8] It cannot be sacrificed in favour of any other order of good. This does not mean, however, that there

---

7 For a good treatment of the meaning of the term 'politics' in Machiavelli, see J.H. Whitfield, 'The Politics of Machiavelli,' *Modern Language Review,* L (1955), 433-44.

8 On Machiavelli's use of the word 'state' see J.H. Hexter's indispensable article, 'Il principe and lo stato,' *Studies in the Renaissance,* IV (1956), 113-39

is no order of good higher than the political. Machiavelli readily recognizes the existence of such good – religious or moral good for example. But it does not follow that because they are higher, the political good ceases to be necessary. Once this difficulty is grasped, namely that the political good is necessary though not the highest, we are half way towards understanding the real point of Machiavelli's political theory.

If the political good and religious/moral good clash, as they sometimes do, Machiavelli the scientific writer is obliged to favour the former. From the theological and moralistic point of view this amounts to favouring sin or moral evil. But Machiavelli sees no logical alternative. All he can caution is that such occasions should be reduced to a minimum, and that moral evil should never be practised if by doing so the political good is likely to be subverted.[9]

Being a Christian, Machiavelli is neither surprised nor frightened by sin or moral evil, for the sacraments presuppose sin and supply the remedy for it. However, this is not the case with political sins or mistakes. Here man must act as though everything depended on him alone. God helps only moral, not political, imbeciles. Hence no man with good sense can deliberately commit a political mistake simply because sin is the only alternative.

The political good is a material good, that is, something to be possessed in this, not the next, life. It consists of honour, glory, riches, liberty, justice, and military security. It is the good of the whole community in which the individual finds his own good, and not the exclusive good of a class or of a particular individual, even the prince.

Finally, the political good is a practical good; actual attainment being one of its essential criteria. In this respect it differs from moral/

---

9 Not being a philosopher in the formal sense, Machiavelli often uses examples to clarify his principles. It is necessary to consult his examples in order to understand the nuances of his thought. Thus to understand his point that the practice of *virtù* need not involve the practice of moral evil we must look for models who accomplish the feat. Such men as Moses and Cyrus practised *virtù* with honour and humanity (*The Prince*, ch. 6), whereas Agathocles, the Sicilian, attained power without honour, and practised 'barbarous cruelty and inhumanity together with his countless atrocities' (*The Prince*, ch. 8). Agathocles subverted both the political and the moral good.

religious good, the plenitude of whose enjoyment is postponed to the next life. But in politics there is no next life. A political mistake, however slight, can mean irreparable damage. The conclusion is simple: the scientific test of political good is success or efficiency. There is nothing political in a statesman who only intends but never accomplishes the intended good.

Necessity, materiality, and practicality being the essential attributes of the political good, it follows that the political actor, if constrained, must be willing to take a neutral stand towards moral virtues and vices. He must be prepared to use them without distinction, provided of course that the intended result is a political good and is actually attained.

Turning to my second set of assumptions, namely that for Machiavelli the study of the political good can and ought to be scientific, it is not difficult to see why he is the Galileo of politics. He secularized its methodology just as his compatriot secularized that of the physical sciences. Machiavelli's fundamental axiom or 'regola generale,' is simple: human nature is the same always and everywhere. Therefore history, more precisely, the history of particular states or political communities, is also the same.[10] States – like men, the sky, the sun, the elements – never change their motion, order, and power.[11] Because of this uniformity it is possible to make comparative analyses, draw valid generalizations, and apply the lessons of the past to the present and the future.

The scientific study of politics is possible only if its principles are derived from fact rather than from speculation. Therefore such study should focus on 'how men live rather than how they ought to live'; on 'republics and principalities' that actually exist rather than on those 'that have never been seen or known to exist': in brief, it should produce 'the truth of the matter as facts show it' (*verità effettuale della cosa*) rather than the imagination of it (*The Prince*, ch. 15). Or as Machiavelli puts it elsewhere, the scientific enquiry of politics involves the nature, origin, development, decay, and reform of politi-

10 'He who considers present affairs and ancient ones readily understands that all cities and peoples have the same desires and the same traits and that they always have had them.' *Discourses*, I, ch. 39

11 *Discourses*, I, preface

cal communities: 'what a princedom is, of what kinds they are, how they are gained, and how they are kept, and how are they lost.'[12]

The scientific way to study facts is inductive, whereby principles are derived from the collation and analysis of relevant data.[13] The data relevant for political analysis, according to Machiavelli, are the examples of history – ancient, recent, contemporary – of states. These examples, he believes, recur in a cyclic or organic pattern:[14] states come into being, they grow and disappear, for more or less the same fundamental reasons. There is a golden age in the history of every state, followed by a period of decline, and, if circumstances are favourable, a period of reform and regeneration. The principle which explains this process is the same everywhere.[15]

In preserving or regaining political vitality, the element of leader-

---

12 Machiavelli, Letter to Vettori, 10 Dec. 1513

13 Machiavelli's induction is not as rigorous as the post-Humean type of induction. For Hume's critical appraisal of Machiavelli's method, see *Philosophical Works*, eds. Green and Gross, 4 vols (London 1882), III, 157ff., IV, 351ff. Walker calls Machiavelli the master of Francis Bacon on induction, *The Discourses of Niccolo Machiavelli*, I, 92; and Butterfield views him as the transitional figure between the Renaissance and modern times in the development of the methodology of the social sciences, *The Statecraft of Machiavelli*, 61.

14 'Prudent men are in the habit of saying ... that he who wishes to see what is to come should observe what has already happened, because all the affairs of the world, in every age, have their individual counterparts in ancient times. The reason for this is that since they are carried on by men, who have and always have the same passions, of necessity the same results appear.' *Discourses*, III, ch. 43

15 'In their normal variations, countries generally go from order to disorder and then from disorder move back to order, because – since Nature does not allow worldly things to remain fixed – when they come to their utmost perfection and have no further possibility of rising, they must go down. Likewise, when they go down and through their defects have reached the lowest depths, they necessarily rise, since they cannot go lower. So always from good they go down to bad, and from bad rise up to good. Because ability (*virtù*) brings forth quiet; quiet, laziness (*tranquillità*); laziness, disorder; disorder, ruin; and likewise from ruin comes order; from order, ability; from the last, glory and good fortune.' *History of Florence*, V, ch. 1

ship – whether of a class or of some extraordinary lawgiver (prince) – plays the crucial role. Without leadership the political good is unattainable. If the community, on its own initiative, does not procure that good, the need for the prince becomes a necessity.[16] The authentic Machiavellian prince is the embodiment of the political good, a man of *virtù*, not a tyrant. If the people are politically virtuous, as in Rome, this is usually because of the healthy tension between classes. In short, institutions, whether monarchical or republican, reflect the kind of leadership available in a political community.[17]

A further element of Machiavelli's method is that valid generalizations, though abstract, must be capable of being used as rules of practical conduct. For politics is action, not contemplation, and political theory must be action-oriented. It is not mere thought; it is what a prince or a people do. It is thought from action, for action. Scientific rules of politics are as much 'remedies' for concrete ills as abstractions. From the storehouse of history, as if from a computer, the successful statesman incessantly draws models for action. Like a de Gaulle he reads or anticipates correctly the pattern of history: the past grandeur is imitated or recaptured.[18]

Machiavelli's principle of corruption and regeneration of political communities influenced the political thought of the eighteenth century. On his influence on Bolingbroke, see Butterfield, *The Statecraft of Machiavelli*, Geoffrey Hart, *Viscount Bolingbroke: Tory Humanist* (Toronto 1965), and Isaac Kramnick, *Bolingbroke and His Circle* (Cambridge, Mass. 1968)
For Machiavelli's influence on the republican tradition in English political thought and on Harrington, see J.G.A. Pocock's excellent study, *The Ancient Constitution and the Feudal Law* (Cambridge 1957), and 'Machiavelli, Harrington, and the English Political Ideologies in the Eighteenth Century,' *The William and Mary Quarterly*, 3rd ser., XXII (1965), 549-84; and Charles Blitzer, *An Immortal Commonwealth: The Political Thought of James Harrington* (New Haven 1960). In France the idea of corruption and regeneration influenced Montesquieu. On this point see Levi-Malvano, *Montesquieu e Machiavelli* (Paris 1912); R. Shackleton, *Montesquieu* (Oxford 1961); and 'Montesquieu and Machiavelli: A Reappraisal,' *Comparative Literature Studies*, I (1964), 1-14
Hence Machiavelli's idealization of Roman history, or his *Romanità*. He does so because he knew that history better than the history of any other nation of similar merit. His idealization does not invalidate his scientific principle.

Successful action, for Machiavelli, is generally the imitation of valid models. It is a creative, not mechanical, act. For he expects the actor to devise his own, 'new,' remedies if old ones will not suffice (*Discourses*, I, ch. 39). Olschki's comments on this point are illuminating:

His examples are paradigms of experience and starting points for his inductive generalizations. They disclose the internal analogies of the historical events he considered typical, significant, or decisive. In that case imitation is not a copy of some given models but materialization of a "regola generale" and the application of a law. It is a sort of experiment that can be realized after some pattern and unlimitedly reproduced by a skilled man who knows the rules and creates the circumstances favourable to their application.[19]

The application of a Machiavellian scientific rule partakes of the features of art. It has only probabilistic, not absolute predictive power, depending on the character of the actor, chance, and circumstances. These latter factors not so much cancel the scientific validity of a rule of action as determine the actual context of its application.[20]

Finally, there is the principle of *fortuna*. The scientific rules of political action are executed in a world half governed by will and reason and half by chance and change. *Fortuna* belongs to the very core of Machiavelli's method, a fact not emphasised by either Walker or Butterfield. As Olschki points out, *fortuna* is the passive, and *virtù* the active forces of political action.[21]

No account of Machiavelli's method would be complete without

---

19 Olschki, *Machiavelli the Scientist*, 47

20 Hence Butterfield seems incorrect in attributing 'rigidity' to Machiavelli's application of the principle of imitation. See *The Statecraft of Machiavelli*, 75-6.
The Prince, ch. 25 clearly supports my suggestion: 'I believe also that a prince succeeds who adapts his way of proceeding to the nature of the times, and conversely one does not succeed whose procedure is out of harmony with the times ...'

21 Olschki, *Machiavelli the Scientist*, 38. See the essays of Flanagan and Plamenatz below.

some mention of civil law[22] and medicine,[23] which he sees as analogues of politics. This attitude is not surprising, for their methodology was inductive and had reached a relatively high level of sophistication in Machiavelli's time: certainly it was superior to that of politics. Thus Machiavelli writes bitterly:

> civil laws are nothing else than opinions given by ancient jurists, which, brought to order, teach our present jurists to judge. And medicine too is nothing other than the experiments made by the ancient physicians on which present physicians base their judgements. Nonetheless, in setting up states, in maintaining governments, in ruling kingdoms, in organizing armies and managing war, in executing laws among subjects, in expanding an empire, not a single prince or republic now resorts to the example of the ancients.[24]

The medical analogy illuminates his organic conception of state and his idea of corruption and regeneration of the political good: the state is like a biological organism, a body, a 'mixed body,' as he calls it, subject to the laws of growth and decay, life and death.[25] Thus

22 On the state of civil law in Florence, and on its influence on Machiavelli, see M.P. Gilmore's valuable study, *Humanists and Jurists* (Cambridge, Mass. 1963).

23 For examples of Machiavelli's references to medicine, see *Mandragola; The Prince*, chs. 6, 7, 13, 26; *Discourses*, II, chs. 5, 30 and III, ch. 1. 0. Tommasini's *Vita* (Rome 1911), II, 37-42 gives an account of the state of medicine in Machiavelli's Florence.

24 *Discourses*, I, preface

25 The text is important: 'And because I am speaking of mixed bodies, such as republics and religions, I say that those changes are to their advantage that take them back toward their beginnings. And therefore those are best organized and have the longest life that through their institutions can often renew themselves or that by some accident outside their organization can come to such renewal. And it is clearer than light that if these bodies are not renewed they do not last. The way to renew them ... is to carry them back to their beginnings: because all the beginnings of religions and of republics and of kingdoms must possess some goodness by means of which they gain their first reputation and

virtù is the principle of health of the body politic.[26] The analogy clarifies his notion of the prince, and the doctrine of ends and means. The prince is to the corrupt political community what the doctor is to the sick patient: a 'saviour' of life, an indispensible person. Medicine (force) should be applied for the sake of the patient, not for the personal satisfaction or gain of the prince. But if the sickness gets worse, the freedom of the prince to do what he thinks necessary increases and that of the patient to determine what is best for him decreases, and the medicine itself becomes stronger. Even purgation and amputation may be necessary for safeguarding the patient's health.

Related to the organic analogy is Machiavelli's conception of the 'migration' of *virtù*. Because of the fundamental law of political corruption and regeneration, no state, however powerful, can maintain itself at the height of its development forever. No matter what the socio-economic structure, the technological and intellectual culture, the basic law of politics will run its inevitable course. Machiavelli is so clear on this point that he does not exempt even Rome, the model, according to him, of political communities. Thus *virtù* migrated in ancient times from Assyria to Media, to Persia and Rome and in his own times reached Turkey, France, and Germany.[27]

their first growth. Since in the process of time that goodness is corrupted, if something does not happen that takes it back to the right position, such corruption necessarily kills that body. The doctors of medicine say, speaking of the bodies of men, that "daily something is added that now and then needs cure."' *Discourses*, III, ch. 1

26 See Felix Gilbert's 'On Machiavelli's Idea of Virtù,' *Renaissance News*, IV (1951), 53-6, where Professor Gilbert points out that in the Italian Renaissance, one of the uses of the term *virtù* occurred in medicine, and that it was quite possible that in Machiavelli's use of this term a medical connotation might have been present. But for a contrary opinion, see Loren S. MacKinney, 'Gilbert's "On Machiavelli's Idea of Virtù,"' *Renaissance News*, V (1952), 21-4, where he argues, I think not convincingly, that Professor Gilbert might be mistaken. In the context of Machiavelli's assimilation of politics to medicine, a medical connotation of *virtù* seems quite plausible.

27 It is clear from this attitude that his *Romanità* needs to be interpreted strictly within the framework of his scientific postulate.

It remains to be pointed out that the secularization of the methodology of politics leads to a secular political ethic. To question the
validity of the one is to question the validity of the other. Only those
who can approve the first, like Bacon[28] and Spinoza,[29] can approve
the second.

The secular ethics of politics does not mean that Machiavelli rejects
or even ignores moral ideals, only that he rejects politics as a means
to them. He does not reject the *fact* of religion and morality, since
he knew very well that the life of politics was an incessant involvement with moral or religious (ideological) issues. What he wanted to
formulate, and did formulate, was a rule of conduct precisely for
dealing with that situation, independently of theology, metaphysics,
and moral philosophy. In doing so he unearthed the scientific basis
of the conflict between politics and morality. He considered it no
part of political theory to work out a solution, yet many critics imply that he should have done so – which is to suggest that he should

---

28 On Bacon's indebtedness to Machiavelli, see N. Orsini, *Bacone e Machiavelli*
(Genoa 1936), and Vincent Luciani, 'Bacon and Machiavelli,' *Italica*, 24
(1947), 26-41. Bacon made three very important uses of Machiavelli: first, he
sought verifications from Machiavelli for his *philosophia prima* (see *Advancement of Learning* in Bacon, *Opera Omnia*, 14 vols, eds. Spedding, Ellis and
Heath [London 1958], III, 348ff.); secondly, he adopted Machiavelli's method
in his enquiry about practical morality (see *Translation of the De Augmentis,
Opera*, V, 56ff.; and thirdly, for inspiration of his own moral theory (see *De
Augmentis Scientiarum, Opera*, I, 729ff.).

29 Like Bacon, Spinoza adopted both the method and the moral theory of
Machiavelli. For example, 'On applying my mind to politics, I have resolved to
demonstrate by a certain and undoubted course of argument, or to deduce
from the very condition of human nature, not what is new and unheard of,
but only such things as agree with practice ... I have laboured carefully, not to
mock, lament, or execrate, but to understand human action ... not in the light
of vices of human nature, but as properties, just as pertinent to it, as are heat,
cold, storm, thunder and the like.' (*Tractatus Politicus*, I, #4) See also I, #1;
V, #7 and X, #1. E. Cassirer observes that 'none of the great modern thinkers
has done more to revise judgement on Machiavelli and purge his name of ob-
loquy than Spinoza,' *Myth of the State* (New Haven 1950), 119.

have written the *Summa Theologica* instead of *The Prince.* Max Weber understood Machiavelli correctly on this point. 'He who seeks the salvation of the soul,' writes Weber, 'should not seek it along the avenue of politics, for the quite different tasks of politics can only be solved by violence.' He goes on to add that that the 'genius or demon of politics lives in an inner tension with the God of love as well as with the Christian God as expressed by the Church. This tension can at any time lead to an irreconcilable conflict.'[30]

From the methodological angle it is necessary to state Machiavelli's positive conception of the relation between religion and politics. He distinguished two things in religion, the immanent and the transcendent. By virtue of the first – rites, ceremonies, anthropomorphic beliefs, discipline, etc. – religion reinforces political institutions and ideologies. In that case religion serves political ends: it is an *instrumentum regni.* The transcendent elements – doctrines, mysticism, aspirations, etc. – lie outside the sphere of politics. Though they indirectly influence it, a scientific analysis of that influence, from Machiavelli's perspective, is not possible. Thus religion lies both within and outside the scope of his method, a fact that many critics and all theologians seem to ignore.[31]

From the foregoing discussion, it should not be difficult to see how and why anti-Machiavellism[32] rests either on a misunderstanding or a

30 Max Weber, *From Max Weber: Essays in Sociology,* tr. H.H. Gerth and C. Wright Mills (New York 1964), 126

31 Thus Chabod writes that Machiavelli was 'ignorant' of 'the eternal and the transcendental' (*Machiavelli and the Renaissance,* 93); and Cassirer that 'Religion no longer bears any relation to a transcendent order of things and it has lost all its spiritual values.' (*Myth of the State,* 139) But the question is not, as I suggest, one of ignorance, but of method. Machiavelli's omission is methodological, and no more than that.

32 I define anti-Machiavellism as the rejection of the validity of Machiavelli's conception of politics and of his method of analysis. The classic anti-Machiavellian tracts are Cardinal Pole's *Apologia* (only parts of it), see below; Gentillet's *Anti-Machiavel,* see below; and Frederick the Great's *Examen du Prince de Machiavel* and Voltaire's edition of it, *Anti-Machiavel: ou Essai de critique sur le Prince de Machiavel.* One should also add Maurice Joly's *Dialogue aux enfers*

disapproval or both of Machiavelli's method. There have been three types of anti-Machiavellism – that of the theologians, of the moralists, and of the Elizabethan dramatists. In this section I shall very briefly comment on each of these types.

The theologians[33] were the first anti-Machiavellians, partly because Machiavelli became the storm-centre of the politics of the Reformation and the Counter-Reformation, and partly of course because of methodological differences. In the eyes of the Roman Catholics, Machiavelli's theory justified the break-up of Christendom, the rise of the new 'heretical' states, and the subordination of the Church to the new princes. To the Protestants, on the other hand, Machiavellism was a theory of plots and deceits, and a source of internal instability and external insecurity.

However, the conflict of method is the fundamental issue. According to the theological method, history is theocentric, and worldly glory is subordinate to the glory of God. Moreover, the human universe is a moral universe, governed by a priori norms of divine law, natural law, and providence. The solution to moral evil is sacramental, not scientific. Thus for Augustine, the state is a consequence of sin, and in the New Law, the *sacerdotium* offers a necessary corrective to *imperium*. Even those who, like Aquinas, recognize the rational basis of politics, cannot go so far as to concede it full autonomy. Consequently, for a Christian, the legitimate state is the Christian state, the true prince is the Christian prince, and valid political ethic must never depart from Christian morality.

As for the theological solution for the conflict between morality and politics, it is casuistic, not scientific. First, there is the distinction between counsels and commandments, the former for those who have a call for sainthood, the latter for all without distinction. Sec-

entre Machiavel et Montesquieu. As for critical studies, R. de Mattei's *Dal Premachiavellismo All 'Antimachiavellismo* (Florence 1969), supercedes all previous ones.

33 The list of anti-Machiavellian theologians is almost endless. They flourished especially in the sixteenth and seventeenth centuries, both in Roman Catholic and Protestant camps. A few important ones are Scipione Ammirato, Giovanni Botero, Tommaso Bozio, Tommaso Campanella, Antonio Possevino, Jeronymo Osorio, and Pedro Ribadeneyra. For a fuller list see de Mattei, cited in n31.

ondly, even the commandments admit of exceptions. Thus killing is forbidden in general, but permitted in particular cases – self-defence, war, the public good, etc.

However, Machiavelli's approach, as we have seen, is neither sacramental nor casuistic but scientific. There is no valid reason why this should make him, as the theologians have alleged, either diabolical, irreligious, or anti-Christian. Cardinal Reginald Pole (1500-58), to take just one example, typifies theological anti-Machiavellism. Indeed he is the first of this school.[34] The source of his difficulty was his repugnance for Machiavelli's method, which he saw as 'satanic.' He is 'the enemy of the human race,' and *The Prince,* though it bears the name of a man as author, is in fact written in the devil's own hand.[35]

It was Pole's search for an explanation of the Henrician revolution that brought him to Machiavelli, who was its true theoretician. Henry VIII was the true new prince, who broke the unity of Christendom (willed by God), introduced a new norm of government (*nova norma regnandi,* p.151), and subordinated the church to the state. Towards religion itself he introduced a Machiavellian via media policy between utilitarian reverence and inoffensive disregard.[36] These radical changes could not have occurred but for Machiavelli and his method. A new norm of politics (*nova norma actionum,* p.114) emerged based on convention and human will (*opinio, voluntas hominis,* p.130), not

34 *Apologia ad Carolum V Caesarem,* written in 1538 and first printed in 1744 in *Epistolarum Reginaldi Poli,* 5 vols (Brescia), I, 66-172. The sections relevant to our purpose occur pp.115-72. The account on Machiavelli is given in the form of a report on a conversation about politics between Thomas Cromwell and Pole. Pole reported that it was Cromwell who first introduced him to Machiavelli, and that the king's minister was in fact the first Machiavellian. Recently some historians have challenged Pole's account from what appears to be an inordinate zeal to whitewash Cromwell, the most prominent among them being G.R. Elton. In my opinion no credible evidence has been brought against Pole, but this is hardly the place to decide on the issue.

35 'Liber enim, etsi hominis nomen at stylum praeseferat, tamen, vix caepi legere, quin Satanae digito scriptum agnoscerem.' All citations from Pole are from the *Apologia.*

36 'Tenenda via media, quam suadet prudentia, ut, cum tua utilitas moneat, religionem observes, cum non suadet, non ita sis scrupulosus, ut ab ea discedas, nec tamen ita temerarius, ut aperte eam rejicias; hoc enim maxime nocet.'

on immutable moral principles. These latter were all right for public profession, but not much else (p.133). Similarly, the source of political theory itself was changed from speculation to experience, from the disputes in the school to actions of political men, from *The Republic* to *The Prince*.[37]

Machiavelli was put on the Index in 1557 by the Council of Trent (1545-63). Though he was removed from it in 1890, there seems to be far less likelihood of a reconciliation between him and the theologians than there would have been between Loyola, Luther, and Calvin.[38]

The moralists have been no fairer to Machiavelli than have been the theologians. The *Anti-Machiavel*[39] of Innocent Gentillet (1532-88) is

37 I give the following free translation of the key text: 'I [Cromwell] am not surprised that you [Pole] do not follow my argument, for only experience can teach it, and only men with some experience [*experti*] can grasp it. And you have no experience in public life. Moreover what I hold would not be acceptable to you because of your own outlook and training in theology. But if only you would leave the ivory tower and its idleness, and take to governmental affairs, especially those pertaining to the king, you would quickly learn what great distance separates knowledge of government learnt from experience and knowledge learnt from the airy disputes of the schoolmen about government. How can anything solid be written about politics and government unless it is not derived from experience? In political science, a brief discourse of a man of experience is worth more than many volumes of impractical speculations of philosophers. If politics should be learnt from books at all, it should be from books which are based on facts, not speculation. I know of such a book, written by an ingenious, penetrating, modern writer. This writer, unlike Plato, does not write about his dreams. The *Republic,* after so many centuries, has been of no practical value. But this new book deals only with those things which are proved to be true by daily experience.'

38 See, for example, Brucculeri's review article, 'Machiavelli e il suo pensiero politico e religioso,' of Alderisio Felice's *Machiavelli* (Turin 1930; Bologna 1950), in the authoritative Jesuit journal, *La Civiltà Cattolica*, no 2434, 1951, 420-30. Brucculeri's rhetoric has a genuine echo from the pages of Ribadeneyra or Possevino, the first Jesuits to attack Machiavelli.

39 The full title of the book is *Discours, sur les moyens de bien govverner et maintenir en bonne paix un Royaume ou autre Principaute. Divisez en trois parties: asauoir, du Conseil, de la Religion et Police que doit tenir un Prince. Contre*

not atypical of the moralist school's attitude. If Pole called *The Prince* the devil's bible, Gentillet called it the 'Koran of the French Courtiers' and the 'Breviary' of the French politicians. Much has been written about *Anti-Machiavel's* denigrating influence,[40] yet no serious attention has been paid to its methodology, to which the preface to the first part is entirely devoted. Only when one understands it will one understand the book itself.

According to Gentillet there are two methods of gaining valid knowledge. First, 'from causes and Maximes men come to knowledge of the effects and consequences'; and secondly, from 'the effects and consequences we come to know causes and Maximes.'[41] The first is proper to mathematics, while in 'the Politicke Art ... wherof Plato, Aristotle and other philosophers have written bookes, men may well use both the ways.' However, unlike mathematicians, political theorists must be endowed with certain moral virtues: 'he that will come to this science ... had need first, to bee endowed with a good and perfect natural iudgement; and secondly, he must be wise, temperate, and quiet, without any passion or affection, but all to publicke good

Nicolas Machiauel Florentin (Geneva 1576). The original edition was anonymous. C. Edward Rathé has brought out a modern edition with the title *Anti-Machiavel*, in *Les Classiques de la pensée politique* (Geneva 1968). The only English translation is that of Simon Patericke (Patrick), Bishop of Oxford, with the title *A Discourse upon the means of wel governing and maintaining in good peace, A Kingdom, or other Principalities, against Nicholas Machiavel, the Florentine,* made in 1577, but only printed in 1602, in London. Da Capo publications, New York and Amsterdam, brought out a facsimile edition of this translation in 1969. The most recent critical study of Gentillet is P.D. Stewart's *Innocent Gentillet e la sua polemica antimachiavellica* (Florence 1969).

40 For example, Irving Ribner, 'The Significance of Gentillet's Contre-Machiavel,' *Modern Language Quarterly,* X (1949), 153-7; Antonio D'Andrea, 'Studies on Machiavelli and his Reputation in the Sixteenth Century,' *Medieval and Renaissance Studies,* 5 (1961), 214-48; and 'The Political and Ideological Context of Gentillet's Anti-Machiavel,' *Renaissance Quarterly,* XXIII (1970), 397-412

41 All citations from Gentillet are from the Patrick translation. Because of the special importance of the Maxims and because of the relative difficulty to obtain the English translation, at least for the general reader, I have given them *in toto* immediately following this introduction.

and utilities; and thirdly, he must bee conversed and experimented in many and sundry affairs ...'

In Gentillet's view, 'the great Dr Machiavelli of the French Court' lacked all these qualities: 'he understood nothing or little of this Politicke Science whereof he speake.' What is worse, 'he hath taken Maximes and rules altogether wicked, and hath builded upon them, not a Politicke, but a Tyrannicall Science': he 'never had parts requisite to know that science'; 'neither hath he any or very little knowledge of hystories.'

To Gentillet then, Machiavelli was an advocate of tyranny, an evil ideologue, not one who wrote scientifically about politics. Thanks to Gentillet's method, he 'proves' the case: if one wants to know why Machiavelli is evil, one has only to look at his effects, namely contemporary French politics.[42] And if one wants to know why French politics is wicked, one has only to look at its causes, namely Machiavelli's maxims.[43]

42 The *Anti-Machiavel* was so blatantly anti-Italian that in 1577 the Italian community in Geneva wrote a spirited pamphlet, *Difesa della città di Firenze et dei Fiorentini. Contra le calumnie et maledicentiae de'maligni*. Gentillet responded by *Declaration pour repondre aux plaintifs d'aucuns Italiens* (Geneva 1577). Antonio Possevino found Gentillet so anti-Catholic that his attack on the Roman Catholic Church was thought to be even more vicious than that of Machiavelli: 'sed ubi hic Catholicam oppugnat Ecclesiam, vel ubi occasio sese dat facile Machiavellum blasphemando aequat et superat' (*Judicium de Nicolai Machiavelli*, 1592, Frankfurt 1608, 4). Gentillet attributed all the woes of France – Italian domination in banking, business, and the court, persecution of the Huguenots, etc. – to Machiavelli.

43 See the table of maxims following this introduction (pp.29-32). On Gentillet's general political stance, Rathé's comments are appropriate: 'La fin que se propose Gentillet devrait être maintenant apparente. Attaché aux traditions françaises, le jurisconsulte [he was by profession a civil servant] veut protéger et mettre en valeur un système politique fondé sur une conception hiérarchique de la vie sociale. Dieu, roi, noblesse, peuple, tous ont leurs droits et leurs responsabilités ... Ce qui lui importe le plus, c'est de refuser catégoriquement de séparer la plénitude de la morale traditionnelle.' *Anti-Machiavel*, 14

The reactionary basis of Gentillet's attack is pointed out by Meinecke: 'Through and through, it [Gentillet's attitude] was still that of a medieval

From Gentillet to Maritain and Leo Strauss the moralists expect the impossible from Machiavelli, namely for him to cease being Machiavelli. Rather than say that they do not agree with his method and therefore reject him completely, they either go on attacking him for what he does not do, such as to claim – as did Gentillet and as do moralists after him – that Machiavelli had a 'positive' aim, namely 'to teach' evil,[44] or attack him from their own methodological standpoint. The moralists neither ignore Machiavelli completely nor represent him fairly.

Turning to the Elizabethan dramatists, we see that Machiavelli fared no better with them than with the other two schools: if anything, English literature of this period has done more damage to his reputation than either the theologians or the moralists. It contributed powerfully to the identification of Machiavellian politics as scheming and plotting, deceiving and self-aggrandising.[45] There is hardly one Elizabethan dramatist who did not make some use of Machiavelli. The following chart may give some idea of the extent of this use.

To what extent the Elizabethan dramatists' concept of Machiavellism is based on an authentic image of Machiavelli is not adequately known despite the vast literature on Machiavelli and Elizabethan drama.[46] To my mind the only reliable study of this specific point is

man who, in the fresh sensuous enjoyment of his traditional and privileged existence, is easily able to bear, even with devoted pleasure, the yoke of clerical and religious power, but the new yoke of an absolutist State, which Machiavelli threatens to impose on him, he will resist with obstinate anger. Neither the Christian in him, nor the knight, wanted anything to do with the cold monster of *raison d'état. Machiavellism,* tr. Douglas Scott (London & New Haven 1957), 56

44 Leo Strauss, *Thoughts on Machiavelli* (Glencoe, Ill. 1958), holds such a view. See Dante Germino, 'Second Thoughts on Leo Strauss' Machiavelli,' *Journal of Politics,* XXVIII (1966), 794-817.

45 See, for example, N. Orsini, '"Policy" or the Language of Elizabethan Machiavellism,' *Journal of the Warburg and Courtauld Institutes,* IX (1946), 122-35.

46 Important critical works are Edward Meyer, *Machiavelli and the Elizabethan Drama* (Weimar 1897; New York 1969); Mario Praz, *Machiavelli and the Elizabethans,* Proceedings of the British Academy, XIII, 1928 (this volume does a good job of updating Meyer); Wyndham Lewis, *The Lion and the Fox* (Lon-

Author	Work	Dominant Machiavellian character
George Chapman 1559?-1634	*All Fools*	Constanzo
	The Conspiracy of Byron	La Fin
	The Revenge of Bussy D'Ambois	Monsieur
John Donne 1571/2-1631	*Ignatius his Conclave*	Machiavelli Ignatius Loyola
Ben Johnson 1573-1637	*Sejanus*	Sejanus
	Volpone	Sir Politik-Would-Be
	The Magnetic Lady	Bias
Thomas Kyd 1558-94	*The Spanish Tragedy*	Lorenzo
Christopher Marlowe 1564-93	*The Jew of Malta*	Barabas. Prologue by Machiavelli
	Edward II	Lighton
	The Massacre at Paris	Guise
John Marstone 1575-1634	*Antonio and Mellida*	Piero
	The Malcontent	Mendonza
	The Bloody Brother	Latorch
Thomas Middleton 1570-1627	*A Game at Chess*	Gondomar Ignatius Loyola
Thomas Nash 1567-1600?	*The Unfortunate Traveller*	The Ugly Mechanical Captain
Shakespeare 1564-1616	*Richard III*	Richard III
	Titus Andronicus	Aaron the Moor
	Antony and Cleopatra	Octavius
	Othello	Iago
John Webster 1580?-1625?	*The White Devil*	Flamineo
	The Devil's Law Case	Romelio

don 1927); Daniel C. Boughner, *Devil's Disciple: Ben Jonson's Debt to Machiavelli* (New York 1968); and three chapters in Frenand Lagard, *John Webster,* 2 vols (Toulouse 1968), I, 501-86; II, 587-741, 755-895. Practically everyone who writes on Elizabethan drama gives the usual nod to Machiavelli, most of them helpful but some of them misleading, such as Sanders Wilburs, *The Dramatist and the Received Idea: Studies in the Plays of Marlowe and Shakespeare* (Cambridge 1968).

that of Bakeless' *The Tragical History of Christopher Marlowe*,[47] which shows that Marlowe misunderstood Machiavelli. Thus:

Machiavellism of *The Prince*	Machiavellism of Marlowe
1 Machiavellism applies only to political affairs	1 Applies also to personal affairs
2 Does not necessarily distinguish between *virtù* and virtue	2 Opposes *virtù* and virtue
3 Advocates *virtù* for the state as a whole	3 Advocates *virtù* for personal ends
4 Admits that *fortuna* ... must be considered	4 Neglects *fortuna*
5 Employs *virtù* for a single purpose	5 Seeks power for its own sake
6 Requires psychological insight	6 Conspicuously lacks psychological insight

On the other hand the Shakespearean critic, Una Ellis-Fremor, suggests, although without the aid of an adequate critical apparatus, that Shakespeare correctly understood Machiavelli but that he found him wanting. According to Ellis-Fremor's interpretation, Shakespeare concluded that Machiavellism (whatever Shakespeare might have understood by this term) 'contained no valid solution of social or political problems,' and that 'he carried forward from his exploration certain conclusions about the nature of individualism and that perversion of individualism which is vaillainy.'[48]

My main purpose here is the explanation of the general opinion that the Elizabethan dramatists misrepresented Machiavelli. The standard argument is that Gentillet was the culprit. Although this statement is true, it overlooks the fact that Machiavelli was known in England before the *Anti-Machiavel*. Furthermore, why did it not produce the same result in the continental literatures, especially since it was available in French (obviously), in Latin (1577), in German (1580), and in Dutch (1637). The point need not be belaboured: *Anti-Machiavel* does not provide the full answer.

47 2 vols (Cambridge, Mass. 1942); the chart in the text is taken from I, 349.
48 Una Ellis-Fremor, *The Jacobean Drama* (London 1936; 3rd ed. 1953), 253

For that answer we must turn to the English political ideology of the times,[49] and the methodology of literature itself. A contemporary view of the latter is found in the classic on literary criticism, *A Defence of Poetry*, by Sir Philip Sidney (1554-86).[50]

The sublime purpose of literature, declares Sidney, is 'to teach and delight' (p.25). It does so by 'moving' the individual to 'imitate' the good as it existed 'before that accursed fall of Adam' (p.25). As a didactic medium, literature is superior to both the other didactic media, history and moral philosophy. The former teaches by examples, the latter by precepts, but neither moves the person to imitate the good it teaches. On the other hand, literature 'moveth one to do that which it doth teach.'[51]

For Sidney, as for other Elizabethans, there is no such thing as value-free literature. In their view, literature has a gravitational pull towards the moral centre. Going beyond mere experience or expression, it transports the individual to the realm of judgement, and initiates in him, through catharsis, a process of internalization of the ideal goodness. In no case, then, can literature remain neutral on the question of vices and treat them as properties like heat or cold.

If Sidney is correct and representative of the Elizabethans, Machiavelli's secular ethic will naturally become an anathema to the literary genius. It will expose him and condemn him by satire and ridicule. But here begins the difficulty. Satire and ridicule can show that Machiavelli's ethic is inferior (being an ethic of the intermediary, not the highest, good) to the ethic of literature as Sidney conceives it. But neither can seriously advance catharsis and voluntary imitation of the good as alternatives to government and its concerns. In all

---

49 For an excellent general survey see Felix Raab, *The English Face of Machiavelli* (London 1964); also a valuable London University D.Litt. thesis (1908), 'Machiavelli in Tudor Political Opinion and Discussion,' by John Wesley Horrocks. For a specific treatment, see B.N. De Luna's brilliant *Jonson's Romish Plot: A Study of Catiline and its Historical Context* (Oxford 1967).

50 I have used the text of J.A. Van Dorsten, *Sidney: A Defence of Poetry* [1580] (Oxford 1966). On Sidney and Machiavelli see Irving Ribner, 'Machiavelli and Sidney's Discourse to the Queenes Majestie,' *Italica*, XXVI (1949), 177-87; 'Machiavelli and Sidney: The "Arcadia" of 1590,' *Studies in Philology*, XLVII (1950), 152-72.

51 Sidney, *A Defence of Poetry*, 39

higher criticisms of the practical ethic there is this tendency towards negativism; and here we see literature sharing it with theology and moral philosophy. Literature does not have a positive doctrine of the practical good: Machiavelli knew this fact better than his Elizabethan critics. Thus, as in the two previous types of anti-Machiavellism, there is once more no meeting of minds.

Anti-Machiavellism, then, rests on an inability to communicate, often made worse by misperception of Machiavelli's method. The question arises, has he made matters worse than before by leaving out the transcendent from the scope of his method? Do we have a case here of more accurate knowledge about the part but less clear knowledge about the whole? Maritain, a contemporary anti-Machiavellian, argues that this is what in fact has happened. The Machiavellian *prise de conscience* was accomplished without the aid of a proper methodology: his 'thorough rejection of ethics, metaphysics, and theology from the realm of practical knowledge and political prudence' led to the perversion of practising moral evil with a sense of duty to *raison d'état*. 'In unmasking the human being,' writes Maritain, 'he maimed its very flesh and wounded it in its eyes,' and thus caused 'the most violent mutilation suffered by human practical intellect and the organism of practical wisdom.'[52]

Chabod, too, believes that Machiavelli's method has caused a split in the unity of human experience. But, with some measure of charity, he also believes that it is the task of posterity, not of Machiavelli, to integrate the new knowledge with that previously recognized.[53] Even after five hundred years posterity has not succeeded in doing so and I doubt if it ever will.

Since the beginning of the nineteenth century, Machiavellian scholarship, abandoning much that was morbid and unscientific in anti-Machiavellism, has taken a new direction. The great pioneers of this development were Tommasini, Villari, De Sanctis, and Burd. Applying the canons of critical scholarship, they were able to see Machiavelli within the framework of his own method. They were followed

52 Jacques Maritain, 'End of Machiavellism' in *The Social and Political Philosophy of Jacques Maritain*, eds. J.W. Evans and L.R. Ward (London 1956), 319-54
53 Chabod, *Machiavelli and the Renaissance*, 142-3

by Meinecke, Croce, Chabod, and Leslie Walker, each of whom explored in great depth some particular aspect of Machiavelli's work. Today the contributions of Bertelli, Ridolfi, Sasso, Hans Baron, Felix Gilbert, Whitfield, and Renaudet, to mention only a few among many, continue to expand the field of sympathetic objectivity. This is not to say that one ignores, or can ignore, the views of Strauss, Maritain, or Butterfield, all of whom belong to the old severe school. They keep alive an important historical tradition associated with Machiavellism, which no serious student of Machiavelli can overlook.

The essays contained in this volume generally follow the course of sympathetic objectivity. They do not search for things not to be found in Machiavelli – a *summa politicae* for example, or a value-free political science, or even the solution to the tension between politics and morality. The volume seeks to present Machiavelli as one who touched on the major issues of politics, including international politics.

The first three essays deal with certain general features of Machiavelli's thought. Wood sees Machiavelli as belonging to the humanist tradition of the Renaissance. His much-wonted pessimism and realism are nothing but starting points for a genuinely optimistic program of political action, the pursuit of the political good. Its precondition, however, is a theory of prudence, the theme examined by Kontos. By means of it the political man can control or anticipate events in a hostile world. Theory is for action, and action cannot succeed without theory. Failure, as Kontos puts it, 'is a kind of theoretical weakness.' It is part of prudence that man appraise his capabilities realistically. Hence Machiavelli's concern for the involvement of psyche and society, the inner world and the outer world. Pursuing this concern, Germino is able to place Machiavelli in 'the great tradition of political theory.' There is consistency and congruence, he suggests, between Machiavelli's assumptions about human nature and his claims of what man can accomplish in society.

The next three essays deal with the key Machiavellian themes of necessity, *fortuna,* and *virtù*. They may be viewed as Machiavelli's explanation of political causation. First, there is the necessity of the political good. The state, argues Mansfield, is a necessary human invention. The process of founding it proves its necessity with abundant clarity. Its existence is not conditional upon the realization of some transcendantal purpose, the recognition and execution of which law of necessity bring man face to face with *fortuna.* In medieval thought, Flanagan points out, the contest with *fortuna* had been a transcendental one, the stake being the salvation of the soul. For Machiavelli, however, the terms of the contest are thoroughly immanent, with success and glory being the desired goal. But not even the immanent goal can be achieved without *virtù.* As Plamenatz points out, this goal is not necessarily opposed to transcendental goodness. What it does is to make political action fully purposive and ethical. It is the efficient cause of success; it is to man's earthly glory what grace is to his heavenly glory.

The great debate on *virtù* centres on its relation to morality. As Gennaro Sasso points out,[54] all the answers given to this question can be grouped under those given by either Meinecke or Croce. Meinecke's answer is sympathetically analysed but rejected by Plamenatz.[55] As the eighth essay of this volume argues, Machiavelli was well aware of the role of higher morality as a fact of life. But he thought of its relation to politics as neither scientific nor dialectical but sacramental. The man of *virtù* is not precluded from finding favour with God, but by means of grace and repentance rather than by means of *virtù.*

Finally, there is D'Amato's essay on Machiavelli and world politics. In order to appreciate what is striking and original in it, one must presuppose Machiavelli's basic teachings on the subject. These, to be very brief, are three: the necessities of the state-system, of force and

---

54 Gennaro Sasso, *Il Pensiero Politico di Niccolò Machiavelli* (Rome 1964), 47

55 Croce's answer, to put it briefly and at the risk of over-simplification, is that *virtù* and higher morality are neither identical nor irreconcilable, their relationship being dialectical. *Virtù* insofar as it is sometimes amoral, is a necessary first step – thesis, if you will – in the evolution of a fully mature moral life: 'without passion, force and authority, there can be no human ascent.' But once the first step has been taken, 'the symbol of the Centaur' will no longer be valid'; what seemed to be the bestial part of man is now found to be the first form of will and action, the necessary premise to any other action. Croce, *Philosophy, Poetry, History: An Anthology of Essays by Benedetto Croce,* tr. and ed. by Cecil Sprigge (London 1966), 659; see also Croce, *La Litteratura Italiana,* 4 vols (Bari 1967), I, ch. 20, 464-70.

war, and of subordinating force and war to political prudence. Concerning the first, there can be no opting out of participation in the international system. As Machiavelli writes, 'even if you prefer to be left alone, others will not leave you alone.'[56] He sees three models of alliance.[57] The first, the imperialist model, turns potential allies into hostile subjects, and ultimately ruins the imperialist. The second, the Swiss federal model, based on perfect equality, is good ideally, but difficult to establish and even more difficult to maintain. It has two advantages, however: 'you do not easily draw wars upon yourself,' and 'all you take, you keep easily.' Finally, there is the hegemonical, Roman model, which for Machiavelli is the best because more easily attainable. Instead of creating subjects or equals, this model creates 'associates' over whom the hegemonical power can exercise command, authority, and initiative.

Machiavelli's conception of the relevance of international law for international relations is strictly pragmatic. International law is useful, but not reliable. Whereas he praised those who respected it,[58] Machiavelli was equally conscious that only few respected it. He did not see it as a restraint on policy, especially when *raison d'état* and nationalism were involved.[59] Hence the tragic importance of force and war. 'Force and necessity ... not writings and obligations make princes keep their agreements.'[60] 'Among private men, laws, writings, and agreements make them keep their word: but among princes nothing but arms keep it.'[61]

56 *Discourses*, III, ch. 2

57 *Discourses*, II, ch. 4

58 For Machiavelli's mention of *jus gentium*, see *Discourses*, II, ch. 28 and III, ch. 1. But read these chapters in conjunction with *The Prince*, ch. 18, esp. 'Experience shows that those princes have done great things who have valued their promises little, and who have understood how to addle the brains of men with trickery; and in the end they have vanquished those who have stood upon their honesty.'

59 *Discourses*, III, ch. 41

60 *History of Florence*, VIII, ch. 22

61 'Words to be Spoken on the Law for Appropriating Money,' *Machiavelli: The Chief Works and Others*, tr. Allan H. Gilbert, 3 vols (Durham, NC 1965), III, 1442

Even though force is primarily directed towards defence and security, Machiavelli's notion of force is sophisticated enough to be of relevance even in the age of deterrence. Deterrence implies a psychological relationship between statesmen which takes them beyond the relationship based on physical military strength. Deterrence implies the capacity to act boldly and plan swiftly, particularly from a position of strength. One gains respect and esteem by display of strength, not by humility, appeasement, or procrastination.[62] Finally, force and arms must be used according to the dictates of prudence. Machiavelli expounds the universal law, applicable to states irrespective of structure or ideology:

> All cities that ever at any time have been ruled by an absolute prince, by aristocrats or by people, have had for their protection force combined with prudence, because the latter is not enough alone, and the first either does not produce things, or when they are produced, does not maintain them. Force and prudence, then, are the might of all the governments that ever have been or will be in the world.[63]

62 *Discourses*, I, ch. 38; II, chs. 13-15
63 'Words to be Spoken ...' 1439

The Index or Table of Machiavels Maximes, confuted in those discourses, divided into three parts

The Maximes of the first part doe handle such Counsell as a Prince should take

---

A Princes good Counsell ought to proceed from his owne wisedome, otherwise, he cannot be well counselled.   1

The Prince, to shun and not to bee circumvented of Flatterers, ought to forbid his friends and Counsellors, that they speake not to him, nor counsell him anything, but only in those things whereof hee freely begins to speake, or asketh their advice.   2

A Prince ought not to trust in Strangers.   3

The Maximes of the second part, handling the Religion which a Prince ought to observe and be of

---

A Prince above all things ought to wish and desire to bee esteemed Devout, although he be not so indeed.   1

A Prince ought to sustaine and confirme that which is false in Religion, if so be it turne to the favour thereof.   2

The Paynims Religion holds and lifts up their hearts, and makes them hardie to enterprise great things: but the Christian Religion, persuading to Humilitie, humbleth and too much weakeneth their minds, and so makes them more readie to be injured and preyed upon.   3

The great Doctors of the Christian Religion, by a great ostentation and stiffenesse have fought to abolish the remembrance of all good letters and antiquitie.   4

When men left the Paynim Religion they became altogether corrupted, so that they neither beleeved in God nor the Divell.   5

The Romane Church is cause of all the calamities of Italie.   6

Moses could never have caused his lawes and ordinances to bee observed, if force and armes had wanted.   7

Moses usurped Judea, as the Gothes usurped a part of the empire.   8

The Religion of Numa was the cheefe cause of Romes felicitie.   9

A man is happy so long as Fortune agreeth to his nature & humor.   10

The Maximes of the third part, entreating of such Policie as a Prince ought to have

That Warre is just, which is necessary: and those Armes reasonable, when men can have no hope by any other way but by Armes. 1

To cause a Prince to withdraw his mind altogether from peace and agreement with his adversarie, he must commit and use some notable and outragious injurie against him. 2

A Prince in a conquered countrey, must establish and place Colonies or Garrisons, but most especially in the strongest places, and to chase away the naturall and old inhabitants thereof. 3

A Prince in a countrey newly conquered, must subvert and destroy all such as suffer great losse in that conquest, and altogether root out the blood and race of such as before governed there. 4

To be revenged of a citie or country without striking any blow, they must be filled with wicked manners. 5

It is follie to thinke, with Princes and great Lords that new pleasures will cause them to forget old offences. 6

A Prince ought to propound unto himselfe to imitate Caesar Borgia, the sonne of Pope Alexander the Sixth. 7

A Prince need not care to be accounted Cruell, if so be that hee can make himselfe to be obeyed thereby. 8

It is better for a Prince to be feared than loved. 9

A Prince ought not to trust in the amitie of men. 10

A Prince which would have any man to die, must seeke out some apparent colour thereof, and then hee shall not bee blamed, if so be that he leave his inheritance and goods unto his children. 11

A Prince ought to follow the nature of the Lyon and of the Fox, yet not of the one without the other. 12

Cruelty which tendeth and is done to a good end, is not be to be reprehended. 13

A Prince ought to exercise Crueltie all at once: and to doe pleasures by little and little. 14

A vertuous Tyrant, to maintaine his tyrannie, ought to maintain partialities and factions amongst his subjects, and to sley and take away such as love the Commonweale. 15

A Prince may as well be hated for his vertue, as for his vices. 16

A Prince ought alwaies to nourish some enemie against himself, to this end, that when he hath oppressed him, he may be accounted the more mightie and terrible.   17

A Prince ought not to feare to be perjured, to deceive, and dissemble: for the deceiver always finds some that are fit to be deceived.   18

A Prince ought to know how to wind and turne mens minds, that he may deceive and circumvent them.   19

A Prince, which (as it were·constrained) useth Clemencie and Lenitie, advaunceth his owne destruction.   20

A wise prince ought not to keepe his Faith, when the observation thereof is hurtful unto him, and that the occasions for which he gave it be taken away.   21

Faith, Clemencie, and Liberalitie, are vertues very domageable to a Prince: but it is good, that of them he only have some similitude and likeness.   22

A Prince ought to have a turning and winding wit, with art and practise made fit to be cruell and unfaithfull, that he may shew himselfe such an one when there is need.   23

A Prince desirous to breake a peace promised & sworn with his neighbor, ought to move warre against his friend with whom he hath peace.   24

A Prince ought to have his mind disposed to turne after every wind and variation of Fortune, that he may know to make use of a vice when need is.   25

Illiberalitie is commendable in a Prince, and the reputation of an handicrafts man, is a dishonour without evill will.   26

A Prince which will make a strait profession of a good man, cannot long continue in the world amongst such an heap of naughty and wicked people.   27

Men cannot be altogether good nor altogether wicked, neither can they perfectly use crueltie and violence.   28

He that hath always carried the countenance of a good man, and would become wicked to obtain his desire, ought to colour his change, with some apparent reason.   29

A Prince in the time of peace, maintaining discords and partialities amongst his subjects, may the more easily use them at his pleasure.   30

Civile seditions and dissentions are profitable, and not to be blamed.
31

The meanes to keepe subjects in peace and union, and to hould them from rebellion, is to keepe them alwayes poore.   32

A Prince which feareth his subjects, ought to build fortresses in his countrey, to hold them in obedience.   33

A Prince ought to commit to another those affaires which are subject to hatred and envie, and reserve to himselfe such as depend upon his grace and favour.   34

To administer good Justice, a Prince ought to establish a great number of Judges.   35

Gentlemen which hold Castles and Jurisdictions, are very great enemies of commonweales.   36

The Nobility of France would overthrow the Estate of that kingdome, if their Parliaments did not punish them, and hould them in feare.   37

TWO

Machiavelli's Humanism
of Action

NEAL WOOD

Western political theorists have been ill-treated by the goddess Fortuna. Whatever the political theorist may have expressed, his thought has often been misinterpreted and transformed into a mythology. So, for example, in the mythology of political theory that has arisen, Plato, Hobbes, Rousseau, and Hegel are totalitarians of the left or of the right; Aristotle becomes a kind of middle-class liberal; Locke is heralded as a defender of popular sovereignty; Harrington is an early historical materialist; Sorel, a fascist; and Marx, a marxist. Moreover, for the purposes of conceptual analysis, the various thinkers have been forced into simplistic dichotomous categories such as mechanist versus organicist, empiricist versus rationalist, individualist versus collectivist, and realist versus idealist.

Perhaps no single political thinker has been so abused by posterity as Niccolò Machiavelli. Ironically, Machiavelli, the dedicated adversary of Fortuna in his writings, was in fact her creature in both life and death. From the time his works were placed upon the Catholic Index in 1557, remaining there until 1890, he has been vilified for being the devil's disciple, a fallen angel, an advocate of immorality, an apologist for absolutism, a political pornographer – in sum, a machiavellian. With the development of the inevitable mythology he has also been stuck with many non-pejorative labels, among them: first modern political philosopher, political realist, political empiricist, power theorist, founder of liberalism, father of nationalism.

In particular, in the mythology that has developed, Machiavelli has been viewed as a kind of precursor of modern political science, a pioneer political scientist of fundamental detachment and objectivity who formulated a power theory of politics free from moral concerns. To the contrary, I would argue that Machiavelli is an impassioned theorist of political action, not the dispassionate scientific observer of political phenomena. Action in his sense suggests self-conscious and purposeful motion, self-directed doing for the accomplishment of the goals upon which the actor has deliberated. For Machiavelli archetypal action consists of the conscious foundation of a new order of things (a new religion, a new state, a new army), the maintenance of an order already founded, or the renovation of an order already established. Reason and experience, conceptual ordering and sensory perception are joined through action. Men are historical creatures because they act, and through action men can purposefully make history instead of becoming the helpless victims of mere circumstance. At the core of Machiavelli's humanism of action, as we shall see, is the conviction that man, in his constant struggle with Fortuna, can to an important extent hold his own and partially control his destiny if he will act with *virtù*. Since action is purposeful doing, values are essential to any act, and Machiavelli's analyses and prescriptions for action are impregnated with values and informed with a notion of the good civic order, admittedly at times rather vaguely and imprecisely articulated.

Even if we consider *The Prince* alone, usually cited to demonstrate Machiavelli's objective, scientific detachment, it is soon apparent that the work is, as Antonio Gramsci has asserted, a 'living book,' 'a true political manifesto' by an 'artist of politics,' a 'partisan with mighty passions.'[1] Furthermore, Machiavelli never discusses power in a vacuum, but always with conscious ends and purposes in mind. He is not only describing and explaining in order to advance knowledge, but also because he is profoundly perturbed by what he finds in his own practical, concrete world, and because he wishes to change it for the better. In his recommendations Machiavelli never espouses or condones personal immorality. His approach to the question of morality and politics is informed with an acute awareness of the crucial moral problem of political action, which Paul Ricoeur has called

1 Antonio Gramsci, *The Modern Prince, and Other Writings,* tr. Louis Marks (New York 1957), 135-6, 141-2, 163

'political alienation,'[2] that estrangement existing between the imperatives of personal morality and the necessities of political action for the sake of human welfare.

Therefore, in what follows, I wish to concentrate upon Machiavelli, the impassioned theorist of action, the radical critic of his own world who would like to change it for the better, and the sensitive human being who is aware of the moral ambiguity of political life. Perhaps my argument that the leit-motif of his political thought is a humanism of action may contribute in a modest way to the demythlogizing of political theory.

The argument that Machiavelli is a humanist is certainly far from novel. Whether he can be considered a humanist or not obviously depends upon the meaning assigned to the term. For example, in a perceptive essay on the Florentine, Merleau-Ponty writes:

If by humanism we mean a philosophy of the inner man which finds no difficulty in principle in his relationships with others, no opacity whatsoever in the functioning of society, and which replaces political cultivation by moral exhortation, Machiavelli is not a humanist. But if by humanism we mean a philosophy which confronts the relationship of man to man and the constitution of a common situation and a common history between men as a problem, then we have to say that Machiavelli formulated some of the conditions of any serious humanism. And in this perspective the repudiation which is so common today takes on a disturbing significance: it is the decision not to know the tasks of a true humanism. There is a way of repudiating Machiavelli which is Machiavellian; it is the pious dodge of those who turn their eyes and ours towards the heaven of principles in order to turn them away from what they are doing. And there is a way of praising Machiavelli which is just the opposite of Machiavellianism, since it honors in his works a contribution to political clarity.[3]

Paul Ricoeur, *History and Truth,* tr. and introd. C.A. Kelbley (Evanston, Ill. 1965), 259-61

Maurice Merleau-Ponty, 'A Note on Machiavelli,' in *Signs,* tr. and introd. R.C. McCleary (Evanston, Ill. 1964), 223. The essay was a paper sent to the Umanesimo e scienza politica Congress, Rome-Florence, September 1949.

In the past 'humanist' has commonly been used in two fundamental ways to describe Machiavelli's outlook. Historians of the Italian Renaissance emphasize his *cultural humanism* as part of the humanistic movement of the period. Thinkers and scholars of a somewhat broader perspective – philosophers of culture and social and political theorists – discover in his thought a *secular humanism.* The two approaches tend to represent differences in emphasis, and are not mutually exclusive or independent. Instead they characterize two closely related dimensions of Machiavelli's humanism. After a brief review of these two dimensions, I shall turn to a third dimension, his humanism of action at which Merleau-Ponty hints in the passage just cited. Together, the three dimensions should constitute a definition of Machiavelli's humanism.

Our term humanist is most immediately attributable to the Latin, *humanista,* widely used in the quattrocento and the cinquecento to refer to a student, a professor, or a teacher of the humanities.[4] Humanists were often wealthy amateurs, secretaries or chancellors of city-states, copyists, and editors and translators of Latin works. They were famous for the composition of orations, for letters, poems, histories often commissioned by their cities and princes, and moral treatises. Their central intellectual concerns were grammar, rhetoric, history, and philosophy, particularly moral philosophy, which were studied by reading, translating, and commenting upon classical Latin, and to a lesser extent, Greek authors. Among the favourites were Isocrates, Xenophon, Polybius, Lucretius, Cicero, Virgil, Livy, Tacitus, and Plutarch. Hence, humanism was very definitely a cultural and educational phenomenon with a distinct literary bias, and should not

---

4 Important sources for a discussion of Renaissance cultural humanism are: Hans Baron, *The Crisis of the Early Italian Renaissance: Civic Humanism and Republican Liberty in an Age of Classicism and Tyranny* (Princeton, NJ, rev. ed. 1966); Felix Gilbert, *Machiavelli and Guicciardini: Politics and History in Sixteenth-Century Florence* (Princeton, NJ 1965); Paul Oskar Kristeller, *Renaissance Thought: The Classic, Scholastic, and Humanist Strains* (New York & Evanston, Ill. 1961 [Harper Torchbooks]); *Renaissance Thought II: Papers on Humanism and the Arts* (New York, Evanston, & London 1965 [Harper Torchbooks]); Eugene F. Rice, Jr, *The Renaissance Idea of Wisdom* (Cambridge, Mass. 1958).

be confused with much of Renaissance learning such as logic, mathematics, natural philosophy, astronomy, astrology, alchemy, medicine, law, theology, and metaphysics, although some of the humanists were certainly acquainted with and involved in these branches of learning.

Humanistic studies during the Renaissance focused upon human values, and proclaimed the dignity of man and his privileged position in the universe, the unique experiences and feelings of the individual. The humanists felt that they had a mission to regenerate man and the civic order by the emulation of what they considered to be the golden age of classical antiquity. History became important not only for its own sake, but also because of the moral lessons which it might teach. Therefore, a humanistic education was thought to be essential in shaping a new man. From the political standpoint one strain of Renaissance humanism has been brilliantly analyzed by Professor Baron as Florentine civic humanism, which characterized the tradition that developed in Florence at the beginning of the quattrocento in response to the threat of the Visconti of Milan. The civic humanists, epitomized by a thinker like Leonardo Bruni, were obsessed with the threat of tyranny and civic corruption and stood for a vigorous republican liberty, communal spirit, civic participation, and social advancement upon the basis of merit.[5] Their approach to war and politics was one of rational calculation in terms of the common good defined as the public utility.

Now it would seem that by these standards Machiavelli is clearly a cultural humanist, albeit a 'vernacular humanist,' since he wrote only in his native Italian. The bridge between his cultural humanism and his secular humanism is perhaps most aptly suggested by Hegel in the *Lectures on the History of Philosophy.*[6] Concluding his discussion of the late middle ages, Hegel refers to the many remarkable men of the period who were not, however, of philosophical persuasion, naming three: Montaigne, Charron, and Machiavelli. These thinkers, Hegel asserts

[5] For a recent pertinent treatment of civic humanism see J.G.A. Pocock, 'Civic Humanism and Its Role in Anglo-American Thought,' *Il Pensiero Politico,* I (1968), 172-89.

[6] G.W.F. Hegel, *Lectures on the History of Philosophy,* tr. E.S. Haldane & F.H. Simson (London 1963), III, 146

have contributed to man's taking a greater interest in his own affairs, to his obtaining confidence in himself; and this is their main service. Man has looked within his heart again and given to it its proper value ...

One significant way in which Machiavelli contributed to the new confidence in man was in his separation of politics from religion and his challenge to the secular authority of the Church. Such is the essence of his secular humanism.

The human activity of politics, Machiavelli believed, can be isolated from other forms of activity and treated in its own autonomous terms. Politics can be separated from the cosmic moral order of natural law. In a word politics can be divorced from theology, and government from religion. No longer is the state viewed as having a moral end or purpose. Its end is not the shaping of human souls, the molding of morally virtuous men according to some trans-historical principle of religious or moral authority, but the creation of conditions which would enable men to fulfill their basic desires of self-preservation, security, and happiness. For Machiavelli, religion has the vital function of personal salvation and from the standpoint of the secular purpose of the state, of serving as an important instrument of social control – a basis for civic virtue rather than moral virtue. Machiavelli did not so much condemn Christianity itself and exalt pagan virtues above Christian values, as he exposed and criticized the corruption of Christianity once it had been institutionalized by a hierarchy of unscrupulous officials with predominantly secular aims. Having attained great temporal power, the Roman Church, according to Machiavelli, played a divisive and debilitating role in the chaotic politics of Italy. Admiring some of the reform movements within the medieval Church, such as the Dominican and Franciscan Orders, he perceived in them an attempt to recapture and return to the elemental principles of Christian personal morality. Although he rejected Savonarola's politics, he seemed to approve of his religious aspirations.[7]

7 The opinion of Machiavelli's friend and contemporary, Francesco Guicciardini, might well be his own: 'I know of no one who loathes the ambition, the avarice, and the sensuality of the clergy more than I – both because each of these

Hegel's great disciple, Karl Marx, who deemed Machiavelli's *History of Florence* a masterpiece,[8] was among the first to recognize the significance of his secular humanism. Machiavelli, according to Marx, conceived of the state as functioning from a human not a theological viewpoint in accord with natural laws which could be understood by reason and experience.[9] Since Marx this has been a favourite theme of marxist literature. So Antonio Gramsci writes:

It should be observed, however, that the direction given by Machiavelli to the question of politics (that is, the assertion, implicit in his writings that politics is an independent activity, with its own principles and laws distinct from those of morality and religion, a proposition of great philosophical importance, since it implicitly originates a conception of morality and religion, i.e. it began a whole conception of the world) is still discussed and con-

vices is hateful in itself and because each and all are hardly suited to those who profess to live a life dependent upon God. Furthermore, they are such contradictory vices that they cannot coexist in a subject unless he be very unusual indeed.

'In spite of all this, the positions I have held under several popes have forced me, for my own good, to further their own interests. Were it not for that, I should have loved Martin Luther as much as myself – not so that I might be free of the laws based on Christian religion as it is generally interpreted and understood; but to see this bunch of rascals get their just deserts, that is, to be either without vices or without authority.' See Guicciardini, *Maxims and Reflections of a Renaissance Statesman* (Ricordi), tr. Mario Domandi, introd. Nicolai Rubinstein (New York, Evanston, & London 1965 [Harper Torchbooks]), Series C, no.28, p.48.

8 Karl Marx and Frederick Engels, *Selected Correspondence,* tr. I. Lasker, ed. S. Ryazanskaya (Moscow, rev. ed. 1965), no.37, Marx to Engels in Ryde, London, 25 Sept. 1857, 98

9 *Writings of the Young Marx on Philosophy and Society,* tr. and ed. L.D. Easton & K.H. Guddat (Garden City, NY 1967 [Doubleday, Anchor Books]), 129. Marx's observation is in the leading article of *Kolnische Zeitung,* no.179, 14 July 1842. Note the comment on this passage as an advance in the conception of human freedom by Shlomo Avineri, *The Social and Political Thought of Karl Marx* (Cambridge 1968), 43.

tradicted today, and has not succeeded in becoming "common sense."[10]

Emphasis is given to the same idea in the *Great Soviet Encyclopedia*.[11] However, liberals as well as marxists appreciate his secular humanism. Recently, the distinguished classicist, Moses Hadas, has related Machiavelli to the thought of Protagoras: 'In government, then, the separateness of the human and divine spheres is necessary, and the return to the doctrine of man the measure is complete.'[12]

Intimately related to the cultural and secular dimensions of Machiavelli's humanism is his humanism of action, centred upon certain assumptions and views concerning violence, freedom, and morality. He believes that history is the story of constant human struggle and conflict. Providing man acts in a consciously decisive and purposeful fashion, he can escape from being the passive victim of historical forces beyond his control. Indeed, to an important extent, man can consciously shape and direct history for human betterment. All such action is fraught with moral ambiguity, but given the necessity of preservation and security in a world of violence, man must act, and act fully aware of the moral implications of the courses of action open to him in a way which will minimize the immoral consequences and maximize the utilitarian results of the intersecting chains of actions and reactions set in motion.

Perhaps more than any other thinker Machiavelli perceived human history as a great arena of strife and dissension involving violence, deceit, and treachery, relieved only now and again by individual and collective acts of heroism and self-denial. The source of conflict within and between states is man's natural egoism, the individual lust for domination and power.[13] The result is inter-state aggression and war,

10 Gramsci, *The Modern Prince, and Other Writings*, 140-1

11 'Machiavelli,' *Bol'shaia Sovetskaia Entsiklopedia*, 2nd ed., XXVI, 106-7. The article describes Machiavelli's *Mandragola* as a satire on the Catholic clergy, disclosing its hypocrisy and greed.

12 Moses Hadas, *Humanism: The Greek Ideal and Its Survival* (New York 1960), 129

13 For a development of these views of Machiavelli on conflict see my following essays: introd., Machiavelli, *The Art of War*, revision of Ellis Farneworth trans-

and domestic turmoil. Within any state conflict takes place between the many who wish to be free from domination and the few who desire to dominate the many. Machiavelli, therefore, offers a theory of conflict which is basically psychological, with economic struggle as simply one of its manifestations. The novelty of the theory, representing a radical departure from the classical-medieval tradition of political thought, lies in the idea that disorder is natural to man, and that under certain circumstances conflict can be controlled and canalized so that its destructive force will become socially constructive.

Internal conflict can have an invigorating and therapeutic effect upon the state, and also serves the vital function of securing and strengthening a citizen's liberties, thereby preventing tyranny. Politics, then, for Machiavelli, is similar to warfare, and the style of the accomplished political leader should be something comparable to the art of war as practised by the skilled general. Nor from the external standpoint should Machiavelli's position be overlooked that conflict and war between states can be a crucial method of unifying a people, of generating civic order and virtue out of indulgent self-seeking and enervating civic corruption.

To Machiavelli violence is the dynamic of this universal chaos of intramural and inter-state contention.[14] In the last analysis, violence

lation (Indianapolis, New York, & Kansas City 1965 [Library of Liberal Arts]), ix-lxxix; 'Frontinus as a Possible Source for Machiavelli's Method,' *Journal of the History of Ideas,* XXVIII (Apr.-June 1967), 243-8; 'Machiavelli's Concept of *Virtù* Reconsidered,' *Political Studies,* XV (June 1967), 159-72; 'Machiavelli, Niccolò,' *International Encyclopedia of the Social Sciences,* IX, 505-11; 'Some Common Aspects of the Thought of Seneca and Machiavelli,' *Renaissance Quarterly,* XXI (spring 1968), 11-23; 'Some Reflections on Sorel and Machiavelli,' *Political Science Quarterly,* LXXXIII (Mar. 1968), 76-91; 'The Value of Asocial Sociability: Contributions of Machiavelli, Sidney, and Montesquieu,' *Bucknell Review,* XVI (Dec. 1968), 1-22.
I wish to define *violence* as the excessive use of physical force so as to injure or damage. It is in this emphasis upon excess and upon injury and damage that violence is to be distinguished from coercion, the use of force to restrain or constrain. In both cases force signifies physical power, as in the force of a blow.

For what follows see the suggestive remarks of Ricoeur, *History and Truth,* 233-46.

has been the source of much of what is meant by civilized life. That some of us live relatively stable, secure, and even luxurious lives pursuing the arts of peace depends, to use Hegel's expression, upon 'the slaughter-bench of history.' The state is the human invention born in violence, nourished by violence, and largely responsible for perpetuating violence. The peace and leisure so necessary for human improvement and welfare rests upon the violence both potential and actual which the state can apply.[15] Machiavelli symbolizes the strange amalgam of the distinctively human and the bestial (law and force, reason and violence), represented by the state and its leadership in the mythological tutor of princes, Chiron the centaur, half man, half beast.[16] Violence renders the collective life of a people possible. From the standpoint of the life of the state, violence can be viewed externally and internally. Externally the violence at the disposal of the state is the ultimate safeguard against foreign intervention, and consequently the basis for the security and well-being of a citizen-body. This is clearly meant by Machiavelli's precept that good arms are necessary for good laws,[17] which he eloquently defends in his introduction to *The Art of War:*

> For all the arts that have been introduced into society for the common benefit of mankind, and all the ordinances that have been established to make them live in fear of God and in obedience to human laws, would be vain and insignificant if they were not supported and defended by a military force; this force, when properly led and applied, will maintain those ordinances and keep up their authority, although they perhaps may not be perfect or flawless. But the best ordinances in the world will be despised and trampled under foot when they are not supported, as they ought to be, by a military power; they are like a magnificent, roofless palace which, though full of jewels and costly furniture,

15 '*Leisure* is the mother of *Philosophy;* and *Common-wealth*, the mother of *Peace*, and *Leisure* ...' Hobbes, *Leviathan*, ch.46

16 *The Prince*, XVIII. Gramsci, *The Modern Prince, and Other Writings*, 161, terms this the 'double perspective' in political action and the life of the state.

17 *The Prince*, XII, XIX; *Discourses*, III, xxxi

must soon moulder into ruin since it has nothing but its splendor and riches to defend it from the ravages of the weather.[18]

The violence of the state used externally for defence and protection in a world of discord may produce the civic virtue, co-operation for the common good, heroism, self-sacrifice, and self-denial of a people whose survival is at stake. Machiavelli continually stresses that under such conditions of necessity, when survival is at stake, a people will often achieve a peak of unity, morale, and civic spirit, and a low point in the pursuit of narrow self-interest, economic aggrandizement, class struggle, and civic corruption in general.[19] As Paul Ricoeur puts it, murder coincides with sacrifices to form an 'ethic of distress' which combines an 'ethic of coercion' and an 'ethic of charity.'[20] Justice and brotherly love are fused; the moral evil of murder results in the moral good of charity and self-denial.

Internally, violence for Machiavelli, given the fact that men are not saints, is the ultimate deterrent of civic disorder and the guarantee of domestic peace and well-being. States are founded in violence; the radical reform of corrupt states must usually depend upon violence; and in order to preserve their liberties, citizens may have to resort to violence against tyrannical rulers.[21] But Machiavelli does not overlook consent in a broad sense as a crucial ingredient in the viable civic order. The capable political leader must always avoid the hatred and contempt of the people, and do everything possible to gain their respect and loyalty.[22] However, Machiavelli suggests that when the chips are down, violence is the final arbiter. Ultimately, because of the selfish nature of man, the justice and authority of the state must rest upon a fear of violence, rather than upon compassion and brotherly love. Ideally, the statesman should inspire fear in the hearts of his people, and win them to his side by acts of humaneness and lib-

18 *The Art of War*, revision of Ellis Farneworth translation, proem

19 *Discourses*, I, i; iii; vi; II, xxv; III, xii; *The Ass of Gold*, V; *History of Florence*, V, i; *Art of War*, II

20 Ricoeur, *History and Truth*, 243-6

21 *The Prince*, VI, XIX; *Discourses*, I, ix-xi; III, i

22 *The Prince*, XVI-XXII; *Discourses*, II, xxiii; III, xix-xxiii

erality, but if he cannot pursue both policies, the former course will suffice, while the latter course to the exclusion of the former will prove disastrous.[23] Machiavelli is fully aware of and addresses much of his thinking to the classic problem of political authority so clearly formulated by Hobbes in the *Behemoth*: 'For if men know not their duty, what is there that can force them to obey the Laws? An army, you will say. But what shall force the army?'[24] And Hobbes' answer in the same work is that the 'power of the mighty hath no foundation but in the opinion and belief of the people.'[25] Machiavelli would certainly agree with Hobbes and add what Hobbes implies elsewhere that the coercive power at the disposal of the ruler and his potential for using violence are essential factors in obtaining 'the opinion and belief of the people.'

It follows from Machiavelli's conception of the world as an arena of violence and conflict, and of the essence of the state as violence necessary for protection against external foes and the preservation of internal unity, that individual and collective action is vital for human security and happiness. Action becomes essential due to the fact that life is so full of danger, and that violence must be pitted against violence. One reason for the basic role of action in Machiavelli's way of thinking is because of his faith that what men become is, subject to the limits of their nature, within their power to determine. Provid-

23 *The Prince*, XVII

24 *The English Works of Thomas Hobbes,* ed. Sir William Molesworth (London 1839-45), VI, 237

25 Ibid., VI, 184. See the interesting version of this position by Hannah Arendt in 'Reflections on Violence,' *New York Review of Books,* XII (27 Feb. 1969), 19-31. A leading contemporary anthropologist, Claude Lévi-Strauss, in *Tristes Tropiques,* tr. John Russell (New York 1967), 308, also agrees essentially with Hobbes: '... Rousseau and his contemporaries displayed profound sociological intuition when they realized that attitudes and elements of culture such as are summed up in the words "contract" and "consent" are not secondary formations, as their adversaries (and Hume in particular) maintained: they are the primary materials of social life, and it is impossible to imagine a form of political organization in which they are not present.

'As a consequence of all this, it is clear that power is founded, psychologically speaking, in consent.'

ing men possess the will to act and to change their world and hence themselves, it is to an important degree within their capabilities to do so since they are basically equal and the products of environmental conditioning. Machiavelli argues that men are essentially the same because they are motivated by similar, insatiable passions. For the most part men are egoistic, shortsighted, and imitative, and once their characters have been formed, inflexible. Hence men remain basically the same from time to time, and place to place.[26] They resemble each other because they are born, and live, and die in a comparable manner.[27] In this sense, therefore, men are roughly equal. But Machiavelli also postulates the fundamental equality of men in a more meaningful way. Although he clearly believes in heroic *virtù*, that a rare few are born with qualities which if reinforced through the proper education will enable them to become extraordinary leaders, he does in general seem to think that the differences between most individuals within the same group and between peoples depend primarily upon differences in social conditioning rather than upon innate racial or ethnic strains.[28] Because of human malleability, within the limits imposed by human nature, much can be done in shaping man by the rational use of childhood upbringing, religion, and military training, and by the rational organization and direction of the civic order.

While we should not labour under the misapprehension that Machiavelli like many of our contemporaries is directly concerned with the issues of racism or of 'nurture' as against nature in accounting for human conduct, no encouragement for a racist position can be inferred from any of his writings. In the main he defends art over nature in the attempt to explain the differences between individuals and peoples. Nothing written by him can be used to defend slavery in terms of the rule of the innately superior over the innately inferior. Nor does he support a theory of climate as a determinant of human life, often linked with a theory of domination by the inherently superior in the thought of his predecessors such as Aristotle. From Machiavelli's standpoint, given the proper organization and education, blacks from torrid Africa and barbarians from the frigid

26 *Discourses,* I, proem
27 Ibid., I, xi
28 *Discourses,* III, xxxi, xxxiii, xxxvi, xliii, xlvi; *The Art of War,* I-III, VI-VII

north can become just as dedicated citizens and courageous soldiers as whites from the temperate regions.

Machiavelli's emphasis upon the malleability of man stems not so much from his desire to see men manipulated and controlled, as from a conviction that it provides the foundation for human freedom. If men are plastic enough to be molded by their social environment, if their selfish desires can be directed toward socially co-operative and constructive ends, they are free within certain limitations to determine their own destinies. One-half of our lives, Machiavelli claims, is determined by the contingent and fortuitous, while one-half is within our power to command. But for it to be so, we must act with *virtù*: decisively, energetically, steadfastly, with courage and rational foresight, carefully preparing for the future.[29] In Machiavelli's portrayal of life as a continuous contest between *virtù* and *fortuna*, the former represents the principle of freedom, of conscious, self-directed energy and movement, whereas the latter symbolizes the unforeseeable and the uncontrollable. By inferential reasoning from Machiavelli's rather imprecise attempts to define *virtù* and *fortuna* and their relationship, one might argue that he offers little support for the prevailing view of twentieth-century behavioural social science that men are not so much the conscious subjects of action as objects of a social or political system to be examined externally. From such a perspective human relations must ultimately be explained in causal, behavioural terms, not in terms of conscious, purposeful action.[30] Man is assigned a role or function in a mechanistic system and thereby transformed from a conscious, purposeful subject into a determined object. Instead, Machiavelli can be interpreted as suggesting that *virtù* constitutes the essence of action, whereas *fortuna* is the principle of behaviour. The man and the people of *virtù* act in a purposeful fashion in order to shape their environment according to their intentions, and insofar as they can do so they are able to determine their own existence. Whoever behaves, ceases to act; unable to seize the initiative

29 *The Prince*, XXV, esp. for the conception of *fortuna*; also *Discourses*, II, xxix; III, ix, xxxi

30 For the distinction between action and behaviour see Hannah Arendt, *The Human Condition* (Garden City, NY 1959 [Doubleday Anchor Books]) 40-2, 295-7.

and create his environment for the attainment of security and happiness, he merely responds to external forces. Not only is he reduced to being the creature of his own uncontrolled impulse, but also he may be readily enslaved by the manipulation of tyrannical power-seekers. Those who place themselves in thralldom to *fortuna* by ceasing to act lose their freedom, and in a very significant way endanger their manhood and their humanity. If this interpretation is correct then Machiavelli simply cannot be thought of as a forerunner of contemporary behavioural social science because he is above all the philosopher of *virtù*, of the mastery of man over *fortuna*.

It can, of course, be argued that this effort to relate *virtù* to action and *fortuna* to behaviour is misleading, insofar as *fortuna* represents the unpredictable, perhaps even the random, while the conception of behaviour used by contemporary social science implies, on the contrary, that the forces to which men are subject are ultimately predictable and even quantifiable. However, the point is precisely that it is man's ability to transcend these forces through conscious, purposeful action which transforms the predictable into the controllable. The idea of behaviour denies action by attributing precise predictability, at least in theory, not only to external forces, but also to human activity itself. Thus, however regular and predictable natural and social forces may be in principle, from the point of view of individual man, it is as if he were the helpless puppet of capricious and uncontrollable forces. Men who simply 'behave,' and do not 'act,' might as well be the creatures of *fortuna*.

Because of the fundamental fact of the violence of the state, the perpetual confrontation of the political actor with the moral ambiguity of his action is a cardinal dilemma of political life. The moral ambiguity of the political arena assumes the predominant form of political alienation,[31] the estrangement or cleavage between the life of the state and personal or family life, between the mode of action called for by politics, and the morality which should characterize relations within the family and between 'friends.' Machiavelli never suggests that the immorality necessitated by the basically violent nature of the state should rule interpersonal relations within the state. He sim-

1 Ricoeur, *History and Truth*, 259-61

ply argues that political alienation is an inescapable part of the human condition. His awareness of the problem of political alienation brings us to the final and perhaps central aspect of his humanism of action.

Machiavelli pleaded for the moral regeneration of his contemporaries, a fact strangely overlooked by many of his critics as well as defenders. To maintain that Machiavelli is a moralist is not to suggest that he constructs a philosophical system of ethics. Obviously, he was not a systematic moral thinker, much less a philosopher in any technical sense. And, certainly, he gives relatively little explicit attention to moral matters. Nevertheless, there is system and consistency to what he does say that may touch – if only indirectly – upon moral questions, in the sense that all his writings – *The Prince* is no exception – are informed by a scathing indictment of his own society and a passionate desire to change it for the better. A continuous thread running through his works is the criticism of the behaviour of his contemporaries, in places coupled with a somewhat fragmentary and imprecise notion of the nature of a good civic order and of the means by which it might be achieved.

A slim volume could be compiled from the passages in Machiavelli's works which together would constitute a direct and challenging denunciation of his times.[32] If the *Discourses* is a brilliant analysis of a people of *virtù*, the *History of Florence* is a penetrating anatomy of the corruption of his own people. Italy is a land torn by war, discord, sedition, and cruelty. Enslaved and oppressed by foreign invaders, the Italians are also mercilessly subjected by native tyrants, both developments aided and abetted by the political machinations of the corrupt Roman Church. And within the various city-states and principalities, Machiavelli is appalled by the intense commercialism, the idolization of prosperity and economic enterprise, by the soft, effete lives of the *grandi* and their sychopants. Von Martin comments that Machiavelli 'saw that bourgeois civilization had seen its spring and summer, that autumn had come and that winter was drawing near.'[33]

32 For example, a few such passages are: *The Prince*, XXVI; *Discourses*, I, proem, x; *The Ass of Gold*, VIII; *The Art of War*, I, VIII; *History of Florence*, I, xxxix; IV, xxxiii; VII, xxiii.

33 Alfred von Martin, *Sociology of the Renaissance*, tr. W.L. Luetkens, introd. W.K. Ferguson (New York & Evanston 1963 [Harper Torchbooks]), 65; also see 66-70.

Machiavelli dwells upon the empty magnificence of the life of the *grandi,* giving themselves up to lascivious pleasures, to insolence and indolent inactivity. Parasites living by the exploitation of the people, they surround themselves with pimps and parasites. Within each state, plagued by a vicious oscillation between tyranny and anarchy, citizen is set against citizen, friend against friend. Informers are rewarded, servants corrupted; nobility and virtue are treated as crimes. Individual life, property, and honour are constantly violated. Evasion of the law and failure to live up to civic duties become accepted practice. A dedication to the pursuit of money and sensual pleasure are normal. A sense of civic spirit and co-operation for the common good has almost completely disappeared. Increasingly corrupted and atomized, Italians have fallen prey to unscrupulous men and predatory institutions. So Machiavelli exclaimed that the 'whole world is rotten.'[34]

But if he was so deeply perturbed by the conditions of his age, what was the standard of evaluation basic to his social and political criticism, and his prescriptions for change? It was simply the standard of utility: what he took to be the need to realize the most widespread fundamental human desires of self-preservation, of security of person, family, honour, and possessions. By means of a properly ordered way of life and a rationally constructed state he believed that these felt desires could be fulfilled, and human happiness achieved. None of this can be found in explicit or systematic form in his impassioned and impressionistic writing, but all the same it is clearly there, a central assumption, waiting for the mind of a Hobbes to regularize and systematize the whole formulation. Machiavelli is a moralist in that he attempts to persuade his contemporaries that their primary felt desires are desirable, and that if they truly wish to attain happiness in terms of the fulfillment of these desires, then they must participate in a social and political regeneration entailing a radical change in their mode of life and political structure. In describing how citizens of the many different city-states of Renaissance Italy thought of their own civic orders as unique entities, Professor Gilbert has recently written:

> Yet this belief in the uniqueness of one's city did not exclude all interest in political experimentation. The norm of a perfect

society at which every city ought to aim always existed. In the fifteenth century the spread of a more extensive knowledge of classical political writings provided new material for attempts to transform the existing political order according to abstract principles.[35]

Machiavelli was certainly not an exception to this tendency. A legatee of the important Florentine tradition of civic humanism, he called for a republican order with an emphasis upon the values of civic virtue, liberty, personal security, and glory.

Of course, the obvious reply to this line of reasoning is that the conception of Machiavelli as a moralist sketched above is quite restrictive. For his so-called moral thought seems only to involve an essential prudential calculation and prudential prescription in a conditional formula derived from human desires, namely: if men desire security and liberty, then men ought to do so and so. What has this to do with morality in the more inclusive sense of self-denying and altruistic action in which each individual is treated as an end in himself rather than as a means for the advancement of self-interest? Machiavelli does not altogether neglect this sense of morality in his few and incomplete suggestions concerning the relationship between prudence and morality. His principal insight is that morality as altruistic self-denial can only be possible in conditions of relative security. Men cannot be expected to act morally, if by doing so they continuously jeopardize their own vital interests. Individual moral action will only occur where there is some expectation that others will act morally, and such an expectation will exist not under the anarchic law of the jungle, but in a relatively secure and stable society.

Now this belief seems to have several consequences. If morality is to be an effective means of regulating social relationships, if morality is to be a meaningful and authoritative regulator, its prescriptions should not be impossible for men to follow. For example, if a fundamental moral precept is the keeping of promises, man cannot be expected to do so if his adherence is tantamount to self-destruction. Or to offer a contemporary example, men cannot be expected to refrain

35 Felix Gilbert, 'The Venetian Constitution in Florentine Political Thought,' in Nicolai Rubinstein, ed., *Florentine Studies: Politics and Society in Renaissance Florence* (London 1968), 464-5

from using artificial means of preventing conception if the result is continued and severe hardship. An effective morality should be intimately connected but obviously not identical with interest, and should never demand the impossible. The conception that the 'moral ought' should always imply the 'prudential can,' is directly premised upon the notion of man as a rather frail reed. Few are willing to martyr themselves for the sake of moral principle, but men do not belong to a race of martyrs, and to be efficacious, morality must be for men, not martyrs.

The irony of Machiavelli's apparent moral position, which he seems to recognize and appreciate, is that the conditions necessary for individual moral action depend ultimately upon the immoral, violent action of the state.[36] If human morality rests upon the security and stability in human relations produced by the violence of the state, then we are confronted with the paradox that historically, morality is wedded to immorality. Such a view, of course, assumes that man is an egoist, and that the violence of the state is necessary in order to control him and to prevent self-annihilation. The consequence is that political alienation is inevitable as long as men are men and not angels.

Machiavelli's stipulations in *The Prince* regarding the action of the political leader have produced the greatest consternation and moral protest among his readers.[37] However, when his words are carefully and calmly examined little which can be called morally frightening or unusual or distasteful is revealed. He begins with the basic assumption that the prince cannot conform to the morality of private men if the existence of the state is to be securely maintained. The prince must not only appear to his subject to be humane, temperate, and virtuous, but actually must be so, otherwise his incaution and diffidence will prove disastrous. However, in order to preserve the state the prince must not only learn how to act immorally, but also must act immorally as required by the particular situation. He must adjust his posture according to every new situation, acting on occasion as

36 When I refer subsequently to the immorality or the immoral action of the state, I have in mind the acts of rulers, particularly those of a violent nature, which violate the canons of personal morality. Obviously many acts of state cannot be characterized in this fashion.

37 *The Prince*, esp. XV-XIX

man – with reason and humaneness – and on occasion as beast – with the cunning of the fox and the ferocity of the lion. Note that Machiavelli never urges private men to act immorally. Immoral means are to be used only for the maintenance of the state, and then, not always, but only when necessary. Neither does Machiavelli grant open license to the prince to act immorally, nor does he state that it is preferable to deceive, be cruel, or employ violence. Machiavelli's preference always is for a prince who combines *virtù* with moral goodness. In passing, Machiavelli postulates a law of human behaviour. Given the fact that men tend always to judge by appearances, they will disregard the means employed, providing an action of state proves successful.[38] He also asserts that in founding a new order of things out of chaotic conditions, the political leader will have to act more immorally than if he is attempting to conserve and maintain an already existing order. Hegel remarks on this point in respect to Machiavelli that:

> Gangrenous limbs cannot be cured with lavender water. A situation in which poison and assassination are common weapons demands remedies of no gentle kind. When life is on the brink of decay it can be reorganized only by a procedure involving the maximum of force.[39]

Finally, and perhaps most significantly, the argument in *The Prince* is in terms of results. Morally good and humane action may produce

38 *The Prince,* XVIII. This particular passage at the end of the chapter is sometimes mistakenly translated into the proposition that the 'end justifies the means.' In discussing the relationship of means to ends Machiavelli never writes in terms of justification. The actual words are: 'e nelle azioni di tutti gli uomini, e massime de' principi, dove non e iudizio a chi reclamare, si guarda al fine.'

39 G.W.F. Hegel, 'The German Constitution,' in Hegel's *Political Writings,* tr. T.M. Knox, introd. essay Z.A. Pelczynski (Oxford 1964), 220-1. Hegel is discussing Machiavelli, and proceeds to say: 'You must come to the reading of the *Prince* immediately after being impressed by the history of the centuries before Machiavelli and the history of his own times. Then indeed it will appear as not merely justified but as an extremely great and true conception produced by a genuinely political head endowed with an intellect of the highest and noblest kind.' (p.221)

evil results, while immoral action may have morally virtuous and humane consequences. Better cruel action, Machiavelli contends, if the result is humane, than humane action eventuating in moral disaster. Obviously, Machiavelli's argument is that in the political arena the actor may have to be tough for the sake of humanity.[40] There is also the intimation that the man of true moral stature is one who has no fear of 'dirty hands' if he feels dirty hands are necessary for humane ends. He who refuses to dirty his hands for the sake of moral purity displays not so much a love of man as a love of principle. He is simply not of man and the down-to-earth human possibilities of solving human problems. In Sartre's well-known play, *Dirty Hands*, Hoederer, the tough, practical-minded party leader, makes this clear to the principled young intellectual, Hugo:

How you cling to your purity, young man! How afraid you are to soil your hands! All right, stay pure! What good will it do? Why did you join us? Purity is an idea for a yogi or a monk. You intellectuals and bourgeois anarchists use it as a pretext for doing nothing. To do nothing, to remain motionless, arms at your sides, wearing kid gloves. Well, I have dirty hands. Right up to the elbows. I've plunged them in filth and blood. But what do you hope? Do you think you can govern innocently? ... You don't love men, Hugo. You love only principles. ... And I, I love them for what they are. With all their filth and all their vices. I love their voices and their warm grasping hands, and their skin, the nudest skin of all, and their uneasy glances, and the desperate struggle each has to pursue against anguish and against death. For me, one man more or less in the world is something that counts. It's something precious. You, I know now, are a destroyer. You detest men because you detest yourself. Your purity resembles death. The revolution you dream of its not ours. You don't want to change the world, you want to blow it up.[41]

---

40 'As sometimes happens, tough politics loves men and freedom more truly than the professed humanist: it is Machiavelli who praises Brutus, and Dante who damns him.' Merleau-Ponty, 'A Note on Machiavelli,' 217

41 'Dirty Hands' (*Les Mains sales*) in Jean-Paul Sartre, *No Exit and Three Other Plays,* tr. Lionel Abel (New York 1949 [Vintage Books]), 223-5

Machiavelli is often criticized for discussing morality in terms of results and consequences instead of moral principles and intentions. However, in the first place it should be repeated that he is not concerned with the systematic analysis of personal ethics, and that he only briefly treats morality as it may relate to political action. In the second place, from the standpoint of social and political action, the only way of arriving at some accurate estimate of the moral principles and intentions of the actor is through the results and consequences of a series of his actions. Whatever the actor may say in regard to his moral principles, the observer must begin with the actions and their consequences, and then attempt to derive moral principles and intentions from them, not, of course, neglecting, but at the same time not relying on the moral professions of the actor. This seems to be such an obvious canon of sound historical analysis, as well as practical politics, that it would hardly appear worth mentioning.

For the sake of analysis I wish to separate what I take to be Machiavelli's views on principle from those on intention. First, then, in respect to principle, it is obvious that he devotes his attention to power rather than to principle. The action entailed by the defence of the state, in its foundation and maintenance, means fundamentally power to Machiavelli: the power relationships between men, between men and states, and between states. Machiavelli himself does not lack moral principle,[42] nor does he, as we have seen, completely omit principle from his political considerations, but his emphasis undeniably is upon the techniques of acquiring, preserving, and enhancing power. Why is this the case? Apparently it is due to his conviction

---

42 It is often forgotten that Machiavelli wrote on penitence, characteristically stressing action through charity. Whoever lacks charity, he asserts, 'must necessarily be unfriendly to his neighbor: he does not aid him, he does not console him in tribulation, he does not teach the ignorant, he does not advise him who errs, he does not help the good, he does not punish the evil.' 'An Exhortation to Penitence,' in *Machiavelli: The Chief Works and Others,* tr. Allan H. Gilbert, 3 vols (Durham, NC 1965), I, 173. The work, probably written in Machiavelli's later years, is called 'the climax of the author's Christian thought' by Roberto Ridolfi, *The Life of Niccolò Machiavelli,* tr. Cecil Grayson (London 1963), 253; 328n2.

that in respect to egoistic, selfish man, moral principle in politics without power is useless and self-defeating, and moral principle with power seldom obligates when interest is at stake and, indeed, may lead to the subversion of all moral principle.[43] The principle of social justice can be employed to justify the most iniquitous and despotic regime as well as the most equitable, and the most principled of rulers may very well create conditions in which all moral principle disappears. As long, therefore, as we live in a chaotic world of conflict and violence, in which men individually and collectively act in a bestial way, considerations of power which relate to the well-being of a community are critical. Such would still be the rule in a world of saints which included only a handful of fallen angels.

Second, in regard to intention, Machiavelli's neglect of the moral intention of the political actor seems to be accounted for by his attitude in general toward moral principle and political power. He most decidedly does not recommend political action without moral intention. His apparent position is that an ethic of intention applies primarily to the sphere of personal morality, that of family and friends, although in any ethic, consequences cannot be overlooked. However, in the greater sphere, with political actors who must provide the conditions of security necessary for a personal ethic to flourish, the paramount concern must be with consequences. The political actor may have the most morally upright and honourable intentions, but unless his actions are rooted in a prudential calculation of the consequences of his actions, he may destroy the very conditions necessary for a thriving personal morality among those whom he governs. If he blindly pursues his moral aims he may run the risk of committing such inhumane actions that his original intentions are completely nullified. It may be better in the long run, for morality's sake, if the ruler has no crusading moral intentions, but is endowed with a discriminating sense of the prudential. Here we are confronted with two more paradoxes which emerge from Machiavelli's writings. The first is that a personal morality of intention cannot exist without a political morality of consequences. The second is that ultimately morality depends upon prudential calculation rather than upon a spontaneous sense of altruism, and unless man is to be undone – rendering moral-

43 See the discussion in Merleau-Ponty, 'A Note on Machiavelli,' 219-21.

ity impossible and consequently meaningless – prudential calculation must be at the root of any viable social and political ethic.

Here, therefore, are the three dimensions of a definition of Machiavelli's humanism. First, from the standpoint of his life and work during the Renaissance he can be called a *cultural humanist* in that he wrote didactic treatises on political life, relying on classical Greek and Latin sources, in which he vigorously condemned tyranny and civic corruption and passionately upheld the virtues of liberty, republicanism, and civic spirit. Second, he was a *secular humanist* in that he separated politics from religion and theology, challenging the secular authority of the corrupt Roman Church. Finally, one can abstract from his writings a *humanism of action* that urges men consciously to direct their lives and to shape their social environments on the basis of human wisdom, and that recognizes, given a world populated by men and not saints, the central moral ambiguity of political life centred upon the perception that the very possibility of personal morality itself entails the necessity of public immorality in the form of the violent action of the state, and the tough and prudential policy of its leaders. Missing from Machiavelli's humanism is any profound overall view of man and his place in the universe and any effort to come fundamentally to grips with the problem of the moral criteria of political judgment and action. In this sense he was always the diplomat, in spirit, the expositor of the art of the possible, and of the balancing of inconveniences, rather than a philosopher. On second thought, perhaps, this is his supreme and timeless value: that he is not a philosopher, but an ardent advocate of action who calls attention to a world usually slighted by the philosopher.

For our own time of troubles in which elders are being seduced by the promise of the affluent society, and the young in reaction to it are wallowing in a permissive romanticism, the message of Machiavelli's humanism is clear. Beware, he says, of tyranny and strive for liberty, remembering that the winning and holding of liberty depends upon the self-knowledge of men acting in concert through the rational creation of institutions and arrangements. Without organization men cannot realize, strengthen, or maintain their liberties. Moreover, in the world of politics men are completely on their own and must assume full responsibility for their actions. Man is free to create a better life, unless he succumbs to the blandishments of false security and indolent pleasure, unless he ceases to act and only responds, an object without purpose, a creature of unfettered impulse, manipulated and determined by forces beyond his control. Although the evil of violence is the way of things, man can never regenerate or fulfill himself through such an evil. Nevertheless, the modes of violence may have to be learned, and if necessary used rationally and instrumentally so that men can live, and live in a more liveable world. Men should strive to be men, should strive to fulfill their humanity and the dreams so essential to it through conscious, purposeful action. In acting men must do so rationally with full self-awareness of the implications of their actions, moral and otherwise. However, in acting, men must replace the false sentimentality of spontaneous anarchy by self-determination through self-discipline and rational social reconstruction. Not to act with conscious, humane purpose, not to recognize the necessity and responsibility of dirty hands, is to be something less than men. The demand for moral purity in a chaotic world requiring radical measures for its very survival amounts to self-deception, if not immorality. The perception of the common predicament of mankind, and 'that what pleases the world is but a brief dream,'[44] does not excuse languishing in the anguish of self-pity.

---

44 Petrarch, *Sonnet 1,* as quoted by Machiavelli at the end of his 'An Exhortation to Penitence.' Gilbert, *Chief Works,* I, 174

THREE

Machiavelli's Thoughts on the Psyche and Society

DANTE GERMINO

That Machiavelli was gifted with profound theoretical insight into politics, few would wish to contest. That he was a full-fledged political theorist or philosopher, is a proposition that many find difficult to accept. Accordingly, although I am personally convinced that he should be included among the ranks of the political theorists – and that, indeed, he was a very great, if untypical, one – I have deliberately employed the word 'thoughts' rather than 'theory' in the title of my paper. It would carry us too far afield from the purposes of this book to discuss the characteristics of political theory,[1] and I do not want to concentrate on the substance of Machiavelli's teaching regarding the psyche and society.

That teaching remains, after half a millennium, of absorbing interest. Indeed, one will find embedded in it many of the concerns of the contemporary discipline of psychology, and especially of social, and what is coming to be called political, psychology. However, to regard Machiavelli primarily from the perspective of contemporary social science – as a kind of precursor of any one of the several currents flowing together to make up what is presently called the 'scientific' approach to political behaviour – would, I think, be inevitably to distort the character of his teaching. We should end by missing what is

---

1 I have sought to discuss this problem in my book, *Beyond Ideology: The Revival of Political Theory* (New York 1967), especially chapters 1 and 2, as well as in chapter 1 of my *Modern Western Political Thought* (Chicago 1972).

Machiavellian (in the good sense) in Machiavelli. It needs also to be stressed that although as a separate discipline among the 'social sciences' psychology is of relatively recent origin, as a topic of speculation – the *logos* on the *psyche* – it is as old as political theory itself, which is to say, at least as old as Plato.

At any rate, it is as an historian of political thought that I seek to approach Machiavelli, and the first (although not the whole) duty of such an historian is to attempt to present the teaching under review in its own terms, even if to a considerable degree he will unavoidably see it refracted through the lenses of present-day concerns.

For Machiavelli, a realistic psychology which could serve as a basis for effective political action rests upon several key propositions: 1/men are basically selfish and anti-social – left to themselves, the agonistic[2] impulses in the psyche predominate over the co-operative ones; 2/nonetheless, the psychological potential for socialization exists in men – they can be influenced to act sacrificially on behalf of the collectivity; 3/the optimal social order is not a systematically repressive one, but one which allows for competition between the two great 'humours' – or collective tendencies – into which every body politic is divided; 4/for a society which is well-ordered to come into being, it is necessary that it be founded by a single superior man or heroic leader, and periodically be brought back to its origins through discipline and severity; and 5/dissimulation and fraud have been indispensable elements of political rule.

There are other implications of Machiavelli's political doctrine with respect to the psyche and society which I intend to discuss in the concluding portions of the paper where I deal with his observations on the role of dissimulation in politics. Machiavelli, I will argue, may have been only imperfectly aware of the full consequences of his teaching. But he was acutely aware of having embarked on a new path of political speculation 'not yet trodden by anyone.' By uncompromisingly exposing the enormous role which he discovered fraud and illusion to have played in politics, he kindled the hope that men might construct a new political world based on relative freedom from illusion. His brutally frank and deliberately shocking account of the

2 Guido Dorso, in his reflections on the psychology of politics, distinguishes between the 'agonistic' (from the Greek *agon*, meaning struggle) and solidaristic passions. Cf. Germino, ibid., ch. 6 for a discussion of Dorso.

role of both violence and deception in politics has indirectly helped to win for man a greater degree of critical self-consciousness. Thus, both the covert implications and the overt conclusions of his analysis of the psyche and society will be considered.

One of the benefits to be derived from concentrating on Machiavelli's psychological teaching is that it will assist us considerably in understanding the distinctive character of his republicanism. The Florentine secretary did not regard his endorsement of a republican regime – and specifically his endorsement of the Roman republic as a model – as an arbitrary preference or an 'idealistic' commitment. Rather, he regarded his republicanism as resting on realistic psychological foundations. The superiority of the republican regime was attributable to the fact that it reflected, ministered to, and mitigated the destructive tendencies of the real psychic constitution of man.

Machiavelli held that human nature was constant;[3] this very constancy enabled those like himself, whose mission it was to 'reason about the state,'[4] to elucidate principles of universal validity that would assist men in understanding their situation more adequately and, within the limits of the possible, in mastering it more successfully. Machiavelli rarely discusses Plato directly,[5] but it is clear that his teaching on the psyche and society is in agreement with Plato on at least one cardinal point: that is, that 'the *polis* is the psyche writ large' – that political institutions do not grow out of rock and wood but out of the minds of men.

Niccolò Machiavelli, *Discourses on the First Decade of Titus Livius,* book I, ch. 39. Tr. Allan H. Gilbert, *Machiavelli: The Chief Works and Others,* 3 vols (Durham, NC 1965), I, 278, hereinafter cited as Gilbert. Except where I explicitly depart from him I have used Gilbert's translation throughout. For the Italian text I have used the edition of A. Panella, 2 vols (Milan-Rome 1939).

Letter to Francesco Vettori, 9 Apr. 1513 in Gilbert, II, 900-1. Gilbert translates *ragionare dello stato* as 'talk about the government.'

In his *Discourse on Remodeling the Government of Florence,* Machiavelli lauds Plato, along with Aristotle and 'many others' (including presumably himself), who, although 'unable to form a republic in reality' have 'done it in writing.' They have thereby sought to 'show the world that if they have not founded a free government, as did Solon and Lycurgus, they have failed not through their ignorance but through their impotence for putting it into practice.' Gilbert, I, 114

Machiavelli begins his exploration of the psychological foundations of politics by emphasizing the aggressive or 'agonistic' passions with which nature has endowed men. We are all quite familiar with his bitter observations on the 'evil' side of man's nature. Thus, we find in the *Discourses* the following famous passage:

Whenever men cease fighting through necessity, they go to fighting through ambition, which is so powerful in human breasts that, whatever high rank men climb to, never does ambition abandon them. The cause is that Nature has made men able to crave everything but unable to attain everything. Hence, since men's craving is always greater than their power to attain, they are discontented with their acquirements and get slight satisfaction from them. Men's fortunes therefore vary because, since some strive to get more and others fear to lose what they have gained, they indulge in enmity and war. These cause the ruin of one province and the prosperity of another.[6]

There are equally striking statements about men's inclinations toward each other elsewhere in the *Discourses*. Thus, we are informed that is is necessary for a legislator 'to presuppose that all men are evil,' that they will always employ the 'malignity of their minds' (*la malignità dello animo loro*) when they have 'free occasion' to do so, and that 'men are more prone to evil than good.' (*Discourses*, I, 3 and 9)

The Prince, as we know, is certainly no truant on this score. In a single chapter of *The Prince* one encounters two of the many observations which have helped over the centuries to earn Machiavelli the reputation as a maligner of the human race virtually without peer: 'we can say this about men in general: they are ungrateful, changeable, simulators and dissimulators, runaways in danger, eager for gain ...' and 'men forget more quickly the death of a father than the loss of a father's estate.'[7]

What is less noticed – partly for the very good reason that it is less visible – is the other side of Machiavelli's teaching regarding human nature. That teaching is not one of unrelieved pessimism about man and his inclinations toward his fellows. Machiavelli, after all, was not

6 *Discourses*, I, 37; Gilbert, I, 272
7 *The Prince*, 17, Gilbert, I, 62-3

a maligner but an analyst of human nature. He found the agonistic impulses so powerful 'in the human breast' because of the peculiar plight of man, a plight for which as a co-participant he had some sympathy. And he did not maintain that man was utterly devoid of social feeling; he only claimed that because of his plight man could not bring his co-operative passions to predominate over his agonistic ones unless pressured by necessity or assisted by society. Even then such predominance would be precarious and provisional. Ambition 'never' leaves men, whom nature has so fashioned that they 'crave everything.'

The following excerpt from his poem, *The Ass of Gold*, shows Machiavelli emphasizing the fragility of man, as he comes into the world, in comparison with beasts, 'born devoid of all protection':

Only man is born devoid of all protection; he has neither hide nor spine nor feather nor fleece nor bristles nor scales to make him a shield.

In weeping he begins his life, with the sound of a cry painful and choked, so that he is distressing to look at.

Then as he grows up, his life is verily short when compared with that of a stag, a raven, or a goose.

Nature gave you hands and speech, and with them she gave you also ambition and avarice, with which her bounty is cancelled.

To how many ills Nature subjects you at starting! And afterwards Fortune – how much good she promises you without fulfillment![8]

Man, for Machiavelli, then, is in some measure a pathetic animal, more to be pitied than censured. He is brought into the world at odds with himself and incapable without external support of fashioning his deliverance. Being born 'without protection' he is in need of a shell of security. Without such a protective shell – that is, the well-ordered state – his constructive and co-operative impulses cannot take root and flourish;[9] with it he is capable of achieving a degree of nobility.

8 *The Ass of Gold*, ch. 8; Gilbert, II, 772
9 Cf. for example, Machiavelli's comment in the dedication to *The Art of War* that 'good customs, without military support, suffer the same sort of injury as do the rooms of a splendid and kingly palace, even though ornamented with gems and gold, when not roofed over, they have nothing to protect them from the rain.' Gilbert, II, 566

The primordial fear which animates men can be assuaged and channelled into constructive endeavours under the shade of the state's security.

Machiavelli nowhere discusses the 'origin of the state' in more systematic fashion than in *Discourses*, I, 2, which is generally held to have reflected extensive borrowings from Polybius. What is interesting about this remarkable passage for our purposes is the stress on 'gratitude' as an emotion natural to man, and as the foundation of a sense of obligation. Once men had 'gathered together so they could better defend themselves' – that is, for security – they gradually evolved notions of justice and respect for law. The basis of their 'understanding of justice,' however, was the inclination of men to have 'compassion' for their benefactor, or chief, to whom they felt 'grateful' for protection. Thus, 'if one injured his benefactor, there resulted hate and compassion among men, since they blamed the ungrateful and honored those who were grateful.'[10] The theme of gratitude vs ingratitude is quite central to Machiavelli's political thought, and it frequently recurs throughout his writings.

Reference to men's capacity for 'benevolence,'[11] 'compassion,' 'gratitude' and even 'love' (of one's fellow-citizens, ruler(s), and country) are too liberally sprinkled throughout Machiavelli's writings to permit their being taken lightly or ignored. Even in *The Prince*, Machiavelli does not fail to point out that if conditions permit, it is most desirable that a prince be loved by his subjects; the model of the fierce Severus need serve only to found a new regime; to preserve one long-established one can afford to follow the gentle Marcus Aurelius, who was himself loved and revered by the people.[12] The ever-present 'malignity' of the human psyche is capable of being mitigated, then, just as is man's total absorption with the self and its aggrandizement. Men can come out of themselves and experience a sense of identification with a ruler or with the *patria* itself.

10 *Discourses*, I, 2, Gilbert, I, 197
11 Cf. *Discourses*, II, 24; Gilbert, I, 293, for a key reference to the 'benevolence' (*benivolenza*) or 'good will' of which men are capable.
12 *The Prince*, 19; Gilbert, I, 76. Even *The Prince*, 17 stresses the relative ease (by respecting the property and women of his subjects) with which a ruler can avoid being hated.

Indeed, in *Discourses*, III, 21 Machiavelli goes so far as to say that 'men are driven chiefly by two things: love and fear.'[13] (Note that love is mentioned first.) *The Art of War* contains some passages which go even farther in the direction of modifying the more famous (or infamous) pessimistic statements about man in Machiavelli; here we are told that 'love of country' is 'caused by nature'[14] and that in any commonwealth where 'something good' remains, it is 'not impossible' to induce men to 'honor and reward excellence [*virtù*], not to despise poverty, to esteem the methods and regulations of military discipline, to oblige the citizens to love one another, to live without factions, to esteem private less than public good, and other like things that could easily fit in with the times.'[15] Presumably, the possibility of influencing men to behave in the above fashion is grounded on certain 'natural' propensities toward co-operation and solidarity in mankind.

In citing these references by Machiavelli to the co-operative and compassionate impulses in man, my purpose is not to 'redeem' the Florentine secretary from the objections that have been raised by countless writers with respect to his excessively 'pessimistic' view of man. In any event, it would not be too difficult to find equally pungent and 'realistic' observations in Augustine or Luther or Calvin or Sigmund Freud. If we must divide political thinkers into pessimists and optimists, Machiavelli could be ranked with either group. But these matters are to one side of my major concern in this paper, which is to enquire into the specific character of his psychological

13 *Discourses*, III, 21; Gilbert, I, 477. 'Therefore a leader can command who makes himself loved, just as he can who makes himself feared.'

14 *The Art of War*, IV (end); Gilbert, II, 662. Gilbert translates this whole passage as 'Love for a man's native land is caused by nature; that for his general, more by ability than by any kindness.' The text is *L'amore della patria è causato dalla natura; quello del capitano, dalla virtù più che da niuno altro beneficio*. Why Gilbert translates *beneficio* as 'kindness' instead of 'benefit' I am at a loss to say. This criticism is not meant to detract from Gilbert's splendid achievement, however. Overall, his translation is the best available.

15 *The Art of War*, book 1; Gilbert, II, 572. Machiavelli adds that by introducing these 'modes' of the ancient Romans, one 'plants trees beneath the shade of which mankind lives more prosperously and more happily than beneath this shade' (i.e. that of contemporaneous Italian modes and orders).

reflections and their relationship to his political teaching. In this connection, it is important to point out more forcefully than is often done that his teaching regarding the psyche is rich, complex, and multi-faceted. Although on balance he found the agonistic passions to predominate in the psyche of the 'generality of men,' his comprehensive teaching also takes the co-operative or solidaristic impulses into account. For Machiavelli, the psyche is a field of contending passional forces, and the inherent instability of politics has its roots in man's psychological instability. Man's unquiet psyche oscillates between the contrasting inclinations and passions of love and hate, fear and courage, the desire for tranquillity and the urge for adventure, inertia and activism, dread of the novel and eagerness for change.

Rather than 'blaming' man and his 'evil' nature for the human predicament, Machiavelli focuses responsibility for political corruption and decay upon the rulers. The anti-social inclinations in human nature are not so powerful that they cannot be reversed by skillful political leadership. The right kind of leadership can create the conditions under which the spirit of sacrifice for the common good, respect for law, and a commitment to civic and military excellence [virtù] flourish. In The Art of War Machiavelli has Fabrizio observe that it is not the people of Italy who are responsible for the corrupt condition in which they then found themselves; rather, it is 'certainly their princes who are to blame.'[16] Elsewhere in the same work he concludes that 'Nature brings forth few valiant men; effort and training make plenty of them.'[17] But it is in the Discourses that he makes his most emphatic statements about where to assign responsibility for failure to achieve a disciplined and well-ordered commonwealth:

By no means should princes complain about any sin [peccato] committed by the people they have in charge, because such sins of necessity come either from a prince's negligence or from his being spotted with like faults ... The Romagna, before Pope Alexander VI destroyed the lords who ruled that district, exemplified the most wicked ways of living, because from the slightest cause

16 The Art of War, book 7; Gilbert, II, 724
17 Ibid., 718

the most serious slaughter and rapine would result. This came from the wickedness of those princes, not from the wicked nature of their subjects, as the rulers said it did.[18]

And again,

So it is truer than any other truth that if where there are men there are not soldiers, the cause is a deficiency in the prince ...[19]

Machiavelli, then, does not advocate either the brutal repression of conflict by a despot or resigned acceptance of the human condition as irremediably anarchic. Rather, he insists that in principle it is possible to manage and control conflict. If either tyranny or anarchy prevails, the fault lies in the society's political leadership and not in the nature of man. Corruption originates at the head of the body politic and then spreads throughout the members.

Just as what we might call Machiavelli's political psychology emphasizes the perpetual warfare that rages within the 'breasts of men' (*ne petti umani*), his 'political sociology' stresses the perennial struggle between rival groups within communities. The roots of societal conflict may ultimately be traced to the agonistic passions of the psyche; the (always provisional) solution of this conflict lies in providing occasion for the expression of the co-operative passions by affording a measure of stability and predictability (the rule of law) in the social milieu *and* by instituting procedures which make it possible for citizens within a given society to 'fight out' their 'enmity' according to 'law' rather than 'force.'

Machiavelli's first mention of what I would call the concept of the 'humouric' struggle is in chapter 9 of *The Prince*, where he observes that 'in every city two opposing humors [*umori*] exist.' These two social formations are the people [*il populo*] and the 'great men' [*i grandi*]. It is suggestive that Machiavelli employs a term with psychological dimensions – 'humours' or 'moods' or 'tempers' – to describe this fundamental division within society. The term *umori* is often lost sight of in the process of translation; Gilbert sometimes renders

18 *Discourses*, III, 29; Gilbert, I, 494
19 *Discourses*, I, 21; Gilbert, I, 247

it 'parties' and at other times 'factions.' But Machiavelli employs the terms 'parts' (*parte*) and 'sects' (*sette*) when referring to what we ordinarily mean by 'factions.' He sharply distinguishes between factions and 'humours.' The term 'party,' on the other hand, makes for difficulties in translation, because of its inevitable confusion with the organized political party, of which Machiavelli, of course, knew nothing, as it was a much later development. His word *parte* could literally be translated as 'partisan group'; 'faction' would be an approximate equivalent.

In *Discourses*, I, 4, Machiavelli observes with respect to the humouric struggle in the Roman republic that 'those who condemn the dissensions' between the nobility and the plebeians are ignorant of the fact that these very dissensions were the 'first cause' for Rome's having remained free. Such critics did not consider that 'in every republic there are two opposing humors, the people and the *grandi*, and that all the laws made in the favor of liberty result from their discord.'

Not only does Machiavelli call the two opposing social currents 'humours,' but he also attributes to them conflicting 'appetites.' Thus we find him proclaiming in *The Prince*, chapter 9, that 'the people desire not to be bossed and oppressed by the *grandi*; and the *grandi* desire to boss and oppress the people.' From these two 'opposing appetites' originate one of these political effects: 'either a principality or liberty i.e., [a republic] or license [anarchy] .'[20]

Machiavelli is sometimes held to be the first political thinker of rank to have emphasized the possibly beneficial results of political conflict. Bertrand de Jouvenel has written of his acceptance and approval of the factional struggle. There is much validity in this statement, although strictly speaking, Machiavelli did not approve of factions (*sette, parte*) any more than did Rousseau after him. While

20 *The Prince*, 9; Gilbert, I, 39. I have altered Gilbert's translation, which in this passage takes considerable liberty with the text, at several points. The original text reads: '*Perché in ogni città si trovono questi dua umori diversi; e nasce da questo, che il populo desidera non essere comandato né oppresso da grandi, e li grandi desiderano commandare e opprimere il populo; e da'questi dua appetiti diversi nasce nelle città uno de'tre effetti o principato o libertà o licenzia.*' Panella, *Discorsi*, II, 39

Machiavelli did not think that the humouric struggle could or should be avoided, he did think this of the factional struggle.

Factions (or 'sects' or 'parties') are based on ambition and narrow group or personal interest to the detriment of the common good. The factional struggle destroys a community; the humouric struggle can preserve it as a strong and vital force. Modern Florence, as Machiavelli frequently points out in both the *Discourses* and the *History of Florence,* is a leading example of a society consumed by intransigent and fanatical factions. Republican Rome, on the other hand, established institutions through which both of the great groupings which divide every society could find regular, legal, and open expression. The interests of the *grandi* were protected by the senate and those of the plebs by the tribunate and popular assemblies, with the consulate first in one camp, then in the other. Now the objective of the *grandi* is to dominate (we could say today to exploit); that of the many, to be free from domination. Put somewhat less harshly, the *grandi* aim to keep their privileged position while the many wish to see them removed. Inasmuch as Machiavelli never openly discusses the problem of economic inequality (although his position on this question may perhaps be implied from his frequent references to a well-ordered republic keeping the citizens poor and the commonwealth rich), we may assume that he regarded a certain amount of economic inequality as inevitable. In any event, he regarded inequities in the possession of power as inevitable; there would always be rulers and ruled. For Machiavelli, then, the humouric struggle was not to be avoided but optimally was to be contained in such a way that the energies resulting from it would benefit the republic – that is, contribute to its collective strength and *virtù.*

The humouric struggle is always present. It will not be harmful but indeed, will be beneficial, if the two humours[21] are provided legal

---

21 In the *Discourse on Remodeling the Government of Florence* Machiavelli speaks of *three* social elements: 'the most important, those in the middle, and the lowest *(primi, mezzani, e ultimi)*.' This classification is apparently based on property. It is not found elsewhere in his writings, to my knowledge. Gilbert, I, 107. In general, socio-psychological factors were rated much more heavily than economic ones by Machiavelli. It could even be said that he unduly neglected the importance of economic motives.

channels through which to express their enmity and defend their interests. When the hatreds that arise between the two groups 'do not have an outlet for discharging themselves lawfully, they take unlawful ways that make the whole republic fall.'[22] One of the incalculable benefits of a genuinely republican form of rule is that grievances may be freely and peacefully voiced.

Machiavelli contended that 'well-ordered states and wise princes with the utmost attention take care not to make the *grandi* desperate, and to satisfy the people and keep them contented.'[23] Beyond this, each side had to be persuaded through 'good education' to accept the legitimacy of the other's existence. If the two social forces become locked in deadly embrace with all their energies concentrated on this contest for complete victory of each other, they are then comparable to 'small birds of prey, who so strongly desire to catch their victims ... that they do not see above them another larger bird that will kill them.' The 'larger bird' in this case is the threat of loss of liberty either through external conquest or internal tyranny. The 'excessive desire of the people to be free' and that of the *grandi* to dominate combine to ensure the loss of liberty for both.

We have referred to Machiavelli's conviction that man's actions can be decisively influenced and to an extent controlled by skillful political leadership. It remains now to examine his views about the psychology of the controllers and the tactics they employ in the art of the 'psychological management' of a populace.

In both *The Prince* (chapter 6) and the *Discourses* (book I, chapter 9) Machiavelli devotes considerable attention to the men of 'very rare brain' who have 'founded new modes and orders.' The 'exceptional' and 'marvelous' men – such as Moses, Cyrus, Romulus, Theseus, Solon, and Lycurgus – were to serve as models for the guidance of future innovative rulers. Since 'men almost always walk in the paths beaten by

22 *Discourses*, I, 7; Gilbert, I, 211. This chapter and I, 9 are particularly relevant to the 'humouric struggle.'
23 *The Prince*, 19; Gilbert, I, 70. Gilbert translates *grandi* as 'the rich.' Such a translation obscures the psychological emphasis of Machiavelli's concept of the humours. It was not only or even principally the property differentials which characterized the two social forces, but questions of status and psychological orientation.

others and carry on their affairs by imitating,' a prudent man 'will always choose to take paths beaten by great men, and to imitate those who have been especially admirable, in order that if his ability [*virtù*] does not reach theirs, at least it may offer some suggestion of it.'[24]

Where most men do good only under necessity – either natural or man-made – these founding heroes spontaneously and out of their own intellectual and spiritual resources (*la virtù dello animo loro*) conceive of great political enterprises and, when fortune presents them the 'occasion,' run every danger and make every sacrifice necessary to implement their designs. These men are able to distinguish between glory and narrow ambition, between the common good and private advantage. They are the true benefactors of the human race.

From his study of the act of foundation in politics, Machiavelli arrives at the following 'general rule':

seldom or never is any republic or kingdom organized well from the beginning, or totally made over, without respect for its old laws, except when organized by one man. Still more, it is necessary that one man alone give the method and that from his mind proceed all such organization. Therefore a prudent organizer of a republic and one whose intention is to advance not his own interests but the general good, not his own posterity but the common fatherland, ought to strive to have authority all to himself.[25]

Machiavelli's praise of rule by a single exceptional individual may seem incongruous in the light of his frequent defence of the people and of their liberty to defend their interests. In other words, it appears that there is a contradiction between his elitism and his populism. This problem is not easy to resolve, although a considerable step toward its resolution may be taken if we do not automatically assume that there is any necessary contradiction between strong leadership in exceptional circumstances and democratic politics.

Although Machiavelli is interested in the general subject of political foundations, it is clear that above all he wishes to demonstrate on principle the superiority of republics – or 'free governments' – over

4 *The Prince*, 6; Gilbert, I, 24

5 *Discourses*, I, 9; Gilbert, I, 218

the various forms of princely rule. His 'best regime' is clearly the republic, and of all previous republics that of Rome best serves as a model for a free society. Therefore, it is not the foundation of societies in general that he discusses in detail but the foundation of Rome.

What Machiavelli professed to discover about the foundation of Rome was that, although Romulus did not spare even the life of his brother in his determination initially to concentrate all power in himself until the new modes and orders were instituted, immediately thereafter he began to share his power with the senate. From this example Machiavelli draws the conclusion that a founder should be 'so prudent and high-minded that he will not leave to another as a heritage the authority he has seized, because, since men are more prone to evil than to good, his successor might use ambitiously what he had used nobly. Besides this, though one alone is suited for organizing, the government organized is not going to last long if resting on the shoulders of only one; but it is indeed lasting when it is left to the care of the many.'[26]

Machiavelli's praise of one-man rule, then, turns out on further examination to be severely qualified and restricted. As is well known, Machiavelli was fiercely opposed to tyranny and he extolled the mixed regime as the best governmental form. He did conclude that exceptional and heroic leaders had periodically arisen in history and that new political institutions – and specifically free political institutions – could be established only through the actions of such exceptional men in whom all power was temporarily concentrated. But his heroic leader was not to be a permanent dictator; in this respect Rousseau's misnamed 'legislator' resembles him.

Except in times of crisis – that is, of grave threat to the state's existence, whether from within or without – Machiavelli was in favour of the dispersion of political power among the conflicting social forces and their representatives as previously described. In the paradigmatic Roman case, the tribunes defended the people and constituted one bastion of power, while the senate defended the 'optimates' (grandi) and comprised another power base. However, Machiavelli did not intend such dispersion to impair the state's capacity for action. He admired the Roman constitutional dictatorship for coping with emer-

26 Ibid., 218

gencies and saw every well-ordered regime as in need of a comparable institution. Furthermore, every sound body politic would need periodically to be refounded or brought back to its first principles (that is, Machiavelli's concept of the 'return to the origins'). For this purpose also temporary consolidation of power in one man was requisite.

The creation and maintenance of republican rule, then, was for Machiavelli an arduous affair, calling for a whole panoply of skills and of diverse personality types. The period of the foundation would have to be sufficiently extensive to mobilize adequate support for the new modes and orders. In the positive sense this would entail the political re-education of the populace in the ways of liberty; negatively, it meant the suppression – by ruthless means, if necessary – of the 'Sons of Brutus,' or of those who sought to bring back the discredited order based on personal rule and privilege. Over the long run, Machiavelli conceived republics to be admirably adapted for survival both in times of crisis and in periods of tranquillity. He attributed the superior survival capacity of republics to the fact that such governments were able to draw upon a variety of personality types for leadership when needed instead of being burdened by a single ruler who might prove himself ill-adapted to the requirements of the times.[27] Thus, the Roman republic could call on the harsh Manlius or the gentle Valerius, depending upon whether circumstances called for the 'arts of war' or 'those of peace.'[28]

The tactics of political rule obviously fascinated Machiavelli, and indeed his observations on this subject occupy a central place in his teaching. This is entirely proper for one who sought to penetrate to *la verità effettuale della cosa* and to examine 'how men live.' The extraordinary richness of Machiavelli's teaching on the 'psychological

[27] 'Thence it comes that a republic, being able to adapt herself, by means of the diversity among her body of citizens, to a diversity of temporal conditions better than a prince can, is of greater duration than a princedom and has good fortune longer. Because a man accustomed to acting in one way never changes ... so of necessity when the times as they change get out of harmony with that way of his, he fails.' *Discourses*, III, 9; Gilbert, I, 453. Cf. also his famous letter to Piero Soderini of Jan. 1513 about the difficulties encountered by individual rulers in adapting to what 'the times' require.

[28] *Discourses*, III, 22

management' of a populace can only be hinted at within the limits of this paper. Certain general remarks might be useful in assisting the reader to view that teaching in perspective, however.

In the first place, Machiavelli is talking about the art of political rule and not about a 'science' of 'social engineering.' He is forever qualifying his observations about men and their behaviour in terms of the specific context. Accordingly, one will find very few 'general rules' in his writings that are not qualified in some way. For those who since Saint-Simon and Comte have been fond of speaking of a 'science of man' that can predict and therefore control human behaviour to the point of virtually eliminating the element of contingency, Machiavelli cannot fail to be a disappointment. His conclusions will be judged to be impressionistic, insufficiently verified, and unsystematic. It may well be, however, that for all its deficiencies there is more of the specific flavour of political reality in his work than in much of more recent 'behavioural' social science.

Secondly, Machiavelli's intentions in discussing the art of rule so exhaustively and in such detail are far from obvious. At first reading he appears to be on the side of mankind's oppressors, as a kind of expert on the tactics of violence, deception, and manipulation. He appears to possess contempt for the masses of men, whom he declares to be always short-sighted and easily deceived and to advocate their cynical manipulation by an unscrupulous elite. In summary, Machiavelli appears as an enemy of human freedom and dignity.

We know, however, that something is very wrong with this portrait. Machiavelli was too ardent a republican and pronounced too favourable a verdict on the people's reliability and capacity to choose wisely under the proper conditions for him to be viewed as a conformist to the legend of 'Machiavellianism.'

But what are we to make of Machiavelli's frequent allusions to successful dissimulation and 'fraud,' as well as his advice to the prince to learn to play the fox as well as the lion? In passages in chapter 18 of The Prince[29] and several of the earlier chapters of the Discourses[30] he seems to have reached the depth of cynicism and to be the advocate of the most unscrupulous manipulation of human beings.

29 The Prince, 18, Gilbert, I, 65, 66
30 Discourses, I, 11, 13, 14; Gilbert, I, 225, 229-33

Before we draw such a conclusion, however, it would be well for 'prudent men,' as Machiavelli himself would say, to examine other possible interpretations of the Florentine secretary's shocking counsels with respect to the use of force and fraud. As with any writer of rank, so with Machiavelli – and perhaps especially with him[31] – it seems reasonable to assume that his words reveal multiple levels of meaning. The concealed or 'hidden,' may well be substantially different from the surface or literal, meaning. One of his persistent themes is the distinction between appearance and reality. Just as he attempts to sort out 'the things which appear' from 'those that are' in political reality, so we must apply the same rule in interpreting his own words, which are, in effect, his political actions.

Machiavelli *appears* to sanction wholesale dissimulation and fraud in politics. Whatever partially effective restraints against adopting such nefarious practices that are present in most cultural environments would presumably be swept away by anyone who seriously follows the literal interpretation of Machiavelli. But what is his intention in repeatedly citing examples of fraud? What is the cumulative effect of such examples on the careful reader? Has he not actually, in the very process of writing about these tactics exposed the *arcana imperii* of countless rulers, ancient and modern? Has not his 'crime' been to discuss openly – *in piazza* – what had previously been uttered largely in secret – *in palazzo*?

It would be foolhardy to claim wholly to have grasped the intentions of so complex a writer as Machiavelli, but I do not think it inherently implausible to conclude that he was motivated by a concern to humanize politics and that his unrelenting emphasis on the role of force and fraud in politics was designed to promote greater awareness of the nature and extent of these practices to the end that they might be mitigated or at least rationally controlled. The shocking examples and counsels, then, were employed for therapeutic effect, to prod men into facing unpleasant realities about human behaviour which must be dealt with before one could hope to establish a free

31 Letter to Guicciardini, 17 May 1521: 'For a long time I have not said what I believed, nor do I ever believe what I say, and if indeed sometime I happen to tell the truth, I hide it among so many lies that it is hard to find.' Gilbert, II, 973

society. It is really quite understandable why Gaetano Mosca said of Machiavelli that as a writer 'he was one of the most honest of all times.'[32]

But Machiavelli was not interested only or even primarily in a kind of indirect muckraking. What was the point of unmasking nefarious practices if such action did not lead to greater comprehension of political reality and an increased ability to deal prudentially with that reality? He clearly regarded moralizing about political evil as worse than useless.

If we study Machiavelli closely, we can learn much from him about the moral ambiguities and practical difficulties inherent in political action. His reflections on the moral ambiguity of action are outside the scope of this paper,[33] but what he discovered about the art of political communication is relevant to a discussion of his psychology.

According to Machiavelli, skill in political rule requires, in part, an awareness on the part of the political elite of the inevitable gap which exists between the apprehension of an act – how it 'appears' to the people – and its real nature. This gap can presumably be narrowed and a new politics be created as men come to take the 'new way' to greater political self-consciousness which he has sought to open up. But a discrepancy of some magnitude between appearance and reality will always exist because, for one thing, of the different perspectives of rulers and ruled, and of the greater proximity of rulers (the political elite) to the particulars of the situation. On the other hand, the critical study of politics – or authentic 'political science' – can provide a general overview of the perspectives of both rulers and ruled. As such, political science itself can be a leavening influence in society, diffusing greater self-awareness – or 'enlightenment' – throughout the body politic. Machiavelli's critical study of politics, then, far from shoring up the position of the political elite and providing them with esoteric 'secrets of rule,' has the effect, if seriously pursued, of democratizing politics through the spread of political knowledge to elites and non-elites alike.

32 Quoted in James Meisel, *The Myth of the Ruling Class* (Ann Arbor 1958), 283
33 I have attempted to characterize his position on the 'ends-means' problem in my article 'Second Thoughts on Leo Strauss's Machiavelli' in 28 *Journal of Politics* (1966), 794-817 at 803-7.

It is in this context that I would evaluate the remarks in *The Prince* and the *Discourses* on the question of judging by appearance or reality.[34] Machiavelli's contention is that rulers must take into account and weigh in the specific context the factors tending to distort the perspectives of those affected by governmental policy. In the light of this consideration, appearances may be more important than reality. A crucial consideration for the wielders of political power has to be the role of illusion in the lives of men. Furthermore, certain myths – above all, those foundational beliefs sustaining the social order and affording the majority of men a kind of anchorage in the world – have their truth. Only the 'strong of heart,' men of 'very rare brain' can perhaps afford to be entirely free of illusion. However – and again here one encounters the multidimensional character of Machiavelli's political teaching – the more an awareness of the role of illusion in human affairs spreads, through the dissemination of the new critical study of politics, the greater becomes the possibility of reducing the reliance on illusion and ultimately of demythologizing politics.

The current political condition based on widespread illusion can be modified. Men are not always deceived. When they have knowledge of particulars they are less frequently deceived.[35] The new critical study of politics will provide them with the knowledge of particulars concerning their political existence.

How else are we to make real sense out of Machiavelli's dramatic announcement in the opening paragraph of the preface to book I of the *Discourses* that he has 'determined to enter upon a path not yet trodden by anyone'?[36] Clearly, by this passage he meant to distinguish himself from the 'generality of men' who 'walk in the paths beaten by others and carry on their affairs by imitating.'[37] Therefore, his political teaching, for all its evident admiration for the ancients, cannot have consisted simply or primarily in an exhortation to follow the ancients.

---

34 *The Prince*, 18; Gilbert, I, 66-7; *Discourses*, I, 25; Gilbert, I, 252; *Discourses*, I, 47; Gilbert, I, 292, 294; *Discourses*, III, 35; Gilbert, II, 509 .

35 *Discourses*, I, 47; Gilbert, I, 292-4

36 *Discourses*, I, preface; Gilbert, I, 190

37 *The Prince*, 6; Gilbert, I, 24

Machiavelli was aware of the many obstacles preventing the emergence of a radically new political universe. 'On account of the envious nature of men,' he notes somberly, 'it has always been no less dangerous to find ways and methods that are new than it has been to hunt for seas and lands unknown ...' Nonetheless, he did not lose hope that, should his attempt fail, others 'with greater *virtù*, eloquence, and judgment' could carry out his 'intention.'[38]

That intention was nothing less than the political re-education of men. Machiavelli attached tremendous importance to the influence of education on the psychological dispositions and conduct of men.[39] However, no more successfully than did Plato could he resolve the problem of the disharmony between philosophy and power. If the new teaching were to be practically efficacious, he believed that it had to be adopted by a reforming prince. He was aware that he, himself, possessed the same disability as had Aristotle and Plato[40] before him in being a man of thought rather than of action and power. And yet, what was the probability of discovering a reforming prince who not only possessed the 'most excellent *virtù*' of founders of previous ages but who was also willing and able to absorb the message of Machiavelli's new understanding of politics and who would lead mankind along the 'new way' to a more self-aware and human political world? Machiavelli's vision of a new political world, in which power and the new self-awareness merged, was, for all its apparent 'realism,' as unlikely of realization as was Plato's dream of the philosopher king. It is no accident that Machiavelli's great contemporary, Guicciardini, found him not to be too cynical or 'realistic' but too impractical and 'idealistic.'

Machiavelli, if he could not achieve the new politics, could at least comfort himself in having shown men the way to recover the prudential wisdom of the old politics – the politics of virtue in the Roman sense. There was, of course, an alternative method of disseminating the new political wisdom. Instead of relying on a prince to fashion the political re-education of a people from the top down, Machiavelli could rely on the gradual, unplanned, and indirect spread of his teaching by those who read and (hopefully) understood him.

38 Ibid.
39 *Discourses*, III, 46; Gilbert, I, 525
40 *Discourse on Remodeling the Government of Florence;* Gilbert, I, 114

Although Leo Strauss has argued with great ingenuity and acumen to the contrary, I can find no evidence to suggest that Machiavelli, despite his fascination with the tactics of conquest and rule as employed by men of power, had worked out a battle plan for men of thought to enable them to effect the re-education of a populace and, indeed, of a civilization. It seems more probable that Machiavelli was convinced he had made a great discovery, and had taken a significant stride forward in man's self-knowledge; and that he was groping to assess the full implications of that discovery and the means of its implementation, which he only obscurely envisaged. Like Plato, Machiavelli failed to achieve the direct impact on political events he initially sought, but he has exerted a more profound indirect influence on the western political consciousness than he could have possibly foreseen. Where an occasional ruler, such as Benito Mussolini, has professed to be guided by Machiavelli, the result has been a parody or downright defamation of the Florentine secretary's ideas.[41] Machiavelli's real followers and successors have been political theorists, and not only those who, like Harrington, Spinoza, and Rousseau, have been directly inspired by him, but also countless other serious students of politics who have imbibed something of his questing and critical spirit.

We observed at the beginning that it did not seem appropriate to link Machiavelli with contemporary social and political psychologists of the 'behavioural persuasion.' In stressing his role as a contributor to the 'great tradition' of political theory, I believe that I have been on firm ground. If we take, furthermore, the works of men like B.F. Skinner, Harold Lasswell, or Hadley Cantrill as – for all their divergences – representative of a leading segment of social and political psychology in recent times, the contrasts between the approaches of these men and of Machiavelli will be even more apparent. For there is a gulf which separates Machiavelli and much of contemporary behavioural social science on the fundamental issue of the constancy of human nature. Machiavelli repeatedly observes that human nature

41 Mussolini, 'Preludio al Machiavelli,' in *Scritti e Discorse di Benito Mussolini*, 12 vols (Milan, 1934-40), IV, 105-10. This was submitted as the Duce's 'doctoral thesis' at the University of Florence. For a discussion of the sources of Mussolini's operative ideology, see my article 'Italian Fascism in the History of Political Thought,' 8 *Midwest Journal of Political Science* (May 1964), 109-26.

is constant at its core;[42] the new 'behavioural' social science is predicated on the assumption of radically 'changing' human nature. Human nature for Machiavelli establishes the unsurpassable limits of political action, whereas in the behaviouralist program, as articulated by its most consistent and self-conscious spokesmen, the idea of limit is disregarded.[43]

Throughout this paper I have stressed Machiavelli's achievements in the area of psychology and politics. I wish to conclude with some brief observations on the deficiencies of his teaching. The deficiencies of his psychological teaching may perhaps best be indicated by a comparison of Machiavelli with two other intrepid explorers of the psyche, Plato and Sigmund Freud. Both the heights and depths of the psyche, we know from these men, are greater than Machiavelli dreamed of in his psychology.

What is largely absent in Machiavelli that is present in Plato is the concept of the psyche as the 'sensorium of transcendence' (Eric Voegelin). To put it another way, Machiavelli presents us with a 'soulless' psychology. As Leo Strauss has noted, Machiavelli almost always employs the term *animo* (mind) rather than *anima* (soul) in his serious political reflections.[44] He, indeed, proclaims himself – and possibly all men, for he employs the ambiguous 'we' – as 'ignorant of supernatural things.' But for Plato, the ignorance (*agnoia*) of the psyche toward the divine could be cured by the 'therapy' of philosophy.

It needs scarcely to be added that the role of reason is also quite diverse in the teachings of the two men. While both Plato and Machiavelli placed a high value on reason – Machiavelli is on record as having thought it 'well to reason about everything' – reason for Machiavelli does not possess the commanding or directing power in the psyche which it has for Plato. As we have seen, the psyche for Machiavelli

---

42 Cf. inter alia, *Discourses,* I, preface and I, 39; Gilbert, I, 191, 278

43 Cf., for example, Hadley Cantril's observation that social science has now reached the stage where we can 'bring about the human nature we want.' 'Don't Blame It on Human Nature,' *The New York Times Magazine* (6 July 1947). For a discussion of assumptions and goals in extreme behaviouralism, see Germino, *Beyond Ideology,* ch. 9, and Floyd W. Matson, *The Broken Image* (New York 1964).

44 Leo Strauss, *Thoughts on Machiavelli* (Glencoe, Ill. 1958)

can best be represented as a horizontal field of conflicting drives rather than, as for Plato, a hierarchical ordering of faculties with reason and 'spirit' in command of the appetites. Reason and intellect (*ingegno, intelletto*) in Machiavelli do not command the passions but help to illumine their nature and to bring their existence, power, and motion to man's self-consciousness. Along with imagination (*fantasia*) and a whole panoply of faculties under the name of *virtù*, reason assists man in obtaining his desired ends, of which the most basic is security and the most exalted, 'glory.' The psyche itself is not oriented toward transcendence but toward the achievement of intramundane desires.

When we confront Machiavelli's reflections on the psyche and society with those of Freud, we are initially struck with certain basic affinities. Freud's positing of two contradictory impulses in man – *eros* and *thanatos* – and his stress on the power of man's destructive, aggressive drives sound very congenial to Machiavelli's analysis. Similar parallels appear to exist between the thought of both men with respect to the relationship of leaders and led and the importance of elites in political rule. Both were concerned, moreover, with enhancing man's capability to deal resourcefully with his problems: in 'exposing,' as it were, the role of the irrational in human behaviour, they hoped for some therapeutic gain to occur. As man grows in self-awareness, the possibilities of rational control of his environment increase. Both thinkers studied the irrational, but neither intended to surrender man to it.

From such a comparison – the barest outlines of which may be indicated here – between Machiavelli and Freud we can also learn more about the limitations of Machiavelli's perspective. We are impressed by the relative narrowness of Machiavelli's psychology. There is in Machiavelli a failure to map out the dimensions and elements of the psyche and to pursue inner human experience to its farthest limits. Freud, on the contrary, follows Plato at least in his continuation of a tripartite characterization of the psyche, although with the Viennese master the terms are different (id, ego, and superego) and the role of reason (as a property of the ego) is a mediating rather than a controlling one. Machiavelli appears to have had little inkling of the depth of the unconscious in man and of the enormity of the problem of bringing repressed desires to the consciousness. The whole area of sexuality and politics remains unexplored in Machiavelli, as it remained, we must in fairness add, for virtually every other 'pre-Freudian' writer. When Machiavelli writes of love, as he frequently does in his letters, it is more often facetiously than otherwise; amorous affairs are seen as welcome distractions from the serious business of politics. Or, alternatively, they can, if pursued on the part of rulers, have adverse political consequences. Rulers should respect not only the property but also the women of their subjects. As we have seen, Machiavelli not infrequently refers to love of fellow men, of rulers, and of institutions – one's country, religion, customs, etc. – but he offers no sustained analysis of love's sources, varieties, and objects. Nor does he adequately explore the relationship between fear and love despite his frequent linking of them together.

Machiavelli, of course, did not utter either the first or last word on the subject of psychology and politics. Much of his analysis is fragmentary and his psychology is restricted as to both range and depth. Yet what he saw, he saw extremely well and we who today attempt further to advance the understanding of man in his political existence owe him our gratitude. He has been a benefactor of humanity. His is only one voice in the continuing 'conversation of mankind,' but it is one that deserves a careful hearing. For his honesty and determination to do all that he could to root out cant and self-deception we are indebted to him, even if many of us cannot but think that a view of political reality which brackets the transcendental dimension achieves clarity at an unacceptable price and is subject to its own distortions and illusions.

FOUR

Success and Knowledge in Machiavelli

ALKIS KONTOS

The great men of history, founders and reformers of states, seem to be Machiavelli's special idols. We frequently hear their names and actions praised, their achievements and respective styles explored with admiration, and time and again we are exhorted to imitate their glorious deeds. His involvement with the heroic personages of history is not simply one of excessive veneration. He identifies with them. In a letter to Vettori, Machiavelli informs us how he dwells upon his imaginary dialogues with the heroes of antiquity. He says, 'I do not feel boredom, I forget every trouble, I do not dread poverty, I am not frightened by death; entirely I give myself over to them.'[1]

The initial impression we receive from Machiavelli's emphasis on historic heroes is that his admiration is reserved exclusively for the glorious few who have triumphed. It is as if only success excites his imagination. My purpose in the present essay is to examine this initial impression. I shall argue that though this first impression reveals an element of truth regarding Machiavelli's genuine concern with success and glory, it does not exhaust the issue. My thesis is that Machiavelli's primary concern is the mode of success rather than success itself; and because the mode of success reflects the presence or ab-

1 Letter to Vettori, no. 137, *Familiar Letters* in *Machiavelli: The Chief Works and Others,* tr. Allan H. Gilbert, 3 vols (Durham, NC 1965), II, 929. Hereinafter cited as *Chief Works.*

sence of the knowledge requisite to prudential action appropriate to the pursuit of success, neither success nor glory are or can be the measure of a man's greatness. Only the possession of that knowledge necessary to the securing of success can be such a measure. Furthermore, since a prudential and knowledgeable course of action can be frustrated by the malevolence of forces beyond the individual's control, failure per se cannot diminish the actor's greatness as long as he possesses knowledge.

A well-known aspect of Machiavelli's political philosophy is his belief that the human condition precludes the possibility of continuous successful action. The goal of political leadership is to establish an environment whereby the basic and immutable tenets of human nature are fully accommodated and utilized, and maintain and stabilize such accommodation as long as possible through the creation of appropriate socio-political institutions.

In a world of constant vicissitude between order and disorder, politics is assigned the role of generating and maintaining order against a natural and inevitable tendency toward disorder. Political power does not have any other function for Machiavelli but to create order within a given place and time. The exercise of political power does not seek order and stability for the world at large but only for one nation at the expense of others.

Since for Machiavelli the specific end of political action is to arrest temporarily the natural and inevitable propensity of a community toward disorder and decline, political success implies the achievement of such arrest revealed in an orderly and dynamic society. Therefore, for Machiavelli not all political goals qualify as appropriate for the use of the state's power, and consequently endeavours with inappropriate goals are disqualified. They are automatically regarded as failures, for they vitiate the notion of politics proper, and it is irrelevant if such wrong political endeavours materialize or not. For example, a successful seizure of power to satisfy a strictly personal hunger for power, a selfish ambition, is indeed the accomplishment of one's own self-assigned political purposes, but such purposes remain alien to the kind of politics Machiavelli had in mind. They are instances of desire for personal aggrandizement whereby private ends take precedence over the public good. It is on such grounds that those who engage in politics only in order to achieve personal power and tyrannize others do not qualify in Machiavelli's terms as great men of history, even though they might have succeeded in their purposes.[2]

Because success relates exclusively to achieving what the very constitution of the world by nature allows in the form of a stable, orderly, dynamic, and victorious state, only attempts to lead one's nation to such a position can be issues of success or failure and call for a serious evaluation of the political actor's greatness. Success is directly related to results. The successful are victorious and victories are recognizable. A testament to a leader's achievement of his historic mission is the state of affairs of his country: its military might and political vitality.

If one is to succeed, he must actively seek the realization of these specific political qualities. Active engagement in their pursuit does not guarantee their achievement. Shunning such engagement, however, does preclude the possibility of success. Once a political leader undertakes this task, his success or failure cannot be judged by the initial outcome of events. The whole spectrum of a man's political reign must be taken into consideration. However, if at any point in time such a leader deviates from either the appropriate ends or means of political rule, he is stigmatized beyond redemption. He can never achieve what Machiavelli regards as success and never gain glory.

As success is directly related to results, so is glory to success. Glory is the natural consequence of success. The vanquished are never granted its splendour.

The glorious men are those who successfully complete their attempt to vitalize their respective societies, to strengthen them militarily, and stabilize them politically. These men are those rare individuals who translate their unique talents into action which yields favourable results. They make history by shaping the destiny of their nations.

Glory is the prize of victory and therefore it cannot be reached but through success. Glory is the culmination of a people's gratitude to and admiration for their benefactor. Yet glory transcends its immediate geographic and historic environment. Though rooted in a spe-

---

2 Niccolò Machiavelli, *The Prince*, in *The Prince and the Discourses* (New York, The Modern Library College Editions 1950), 32. Hereinafter cited as *The Prince* and *Discourses* respectively.

cific national soil and historic hour, it becomes universal, if not in terms of gratitude, in terms of admiration. Glorious men are the property of mankind but nationally generated.

A leader's glory shines in posterity yet its origins must be present during his lifetime. The events must and do indicate his achievement, his progress against disorder, his mark on history. Glory cannot be granted where fame, honour, and reputation were totally absent.

To Machiavelli, the pursuit of glory is clearly motivated by ambition but is to the advantage of all. Glory as a reward for success is a bond between the great and the ordinary men, those who are bent on making history and those who are the instruments of such political creation. It is the compatibility between the successful results of the intentions of great men and the quality of the life of ordinary citizens thus ensuing that permits glory to perform a politically cohesive role. Such a role is derived from the mutual advantages of the leader and the community. It is here that selfish ambition deviates from public spirited ambition, for whilst the latter demands and offers a unity between exceptional individualism and collective life, the former warrants the subordination of the many to the whim of the one as an end in itself.

As Machiavelli tells us, to gain power is one thing and to gain glory another.[3] Without power there is no possibility for glory, yet mastery of power is only the beginning. To Machiavelli there is a clear distinction between true glory and false glory that results from tyranny, misuse of political power, or its seizure by inappropriate methods.[4] To pursue one's selfish interests in matters of state is ultimately nothing but failure, for by tyrannizing when it could be avoided is not to perceive 'how much glory, how much honor, security, satisfaction, and tranquility of mind' has been forfeited, whilst 'infamy, disgrace, blame, danger, and disquietude' have been incurred instead.[5] 'To esteem private less than public good' is to Machiavelli a good political practice, one of his political ideals.[6] It is also a prerequisite for true glory. It is here that tyrants fail.

---

3 Id.
4 *Discourses*, 142; *The Prince*, 32
5 *Discourses*, 142
6 *The Art of War* in *Chief Works*, II, 572

Success serves a dual function. It salvages one from anonymity during life and then preserves the great man's memory for posterity. The psychological urge to be remembered and, conversely, the fear of oblivion are regarded by Machiavelli as significant human motivations. Fulfillment of this drive does not come about only through glory, for glory is only one kind of remembrance. Thus, though great men deserve and do achieve 'eternal glory'[7] through success, evil political rulers can and do achieve 'eternal infamy.'[8] And though it might be preferable to be remembered positively rather than infamously, if no avenue to glory is available, then men's desire to maintain their names in perpetuity leads them to strive to gain fame 'with blameworthy actions' rather than surrender fame altogether because it cannot be gained by 'praiseworthy deeds.'[9]

Haunted by the fear of oblivion or propelled by a passion for fame, men seek glory in matters of state, yet many err on issues of substance and either lose sight of true glory and its demands, or intentionally opt for fame irrespective of its quality. Men are capable of differentiating the qualities that are praiseworthy and those which deserve blame, and do praise the first and condemn the second, but in action fail to maintain the distinction either knowingly or because of ignorance.[10]

Whatever the pressures of oblivion, whatever the motivating force of fame and the impending dangers of mismanagement of political power, to Machiavelli there clearly exists a simple, unambiguous relationship between success and glory. For Machiavelli, success, appropriately achieved and securing the politically proper ends, brings glory. But because success equals glory and because the glorious are great, achievements and glory are still not the measure of greatness.

The glorious men of history are indeed great men, extraordinary individuals who impose their will upon human destiny within existing permanent limitations. These men are born with talents and abilities superior to those of ordinary men. Granted this initial natural superiority, great men succeed either 'by ability or by good for-

7 *Discourses*, 142
8 Ibid., 145
9 *History of Florence*, in *Chief Works*, III, 1032-3
10 *Discourses*, 142

tune.'[11] Success achieved through ability allows a greater degree of autonomy to the individual in that it reduces his dependence on external factors. With success achieved by good fortune, the reverse holds true. Where the role of external forces is minimized, then clearly such men of great ability when successful owe 'nothing to fortune but the opportunity which gave them matter to be shaped into what form they thought fit ...'[12] Nothing beyond the opportunity and that initial natural ability is derived from the outside world.

It is here that the simple and direct connection between success, glory, and greatness breaks down. For here results, success, in the case of fortune providing only the initial opportunity, are directly dependent on the individual's ability. On the other hand, success achieved totally as a result of fortunate circumstances or where ability plays only a minor role, could obscure the real degree of greatness, for greatness no longer relates directly to the magnitude of success achieved. That is, a man with lesser ability might outshine a man with greater ability.

Not only does success per se not tell the full story of a man's greatness, but failure in no way automatically reflects the absence of ability, though it does not allow for glory. Different circumstances could lead one man to success and another to failure without either having been 'caused by the greater or lesser ability' of the men involved.[13] Neither success nor failure can in and of themselves mirror human greatness or weakness fully. Comprehension of the true dimension of human greatness demands an understanding of the grounds of one's success or failure.

The confrontation of ability and external forces must be examined on the basis of how much or how little, if at all, was left to chance. The quality of a man's talents is best shown when nothing that can be controlled by his power is left outside his jurisdiction. Ability is the exercise of control anywhere and any time that circumstances permit. This presupposes the presence of knowledge, of what can and cannot be controlled, and of how to exercise such control effectively. Such knowledge constitutes the essence of Machiavelli's political the-

11 *The Prince*, 24. See also 20.
12 Ibid., 20
13 Ibid., 17-18

ory and represents the results of his scrutiny of history and experience.[14]

Only from the vantage point of such theoretical penetration of reality and its immutable character can one accurately evaluate the human ability to wield political power. Results alone can disclose only partial truths. Though success is important, the theoretical principles and guidelines of action would be far more crucial.

Machiavelli believes that if human conduct could constantly shift according to the requirements of the times, then success could be permanent. He says, 'I have often reflected that the causes of the success or failure of men depend upon their manner of suiting their conduct to the times.'[15] Elsewhere he states that 'if one could change one's nature with time and circumstances, fortune would never change.'[16] But this is an impossibility because to do so one would have to be able to change human nature, exactly what Machiavelli holds as permanently fixed. Therefore, change of circumstances sooner or later will catch men unprepared. What is more important is that even the highest degree of preparedness and alertness is doomed, for there is an inherent limitation in how far men can prepare themselves, and there are also certain eventualities that cannot be prepared against. In other words, there are two kinds of defeat by external forces: to be confronted by a situation for which one could have prepared but did not; and to be confronted by events one could not possibly have conceived of or having conceived of could do nothing about.

Unpreparedness is a form of theoretical weakness. It is failure to cope with reality when it is possible to do so. Manifestations of such weakness are: repeating past conduct because its past success induces one to assume it a valid mode of action in the present;[17] a trust of hope rather than one's resources;[18] and a pursuit of a middle course of action rather than a more decisive one.[19] Machiavelli rejects the middle course of action as ruinous because it cannot rise to the occa-

14 Ibid., 3; *Discourses*, 101, 103-4
15 *Discourses*, 441
16 *The Prince*, 93
17 Ibid.; *Discourses*, 443
18 *Discourses*, 378
19 Ibid., 184, 362, 527

sion. He draws three distinctions regarding action: the positive, decisive action which he clearly prefers;[20] the middle course of action which he rejects;[21] and the perfect course of action which, though conceivable, cannot be actualized. This latter type of action he calls the 'precise middle course'[22] or the 'just middle course.'[23] Its theoretical perfection warrants an absolute correspondence with the demands of any given situation which, in turn, would succeed in preserving a perfect political order, an 'equilibrium' which would guarantee tranquillity and security.[24] Such a course of action is not possible for it requires the constant modification of human behaviour to an impossible degree. If it were possible, the 'precise middle course' could negate the power of fortune. Such negation would necessitate the anticipation of every single future event. But there is a limit to how far ahead one can anticipate, to what extent one can be liberated from past experience, and what human action can prevent.

Machiavelli does forfeit his notion of the perfect political action. He contents himself with the decisive action, the heroic mode of leadership which maximizes what is humanly possible and which intends to create the best possible political organization doomed to be superseded finally by disorder.

Machiavelli concentrates on the creation of political theory as a guideline to political action aiming at the successful exercise of political control in its maximum possible degree within the prevailing circumstances. The foundations of such theory expressed in terms of prudential maxims are derived from his study of history and experience. Exploring comparatively the successes and failures of great men, Machiavelli establishes a theory of political action and a philosophy of life. His political philosophy claims, in my view, to have embodied that unique understanding of reality, that historical and experiential knowledge which facilitates successful political action by prudentially, decisively, and courageously manipulating one's political resources, primary among them being people, and which knowl-

20 *The Prince*, 94
21 *Discourses*, 184, 362, 527
22 Ibid., 129
23 Ibid., 441
24 Ibid., 129

edge precludes failure as far as human capabilities allow. It means to leave nothing to chance that could be controlled.

It is crucial in this context to appreciate Machiavelli's concern with such knowledge as one that goes beyond success. His interest lies in a mode of action which discloses the presence or absence of the requisite knowledge irrespective of results. Results obviously have an imminent political relevance and significance. But only results yielded under the influence of prudential action guided by a knowledge of reality can be of lasting importance and use; only such results can serve as models of political practice.

For example, Machiavelli claims that resorting to divine authority is a method for strengthening political authority and is something which has been practised by the most remarkable of lawgivers.[25] Two cases in point are Lycurgus and Solon. Both resorted to religion. But Lycurgus, besides resorting to religion, showed his political acumen by organizing the government of Sparta in a manner permitting king, nobles, and people to share power.[26] Solon failed to do so and established a popular government which turned out to be of short duration.[27] In Machiavelli's view, both lawgivers acted with a realistic evaluation of the political utility of religion. Yet reality warranted further implementation of political maxims of prudence. It demanded the establishment of specific institutions to maximize what opportunities resorting to religion had opened to the respective lawgivers. Lycurgus knew this and so practised and succeeded. His institutional arrangements had created a government that lasted 'over eight hundred years in the most perfect tranquility, and reflected infinite glory upon' him.[28] Solon failed to utilize fully what his uses of religion made available to him.

Another example is that of Romulus and Numa. Romulus established Rome and is praised for his valour.[29] Yet Romulus' rule suffered from a certain insufficiency.[30] He ignored religion. Numa did

25 Ibid., 146-7
26 Ibid., 115
27 Id.
28 Id.
29 *Discourses*, 172, 174
30 Ibid., 145-6

not, and of the two Rome is indebted more to Numa than to Romulus.[31] Though Numa had introduced the vital feature of religion into the political life of Rome, a feature ignored by Romulus, he erred in his turn for he relied exclusively on the power of religion and provided no adequate institutional structures, thus leaving himself and his people vulnerable to chance.[32] Rome still remains indebted to him for introducing religion, and from him we learn the need for religion. But to imitate him precisely, that is, to rely only on religion, is still to be at the mercy of chance. From Romulus we learn of courage, need for violence, and concern with the general good as opposed to gratification of the leader's own ambition.[33] We also learn about his negligence of religion. Thus, neither Numa, who relies too much on chance, nor Romulus, who is deficient in prudence though not as much as Numa, is to be imitated. What is exemplary is a combination of valour and prudence.[34] Neither Numa nor Romulus achieved such a combination. Yet Machiavelli points more favourably to Romulus,[35] for indeed it is easier to rectify his deficiency than Numa's error.

Another case in point is that of Sparta and Rome. Sparta achieved longevity because of Lycurgus' political organization. But Sparta had not provided for expansion.[36] Venice was in the same predicament.[37] The longevity of the small state depends substantially on chance. Only good fortune can save it from the need for expansion, which its size precludes as a possibility. Even if saved from the need to expand, the small state is still subject to internal erosion resulting from the ill-effects of domestic and external tranquility.[38] Thus, the small state depends excessively on chance and also creates the conditions for its own disintegration. Rome is the preferable model; no middle course between Rome and any other republic can be found.[39] There-

31 Ibid., 146-7
32 Ibid., 174
33 Ibid., 139
34 Ibid., 174
35 Id.
36 *Discourses*, 128
37 Id.
38 *Discourses*, 129
39 Ibid., 129-30

fore, it becomes a choice between the real advantages of Rome's em-
pire-building, and the deceptive advantages of small states like Sparta
or Venice.

What this comparative analysis of Sparta, the small state, and Rome,
the empire, demonstrates, is that Lycurgus, though superior to Solon,
still erred by allowing Sparta to be unprepared against what should
have been expected and prepared for. Sparta's longevity is more the
result of good fortune than Lycurgus' political skill. Much was again
left to chance that should have been under political control. The inadequacies of Romulus, Numa, Lycurgus, and Solon are not identical. They vary substantially in degree. Rome becomes the ideal model
not in its actual historical experience but in a theoretic synthesis
whereby the best of what has occurred is supplemented by what
should have happened. The historic record is rectified.

Case study after case study reveals for Machiavelli the constant and
irreducible struggle between human action and chance over man's
destiny. According to Machiavelli, it is true that no socio-political
organization can and will endure forever. It is equally true that there
are certain courses of action which could eliminate its decline and
failure due to human error, and which in turn could lead to its relative permanence and success. The possession of the theoretical guidelines of such courses of action reveals a man's greatness and true stature irrespective of results. The most fortunate manifestation of such
knowledge is successful political action, which for Machiavelli is tantamount to the founding or the reforming of a political society. And
if the opportunity for action does not offer itself (thus condemning
this knowledge to inertia), or if it does and the action fails (by chance
but not due to error), the greatness of the possessor of this knowledge is not lessened, though he will be denied glory. Machiavelli argues in favour of prudential control of things political, as opposed
to leaving them to chance. Knowledge of how to do this is greatness
itself.

Concurrent with Machiavelli's references to history and the work
of historians runs Machiavelli's own interpretation of history, his own
analysis of events and issues. For example, he begins the *History of
Florence* by informing us that the historians he was to use as his pro-
totypes, 'two very good historians,' turn out, after careful examina-

tion of their works, to be inadequate.[40] Machiavelli intends to remedy their inadequacies. Elsewhere he says that 'Livius as well as all other historians affirm that nothing is more uncertain and inconstant than the multitude ...'[41] And he continues by undertaking to deny this 'against the accusation of all writers ...'[42] Again Machiavelli tells us that many authors, among them such eminent ones as Plutarch and Livius, claim that the Roman empire was more indebted to good fortune than merit; and Machiavelli proclaims, 'I do not share that opinion at all,' and proceeds to state his case.[43] Thus, his position runs contrary to the established view of historians. Each of his historical examinations ultimately is resolved into a principle, aphorism, or rule which reflects Machiavelli's concluding interpretation of the event or issue and not necessarily a restatement of what is already accepted. Even when the great men are recalled by name, Machiavelli does not say that Moses, Cyrus, etc. are regarded as the greatest. He rather says, 'I regard as the greatest ...'[44] The examples of Romulus, Numa, Solon, and Lycurgus are again instances of such reinterpretation.

Concerning in particular the study of the past as opposed to the study of contemporary experience, Machiavelli says that the past can never be wholly known; the sheer passage of time renders the past less amenable to perfect knowledge than the present.[45] One of the reasons why the past is partly lost is because 'very frequently writers conceal' historical reality.[46] As for the present, we 'ourselves are either actors or spectators,' which helps us to gain a more perfect knowledge of it.[47]

He is also aware that historians might have to conceal their true position out of fear, and that as such, history should not be taken at face value but read critically.[48] Historic truth and knowledge of

40 *History of Florence*, 1031
41 *Discourses*, 260
42 Id.
43 *Discourses*, 277
44 *The Prince*, 20
45 *Discourses*, 271, 273
46 Ibid., 271
47 Ibid., 271-2
48 Ibid., 142-3

reality through experience are not easily come by. They are concealed, partially lost; they require relentless, persistent, and systematic examination if one is to discover their secrets. Indeed such a
search for truth extends over a 'course of many years.'[49] Machiavelli
obviously sees himself as possessing such knowledge. By means of it,
he feels he can distinguish appearance from reality and consequently
become a judge of human greatness.[50]

In a discussion of the two methods by which a private citizen may
become a prince, namely, through great ability and good fortune,[51]
Machiavelli mentions two cases, those of Sforza (a case of ability),
and of Borgia (a case of good fortune). The discussion on Borgia centres on the fact of failure in spite of ability.[52] Borgia does come to
power through good fortune, but he fails through a misfortune that
no human ability could prevent. For even a combination of valour
and prudence can be defeated.[53]

Borgia had adopted every measure and had done everything 'that
a prudent and capable man could do to establish himself firmly in a
state that the arms and the favours of others had given him.'[54] In
spite of failure, he still displayed ability. His knowledge of the right
course of action was frustrated only by events he could neither foresee nor control, namely 'that at his father's death he would be dying
himself.'[55] True, Borgia did not foresee his failure, but this by itself
does not tarnish his ability. The cause of his failure was not lack of
foresight but external circumstances. And the only accusation that
can be brought against him, the only error that he committed was
'that in the creation of Julius II he made a bad choice.'[56]

Failure, when it is due to the premature termination of excellence,
only reveals the tragic predicament of men and the ruthless omnipo-

The Prince, 3
Discourses, 182
The Prince, 20. See also 24.
Ibid., 24. Borgia failed 'through no fault of his own but only by the most
extraordinary malignity of fortune.'
Discourses, 174
The Prince, 24
Ibid., 29
Id.

tence of fortune. It does not diminish the stature of a great man, one who knows how to act politically. Precisely because fortune is omnipotent, results cannot be the basis for evaluation of political ability. That fortune, in the eyes of Machiavelli, often appears as omnipotent, we should have no doubt.[57]

In discussing Castruccio's life, Machiavelli indicates that it reveals the power of fortune beyond and above the capacities of prudence.[58] Machiavelli tells us how fortune 'hostile to his fame, when it was time to give him life, took it from him and broke off those plans that he for a long time before had been intending to put into effect ...'[59] And the way Castruccio contracts his mortal illness does not indicate error, for he did what he had done in the past under similar circumstances.[60] Castruccio in full awareness of his impending death speaks of fortune as the admitted 'arbiter of all human things ...'[61] Castruccio decries the absence of sufficient judgment on his part to understand the machinations of fortune early enough so as to confine his political activities to the creation of a state more secure than what he now leaves behind.[62] He also decries the lack of time through which he could achieve all that he wanted to.[63] Not to fail, as Castruccio obviously does fail, is possible by attempting a much more moderate task of political leadership. Castruccio's statements are deceptive because they suggest that a viable alternative is to engage in consciously limited political goals. But the greatness that propels the individual to plunge into the vast task of its implementation precludes such re-

---

57 Indicative but not exhaustive are the following: 'I repeat then, as an incontrovertible truth, proved by all history, that men may second Fortune, but cannot oppose her; they may develop her designs, but cannot defeat them.' *Discourses*, 383. See also *Tercets on Fortune*, in *Chief Works*, II, 745-9; *The Life of Castruccio Castracani of Lucca*, in *Chief Works*, II, 534, 552-3; *The Prince*, 24; *Discourses*, 174. Machiavelli's words on fortune in *The Prince*, 91, 94, in no way refute the tenor of the above references.

58 *The Life of Castruccio*, 534

59 Ibid., 552

60 Id.

61 Ibid., 553

62 Id.

63 Id.

straining. To know that one might fail need not force one to shrink from the task ahead and veer to something less ambitious and more secure.

What Castruccio needs is time to fulfill his greatness. For the very presence of greatness commands him to go beyond the politically limited. The message Machiavelli delivers through Castruccio's story is not simply one of the power of fortune over prudence, but of the presence of greatness which once activated is subsequently thwarted prematurely by fortune. Machiavelli's writing on Castruccio is his single most eloquent statement on failure through fortune's malevolence despite which a man's greatness can still shine. This becomes apparent in the concluding passage of the story. 'He lived forty-four years and in all fortunes he acted the prince.'[64] This alone is a sign of greatness, for Machiavelli insists that 'a truly great man is ever the same under all circumstances ...'[65]

Machiavelli continues praising Castruccio by comparing him to Philip of Macedon and to Scipio of Rome, who also died at the age of forty-four. In comparison, Machiavelli finds Castruccio not inferior to them; indeed, he appears to be even superior to them, for Machiavelli says that 'without doubt he would have surpassed both if instead of Lucca he had had for his native country Macedonia or Rome.'[66] The full meaning of fortune's power is revealed to us in this last statement. Not only does Castruccio die prematurely but also his greatness warranted a vehicle of expression superior to Lucca, something which fortune denied him from the very beginning.

It is in this complex area that Machiavelli's notion of greatness as knowledge and success, glory, and failure meet. It is here that the people at large are denied the role of ultimate judge and such privilege is extended exclusively to the theorist, he who has the knowledge to determine in others its presence or absence and its prudential application or reckless abandon. It is in this sense that Machiavelli can speak of men who know how to govern states, as opposed to 'those who have the right to govern, but lack the knowledge.'[67] Ma-

4 Ibid., 559
5 *Discourses,* 500
6 *The Life of Castruccio,* 559
7 *Discourses,* 102

chiavelli's whole political philosophy is his claim to possess such knowledge, which he defines as the 'real knowledge of history,' the true sense or the spirit of it.[68]

To Machiavelli this kind of historical knowledge is tantamount to a full understanding of reality. If acted upon whenever the opportunity presents itself, one might succeed, if circumstances so permit, then that individual will be glorious. If circumstances do not appear to be so benevolent, then the individual is barred from being glorious but not from being recognized as great. And finally, if no opportunity is available, if all his knowledge is condemned to remain theory, it need not remain unrecognized. For where action is ruled out, the possessor of that special knowledge is still under its compulsion; and where action is precluded, then, as Machiavelli puts it, 'it is the duty of an honest man to teach others that good which the malignity of the times and of fortune has prevented his doing himself ...'[69]

Elsewhere Machiavelli states that even theoretical writings of politics can bring glory to men, 'when unable to form a republic in reality, [they] have done it in writing, as Aristotle, Plato, and many others, who have wished to show the world that if they have not founded a free government, as did Solon and Lycurgus, they have failed not through their ignorance but through their impotence for putting it into practice.'[70] Machiavelli himself falls into this category. And though glory is never to be underestimated as a motivating force that activates human excellence, it must be remembered that success that goes beyond mere chance is the crucial issue. Failure, as long as it results from anything but ignorance, does not affect the stature of a great man, though it will never grant him glory.

Machiavelli himself, ostracized from the corridors of power, in despair and loneliness, remained faithful to his notion of greatness manifested at least in a theoretical treatise. Though he might prefer to see a theorist as prince or a prince who becomes a theorist, he sees a third alternative, that of the counsellor-theorist. His political philo-

68 Ibid., 104
69 Ibid., 274-5
70 *A Discourse on Remodeling the Government of Florence,* in *Chief Works,* I, 114

sophy being action oriented allows him to settle for less than full power if he can have the ear of the powerful. This attitude once again reaffirms that however genuine his concern with success and glory, however pivotal they might be in his thought, beneath them rests the more significant issue of political knowledge, the true and sole basis for greatness and political excellence.

Machiavelli believed that he was reviving the grandeur of antiquity; yet in reality he does not echo the past pure and simple. Standing between a dying, if not already dead, past and an as yet unborn political tomorrow of which he could have only vague premonitions, he speaks a language that of necessity remains enigmatic, intriguing, and incomplete. He speaks the language of political transition, the very substance of which prevents full articulation and lucidity. It is in this language that rests the secret of the perennial fascination with his thought and its perplexing quality.

Obsessed with antiquity, confronted with the political degeneration of his world, Machiavelli could only become at best a heretic, a reinterpreter of past glories and their inner meaning. Only the pronouncements of Hobbes would establish modernity by fully disassociating from the past, intentionally ignoring it, whereby the remnants of the heroic and the lure of glory still lingering in Machiavelli would disappear, where the knowledgeable and the ignorant would no longer be meaningful categories, and where the fear of sudden and violent death presumably would force men to understand the rationality and consequent need of trading freedom for security, power for peace. Thus, the market logic dethrones fortune, rules out the heroic, and ushers in the pattern of bourgeois life.

Machiavelli's notion of theory and its emphasis on action we cannot but heed. Yet its very content must be scrutinized carefully, for in spite of the fact that its author prides himself on possessing a full grasp of reality and an immunity to appearance, it is the deceptive character of appearance always to manifest itself as reality.

Machiavelli insists that to decipher reality and avert illusion, one must examine what men do. In order 'to go to the real truth of the matter than to its imagination,' we must examine what is done.[71] Men might be what they do but Machiavelli's failing was that he took

The Prince, 56

for granted that what men do must and does reveal what is permanent, eternally valid, and immutable in them, hence a fixed concept
of human nature. Whenever we are to examine what men do, which
we must, we should always bear in mind that human behaviour mani-
fests itself in and through socio-economic structures. To forget the
presence and role of concrete social conditions is to enter the laby-
rinth of illusion in the name of reality, exactly what Machiavelli
wished to avoid most and believed he had escaped.

FIVE

Necessity in the Beginnings of Cities

HARVEY C. MANSFIELD, JR

In the first of his *Discourses on Livy* Machiavelli considers 'what have universally been the beginnings of any city whatever.' In doing so he brings up the question of how much men can live by their own choice in a regime constructed to produce a certain way of life and how much they must be ruled by the necessity of their site. 'Virtue,' he says, 'is seen to be greater where choice has less authority.'[1] But he says nothing of God or religion, even though they are connected to the beginnings of cities; for men who believe they are ruled by God or gods always trace their connection to divinity through their beginnings or the beginnings of their cities. Thus Machiavelli discusses necessity and choice rather than religion, and this choice we need to understand. To understand it, we must suppose it no accident that Machiavelli begins the *Discourses* with a discourse on beginnings. The difficulties to be overcome by his rhetoric in persuading us to adopt his 'new ways and orders' reflect and reveal the problem faced by the founder of a city: Machiavelli's literary problem is the same as the fundamental political problem.

For some recent scholars of Machiavelli, the literary problem of the *Discourses* is the question of when it was written. Nobody knows for

Discourses on the First Ten Books of Titus Livy (hereafter *Discourses*), I, 1 (I, 127). Numbers in parentheses refer to Niccolò Machiavelli, *Opere Complete*, 8 vols (Milan 1960-7).

sure, since Machiavelli did not say when he wrote the *Discourses* and the date of first publication (1531, posthumously) gives no clue to an exact dating of the writing. *The Prince,* which seems to have been completed in 1513, contains an allusion which seems to refer to the *Discourses* as if it were completed;[2] yet the *Discourses* contains comments upon events that occurred as late as 1517.[3] There is no manuscript evidence on this matter to hinder conjecture, and even the one letter which explicitly refers to *The Prince* as if it were complete, is nevertheless ambiguous.[4] Moreover, Machiavelli claimed to present everything he knows only, but equally, in *The Prince* and the *Discourses.*[5] Since they were written at about the same time, and since the former seems favourable to princes and the latter to republics, one must conclude either that Machiavelli presented everything he knew in two ways or that he changed his thought entirely very rapidly. With this much scope for discovery, and with competition on a common problem, these scholars have exercised their faculties to the utmost and produced impressive results in a body of controversial literature that is still growing in size.[6]

One scholar has used the techniques of textual criticism to suggest emendations of what he considers to be Machiavelli's loose insertions in favour of what he considers to be Machiavelli's settled intention.[7] Another has used Machiavelli's references to Livy to form a sequence which qualifies the stated plan of the *Discourses* and reveals two stages of composition, the first when Machiavelli had one conception and the second when he had another.[8] A third scholar has found by

2 *The Prince,* 2 (I, 15). Federico Chabod, 'Sulla Composizione de "Il Principe" di Niccolò Machiavelli,' *Archivum Romanum,* XI (1927), 330-83

3 Felix Gilbert, 'The Structure and Composition of Machiavelli's *Discorsi,*' *Journal of the History of Ideas,* XIV (1953), 139; L.J. Walker, ed., *The Discourses of Niccolò Machiavelli,* 2 vols (London & New Haven 1950), I, 40-5

4 Machiavelli has 'composed a little work' but is sending it to his friends for comment; letter of 10 Dec. 1513 (VI, 304).

5 *The Prince,* epistle dedicatory; *Discourses,* epistle dedicatory

6 It is well summarized by Sergio Bertelli (I, 109-16).

7 Hans Baron, 'The *Principe* and the Puzzle of the Date of the *Discorsi,*' *Bibliotheque d'Humanisme et Renaissance,* XVIII (1956), 405-28

8 Felix Gilbert, 'The Structure and Composition of Machiavelli's *Discorsi*'

study of Machiavelli's sources that Machiavelli waited until 1515 to compose book I of the *Discourses*, so that he could appropriate an important part of it from the translation of the sixth book of Polybius made by an obscure, itinerant Greek.[9] But no report can convey the subtlety of the arguments merely by giving their results. They must be seen to be believed, for they gain solidity by building on one another and against one another.[10]

Therefore, when one decides not to join this controversy, he may think himself obliged to explain. It would be easy to say that some are interested in the dating of Machiavelli's works, and others in his meaning. This is insufficient because those interested in the dating are also interested in the meaning; they are not disputing over bibliographical detail. Indeed, their inquiries begin by taking note of obscurity in Machiavelli's meaning, state as their purpose the clarification of his meaning, and then conclude with a statement of clarification. But to see the starting point of their inquiries is enough for our purpose. We must have, Felix Gilbert says, 'otherwise inexplicable contradictions in our source material.'[11] When contradictions appear in Machiavelli's text that cannot be explained in the text or on the basis of the text, then we must seek explanation or elucidation in what Machiavelli did not say. For example, Gilbert finds a contradiction between the 'political realism' of *The Prince* and the 'political idealism' of the *Discourses*, and by means of his researches on the

J.H. Hexter, 'Seyssel, Machiavelli and Polybius VI: The Mystery of the Missing Translation,' *Studies in the Renaissance*, III (1956), 75-96

Baron, 'The *Principe* and the Puzzle of the Date of the *Discorsi*,' 406-8 and 'Machiavelli: The Republican Citizen and the Author of "The Prince,"' *English Historical Review*, LXXVI (1961), 217n; Hexter, 'Seyssel, Machiavelli and Polybius VI: The Mystery of the Missing Translation,' 95; Gilbert, 'The Structure and Composition of Machiavelli's *Discorsi*,' 152; Gennaro Sasso, 'Intorno alla Composizione dei "Discorsi" de Niccolò Machiavelli,' *Giornale Storico della Letteratura Italiana*, CXXXV (1958), 257

Gilbert, 'The Structure and Composition of Machiavelli's *Discorsi*,' 143, 150; 'loose structure' according to Baron, 'Seyssel, Machiavelli and Polybius VI: The Mystery of the Missing Translation,' 406, 413, 419; J.H. Whitfield, 'Discourses on Machiavelli VII, Gilbert, Hexter and Baron,' *Italian Studies*, XIII (1958), 43-6; Gennaro Sasso, *Studi sul Machiavelli* (Naples 1967), 112-13

dating of those works, concludes that it can be explained as 'an intellectual development,' not as 'an expression of a tension in Machiavelli's mind'[12] (not to mention a consistent intention). Not only this conclusion but the motive for the researches depend on the finding that Machiavelli's political realism contradicted his political idealism in the 'source material.' The motive depends on the finality of this contradiction in Machiavelli's text; that is, it depends on the failure of every attempt to resolve the contradiction in the text. After these failures it became necessary to resort to the 'intellectual development' unavowed by Machiavelli for an explanation. Gilbert's starting point, then, was a certain understanding of Machiavelli's meaning which was definitive as regards the text, and his conclusion was a better understanding.

What is omitted in this procedure is the attempt to clarify the obscurities and contradictions in Machiavelli's meaning – whose existence everyone admits – under the hypothesis that they were deliberately intended as rhetoric. This hypothesis, even if seemingly remote from the truth, takes precedence over an attempt to establish Machiavelli's meaning from the 'otherwise inexplicable contradictions.' It would forestall an appeal to sources outside Machiavelli for the purpose of understanding him, and it would eliminate the need to apologize for the unsystematic character of his thinking.

Obviously, Machiavelli was a penetrating and sagacious thinker, but obviously too, his writings contain many inconsistencies and errors, not only in a comparison of *The Prince* and the *Discourses,* not only in widely separated parts of these works that might constitute different 'stages of composition,' but even on the same page of these and other works. Perhaps this makes him a poet rather than a philosopher – if a poet is a man whose thought is held in the grip of his imagination, instead of the reverse; and if a philosopher is defined, in contrast to Machiavelli's favourites, Lucretius and Xenophon, as a man who intends 'to outline a philosophical system' or 'to introduce new philosophical terms.'[13] But what is it to be systematic?

12 Gilbert, 'The Structure and Composition of Machiavelli's *Discorsi,*' 156
13 Felix Gilbert, *Machiavelli and Guicciardini: Politics and History in Sixteenth-Century Florence* (Princeton, NJ 1965), 193. Ridolfi says Machiavelli was a

A strictly systematic book would consider every subject once in one place, and to be sure of this result, would deduce every proposition from distinct and irreducible propositions or axioms 'in a geometrical manner.' Spinoza's *Ethics* is almost such a book. An author can afford to be systematic in this way if his audience is open to every new opinion and not partial to the opinions it holds. In this case, strict system is the most economical way of presenting one's thoughts, for one could speak to others as to oneself. But if the audience is partial to its own opinions, and more retentive than receptive, then rhetoric is required for introducing new thoughts. Rhetoric is the deliberate distortion of system in deference to the opinions of the writer's audience. Nowadays 'systematic' is often said loosely to describe an author who looks consistent. But looks consistent to whom? – to the casual or to the careful reader? An author can be consistent without being systematic when his distortions, his apparent errors and inconsistencies, are made deliberately with an eye to his audience. This author has his own order; he treats each subject 'in its place,' as Machiavelli says. His order is part of his rhetoric; so he only hints at it, and sometimes does not seem to follow the plan that he does set for himself, as Machiavelli does not seem to follow the plan he gives at the end of the first chapter of the *Discourses*. This author is subtler and more difficult than the systematic author because the purpose of his rhetoric must be discerned through his rhetoric.

It may seem arbitrary to attempt to distinguish an author's rhetorical statements from his true intention, but in truth it is difficult and uncertain. If the attempt is not made, one must assume that the author did not use rhetoric. This assumption – that every speaker is 'sincere' and every statement literally intended – is truly arbitrary. Machiavelli tells us, indirectly of course, that it does not apply to himself. He says in the preface to book I of the *Discourses* that he is bringing 'new ways and orders,' and in the epistle dedicatory, that he deserves to be loaded with honours by men who deserve to be

poet, and 'there can be no real wickedness [tristizia] where there is poetry.'
R. Ridolfi, *The Life of Niccolò Machiavelli,* C. Grayson tr. (Chicago 1963), 13, 107, 168, 252

princes. In the twenty-sixth chapter we are told that he who becomes a new prince must make everything anew, so that 'no rank, no order, no condition, no wealth is held by anyone that is not acknowledged as from you.' Then how does Machiavelli make his way as a potential new prince or an adviser of potential new princes?

In a moment of doubt, Ernst Cassirer once said that Machiavelli was 'perhaps one of the most sincere political writers,'[14] and in a moment of sincerity, Machiavelli said the following about rising from low to high fortune: 'I do not believe that anyone can be found placed in low fortune who arrived at great power only by open force and ingenuously, but indeed it has been done by fraud alone ...'[15] If Machiavelli is a new prince, or an inspirer of new princes, he must make his way by fraud at least in part, and since he himself is unarmed, wholly by fraud. Indeed, Machiavelli goes on to say that fraud 'has always been necessary to use by those who wish to rise from small beginnings to sublime heights.'

What then is rhetoric but written fraud, when the object of the writer is to rise in the world by the reputation or influence of his writings? In this chapter (II, 13) Machiavelli gives three examples of fraud in rising from small fortune to great as given by two writers, Xenophon and Livy, concerning two princes and the Roman republic. Then he exposes a technique of fraud in writing used by Livy to describe the Roman fraud, which is to put the writer's criticism of a powerful enemy in the mouth of an enemy of that enemy. Machiavelli seems not only to comprehend the writer's rhetoric under fraud, but to have it in mind more than any other kind of fraud.[16]

He also invites us to direct this reasoning to himself. At the end of the preface he says that he undertakes to induce men away from the error of believing that the politics of the ancients cannot be imitated today: 'And although this undertaking may be difficult, nevertheless, aided by those who have encouraged me to take up this burden, I believe it may be carried in such a way that a brief journey will be

14 *The Myth of the State* (Garden City, NY 1955), 149
15 *Discourses*, II, 13 (I, 311)
16 On this chapter see Leo Strauss, *Thoughts on Machiavelli* (Glencoe, Ill. 1958), 138-9.

left to some other to carry it to its destination.'[17] This is as plain a statement as one could have that Machiavelli has concealed his intention in the *Discourses,* leaving it to be discovered by 'some other' who can complete or execute it.

Machiavelli retains his distinction between the new prince and his adviser, between the man who has a short journey to the destination and the man who first takes up the burden and carries it most of the way; but this distinction is the essence of his rhetoric. If he could accomplish his undertaking 'at one stroke,' he would not need to advise others to adopt his 'new ways and orders.' But his undertaking consists precisely in overcoming the prejudice of his times that ancient politics cannot be imitated. Princes need advisers and advisers need princes for the same reason, because prejudices need to be overcome; they cannot be overcome except by fraud practised upon both the prince and his people, for open and ingenuous force cannot succeed unless it is stronger than the existing order and all those whose rank, condition, and wealth are owed to the existing order. Open and ingenuous force is the weapon of the existing order; it keeps the existing order, rather than some other, in existence; it constitutes the existing order. Fraud creates and conceals a force against the existing order that does not seem to oppose it openly because the fraud does not seem to challenge the power of the ruling prince or government. Such fraud must be conceived and perpetrated by someone who does not seem to profit from it directly, or who is content to wait for that highest glory which comes only after one's lifetime, an adviser who is willing to remain an adviser and not become his own prince. Machiavelli, holding 'the office of a good man' and in his 'natural desire' to bring 'common benefit to everybody,' wishes to offer a teaching useful to humanity, not a mere fraud for the purpose of self-promotion. But his teaching includes a new praise of fraud and cannot succeed without the use of fraud and without bringing glory to himself.[18]

With the understanding that Machiavelli's rhetoric is the language of the weak to the strong, of the weak gaining in strength to the

---

17 *Discourses,* I, preface; cf. I, 9 on Agis and Cleomenes.
18 *Discourses,* I, preface; II, preface; III, 1, 8, 35, 37

unwary strong, one might begin to see the difference between *The Prince* and the *Discourses* by considering the different rhetorical situations indicated in the dedicatory epistles of those works, the former dedicated to an actual prince, and the latter to two men who deserve to be princes but are not. The reference to 'reasoning about republics' in *The Prince* and the references to *The Prince* in the *Discourses* might then be understood as cross references by a writer who has put 'everything he knows' into two books from the two essential points of view and who, knowing the malignity of his times and the strength of his enemies, and eager for the glory of fame after his lifetime, remains indifferent to the exact dating of those books.[19]

We can now consider the first chapter of the *Discourses* with the hypothesis that Machiavelli, in seeking to gain adherents to his 'new ways and orders,' will not say everything about one topic in one place, but will develop his meaning through the whole work. Although he begins with the topic of beginnings of cities, he will not give the final, unqualified truth about them in his first statement, especially in view of the connection between the topic of beginnings and writers who wish to propagate a new conception of politics. In fact, we find that Machiavelli returns to the topic of beginnings later in the *Discourses* to propound his celebrated thesis that states can survive only by periodic reversions to their beginnings.[20] Again Machiavelli's rhetoric duplicates his political teaching; he returns to the topic of beginnings to teach that states must return to their beginnings. After examining the text of the first chapter, we must see how it is provisional and why it is necessary to return to the topic and the events of the beginnings of cities.

According to the chapter title, the first chapter is about the beginnings of all cities and of Rome. It is not explicitly about the beginnings of man simply, like the Book of Genesis; but, as we shall see, Machiavelli seems to imply that man's political beginning, rather than his creation by God, is the beginning that rules his life. The first sentence of the chapter distinguishes between the beginning of the city

---

19 *The Prince*, 2; *Discourses*, II, 1; III, 19, 42; see Strauss, *Thoughts on Machiavelli*, ch.1.

20 *Discourses*, III, 1, 8, 22; cf. I, 2, 17

of Rome, on the one hand, and its legislators and how it was ordered, on the other. The discussion in the first chapter moves from the kind of beginning Rome had to the virtue of legislators as shown first in the choice of site and second in the ordering of the laws. As a whole it justifies the distinction between the beginnings and the regime, because it shows that at the beginning, the legislators of a city cannot determine its regime or how it will be ordered.

'Intending first to discuss the birth of Rome, I say,' says Machiavelli, 'that all cities are built either by men native to the place where they are built or by foreigners.'[21] What is the importance of this difference? Considering Machiavelli's examples, we see that Athens and Venice were begun by natives gathering together to resist attack, Athens under Theseus and Venice under no single legislator. A city may be built by natives whether they build 'by themselves or under someone who has greater authority among them.' When we come to cities built by foreigners, we find that some were built by free men and others by 'those who depend on others.' Examples of the latter are colonies built by 'the Roman people,' Alexandria built by Alexander for the sake of his own glory, and Florence built 'by soldiers of Sulla or perhaps by inhabitants of the mountains of Fiesole.' By contrast, free men build cities when forced to abandon their native land and find a new seat, and either inhabit cities which they find in the lands they have acquired, like Moses, or build anew, like Aeneas. Free men may be either 'under a prince' like Moses or Aeneas, or 'by themselves'; here again Machiavelli expresses indifference to the regime. He then drops the discussion of native and foreign builders until the end of the chapter, when the difference reappears in order to be dismissed: 'Whoever examines, then, the building of Rome, if Aeneas is taken for his first progenitor, will put her among those cities built by foreigners; if Romulus, among those built by men native to the place; but in any case, he will see that she had a free beginning without depending on anyone ...'

Men make a free beginning not by virtue of the regime or form of government but by not being dependent on others. Machiavelli uses the distinction between native and foreign builders or legislators to introduce a different distinction between peoples with a free begin-

21 *Discourses*, I, 1 (I, 125)

ning and those that begin dependent on others. Surprisingly, he at
first identifies the free beginning of a city as a kind of foreign rather
than native beginning. The foreign builder either conquers or builds
anew, and thus his people does not depend on the prior or native
inhabitants for their beginning. But the native inhabitants, he has
said, build their own city in self-defence against foreign enemies, and
therefore, it would seem, they build to avoid becoming dependent
on others.

Moreover, natives as well as foreigners have to move in order to
found a city, according to Machiavelli's own account. Athens was
built 'under the authority of Theseus' by a scattered population, and
the Venetians had to move, as we learn in the *Florentine Histories,*
from fertile lands around Padua and Aquileia to make their new
home in a swamp. Leaving – if not leaving the old site, at least leaving the old ways and orders – seems to be characteristic of all beginnings. Machiavelli is reticent about the reasons that these men may
have had for leaving their native lands, but we may supply the defect
from his other writings and from other places in the *Discourses.* The
Venetians are said here to have come together 'because of the coming of new barbarians after the decline of the Roman empire.' In the
Florentine Histories we learn that the Venetians not only left their
old homes; they were in fact the former inhabitants of Aquileia and
Padua driven out by Attila King of the Huns, who burned their cities
and many others besides, and who refrained from destroying Rome
only at the Pope's request.[22] In *The Prince* we are told not that
Athens was built by its scattered inhabitants under the authority of
Theseus, as here, but that Theseus had to find the Athenians dis-
persed in order to demonstrate his virtue in acquiring or founding a
new kingdom.[23] In this chapter, again, Moses is said to have built a
city by conquering one when the people under him was forced to
abandon its native country; later it appears that Moses killed the former inhabitants of Syria (or 'countless men'), seized their property,

22 *Florentine Histories,* I, 3, 29. Respect for the pope did not prevent Attila from
killing Bleda, his brother, in order to be sole ruler; but since he left Italy, this
respect did prevent him from founding an Italian city after the example of
Romulus. *Discourses,* I, 9, 18

23 *The Prince,* 6, 26

and set up a new kingdom with the new name of Judea.[24] Aeneas was of course forced to leave Troy, although Machiavelli does not mention it. Thus, leaving is the result of being forced out, and both 'natives' and 'foreigners' may be forced out – of their homes or their names if not their land.

The distinction between native and foreign beginnings with regard to freedom does not survive an inspection of the examples that Machiavelli brings up to illustrate it. Rome, he concludes, had a free beginning regardless of the nativity of its 'first progenitor,' who was either the native Romulus or the foreigner Aeneas. Whether the first legislator was native or foreign does not matter because he must be both. As a native who builds anew and reorders the city completely for the sake of self-defence, he makes himself a foreigner to the old ways of that city. As a foreigner he makes himself the first native of a new regime. Having been first in war and hence first in peace, such a founder easily makes himself first in the hearts of his new countrymen. Contrary to Machiavelli's first statement but consistent with his intention, native beginnings can be free beginnings. To see them as such, we must understand that natives build their city to become foreigners to their enemies, while foreigners become natives by leaving their former native land and starting again.

One may suspect that Machiavelli stresses the foreignness of free beginnings not to favour the pretensions of the adventurer or the conqueror (he does not deny them), but to make a deeper point. A beginning is a leaving, not an arriving; it is leaving blasted hopes, not arriving to a hope fulfilled. Though Machiavelli mentions Moses and the city he built, he does not mention the promised land toward which Moses led his people; he does not mention God or the gods in this chapter. Machiavelli does not give Moses a special status as founder here, but in *The Prince* he calls him 'the mere executor of the things that were ordered by God' and the pupil of God in one chapter, so that we know he is aware of his claim to special status, and rudely cancels that status in another chapter, so that we know he rejects it.[25] Moses merely combines the religious aura of Aeneas (the son of a goddess) and perhaps the religious laws of Numa with

24 *Discourses*, II, 8; III, 30
25 *The Prince*, 6, 26

the ruthlessness of Romulus, who killed his own brother in order to found a city by himself.[26]

In this chapter the clearest allusion to Christianity is a remark about Florence, one of the two cities said to have begun depending on others, 'because (whether built by the soldiers of Sulla or perhaps by the inhabitants of the mountains of Fiesole, who, trusting in the long peace which was born in the world under Octavian, took refuge to live in the plain by the Arno) she was built under the Roman empire, and could not at her beginnings make other advances than those which the courtesy of the prince allowed her.'[27] The art of this sentence is to suggest an ambiguous source of protection and dependence, the prince who was son of Caesar or son of God.[28] Although silent about religion in this chapter, Machiavelli implies a conclusion about the promised land and the city of God; for the distinction between native and foreign beginnings leads to the question of the scope and use of human choice. Whether native or foreign, a true beginning is a free beginning; and a free beginning is an independent beginning – a human beginning. Men are forced to leave their old site or their old way of life to make a new life that is independent. Their old protection has failed them, as will every protection, including divine favour, and they must make themselves natives against the foreigners menacing their existence. This necessity sets men free, or rather forces them to free themselves, and it is to their own recognition of this necessity that they are indebted, not to their creator.

In the *Florentine Histories,* Machiavelli tells more about the dependent beginning of Florence than he does in the *Discourses,* and a brief excursion to that discussion will clarify the meaning of a free

26 *Discourses,* I, 9, 18

27 *Discourses,* I, 1 (I, 126); cf. *Florentine Histories,* II, 2, in which it appears that 'the reputation of the Roman republic under the Roman empire' was responsible for the early security of the site of Florence and that Florence was laid waste later by Totila, king of the Ostrogoths.

28 Venice, the other Christian city mentioned here, needed the long repose of a safe site; *Florentine Histories,* I, 29; II, 1. Guicciardini's criticism that a colony need not be dependent on its mother country would be pertinent if Machiavelli were not thinking of man's dependence on God; Francesco Guicciardini, *Considerazioni intorno ai Discorsi del Machiavelli sopra la Prima Deca di Tito Livio, Opere,* 2 vols (Milan 1941), II, 430.

beginning. There he begins his account of the origin of Florence by praising the 'great and marvelous orders of ancient republics and principalities' for building at all times new lands and cities. These orders, which have disappeared 'in our times,' consisted in the practice of sending into conquered or empty countries 'new inhabitants whom they called colonies.'[29] By this means conquered provinces were made more secure for the conqueror and the empty places within them filled with inhabitants. It is important to fill the places in a land that are not naturally healthful or productive because if this is not done, the fertile spots acquire an excess of inhabitants, who become poor. Machiavelli gives two examples of modern cities, Venice and Pisa, in which human 'industry' made unhealthful places healthful. Then, he cites the city of Florence as the example of the ancient method, now vanished, of building new cities by sending out colonies. Florence had an ancient beginning under the protection of Rome, and also a beginning in the ancient manner as a colony.

Thus the modern city, Machiavelli's own, which serves him as the exemplar of modern weakness in the *Florentine Histories,* is first presented as the example of the praiseworthy ancient method of building anew. Florence was built by merchants from the city of Fiesole under the Romans and further colonized by Romans, yet, we are told, it was built 'anew.' How can a colony be considered a new beginning? In this aspect, the method of a new beginning is to send colonies from an established state; it is an act of established power creating new power for itself. It would seem that every beginning of a city is both native, as an extension or a survival of some established power, and foreign, as a creation of power by intrusion into another land. Machiavelli says that colonies were sent into 'conquered or empty countries,' but what is the difference? By sending out colonies, the ancients filled up their lands; so if they still had empty lands to colonize, and if no natural disaster had occurred, the lands must have been emptied by conquest. This is what happened at the founding of Venice; and Pisa, too, was filled only after Genoa and its shore were laid waste by the Saracens.

One could infer the necessity of conquest from the identification of new building as colonizing, for the colonists would force the old inhabitants into the barren and unhealthful sites. These old inhabitants would in turn become new colonists of the sites they were forced to occupy. The best sites are always occupied by the dominant powers, and they must be ousted or obeyed. Every new beginning is either the growth of an established power or an attack on an established power, in fact an attack either by or upon an established power; it is not a voluntary, unhampered growth in empty places. Some empty places must remain in the world for the health of mankind, since men must be able to move and change; and when the world becomes filled, heaven or nature must empty it with floods, plagues, and famines. But as the survivors of such a disaster descend from their mountain refuges, 'few and battered,' they must occupy the best sites and make ready for contention with other men.[30]

Yet Florence, it seems, had a protected beginning. It was begun by ancients in the manner of the ancients, but with a difference. At first, it was a market on the plain for the merchants of Fiesole (situated on the summit of a mountain), which thrived after the Roman conquest of the Carthaginians made Italy secure. Later, it was colonized as a result of the peace that 'descended' after Rome's civil wars. Florence was created not of necessity but 'at the call of convenience' in an empty place that would have been exposed to attack had it not been protected by the power of the Romans.[31] The beginning of Florence was not a true beginning because it was derived from Rome. Florence was made for the convenience of local merchants without any necessity of its own; it was made possible by the necessity that pressed the Romans to defeat their enemies. Machiavelli cites Florence as the example of one method 'among the great and marvelous orders of ancient republics and principalities,' but in the first sentence of the first chapter of the *Discourses,* he says that those who read of Rome's beginning, its legislators, and how it was ordered, will not marvel that so much virtue was maintained for so long. Florence's beginning is derived from a marvelous Roman order, but Rome's ability to protect Florence is not marvelous. It is a consequence of Roman virtue. Florence's beginning revealed as little virtue as necessity of its own, so it points to Rome's beginning, which was typical of beginnings as well as the ultimate beginning of Florence. From the

30 *Discourses,* II, 5 (I, 294)
31 *Florentine Histories,* II, 2 (VII, 139)

Florentine Histories we are led back to the fundamental discussion in the *Discourses,* confirmed in the understanding that every true beginning is free in the double sense of independent and unprotected. Every true beginning is thus native and foreign.

In the first chapter of the *Discourses* Machiavelli does not assert that the difference between native and foreign is conventional, and subject to swift and ruthless change; one must reach for this conclusion elsewhere in his writings. Here he wishes to show that men are forced to make this fundamental, political distinction when they build cities. If they could rely on the protection of nature or God, they would not have to separate themselves in this distinction. If they could consider themselves natives of a mother earth or of an intended home, they could regard themselves as brothers. But necessity forbids it, and Machiavelli now brings up the topic of necessity in the legislator's choice of site.

Machiavelli has said in the first sentence of the chapter that those who read of Rome's beginning, its lawgivers, and its ordering will not marvel at its virtue. Then, after discussing native and foreign beginnings, he speaks of free builders of cities, like Moses and Aeneas, who are forced to leave their native land to find a new seat; in their case 'one can recognize the virtue of the builder and the fortune of what he builds, which is more or less marvelous as he is more or less virtuous who has been the beginning. His virtue is made known in two ways: the first is the choice of site, the other the ordering of the laws.' We see that the lawgivers of Rome have become a single builder who is the cause of both the beginning of the city and the ordering of the laws. Virtue in a city seems to be caused by and visible in the builder; the fortune of Rome, which seems marvelous to the untutored, can be accounted for by the virtue of the builder. The builder chooses the site and orders the laws, whereas the lawgivers in Machiavelli's first expression (*latori di leggi*) might have been lawbearers, perhaps from above. What is notable is building, human building in a site chosen by men.[32] Men do not receive a place or home from God.

---

32 *Latori di leggi* occurs in a similar context in *Discourses,* I, 42, and II, 1 (I, 275), as opposed to *legislatori* in I, 6 (I, 143), *ordinatore,* which first occurs in I, 2 (I, 130), and *fondatore,* first appearing in I, 9 (I, 153). To signify the human,

In the second chapter we are told immediately that Rome did not have one 'orderer,' and later we learn that this was very much to Rome's advantage. The first chapter exaggerates the scope of the single human builder in order to make human choice its theme.

What does the legislator choose? Machiavelli uses the answer to reduce the power of human building, just after he had seemed to raise human power by omitting all mention of divine power at the beginnings of cities. He says that the virtue of the legislator is made known first in the choice of site and second in the ordering of the laws – as if these were separate questions. As regards the site, Machiavelli asks whether the legislator should 'choose' a barren or a fertile site.[33] This is a surprising question from him, for it was part of the utopianism of classical philosophers that they discussed this question under the very unrealistic assumption that the legislator would have the opportunity of choosing the site.[34] Machiavelli uses the assumption momentarily so as to make a turn in his argument.

A barren site has the advantage that men are 'forced to keep at work, less occupied with laziness, living more united, having by the poverty of the site less cause for discords ...' This choice would be most wise and most useful if men were content to live on their own and did not wish to command others. But since men cannot secure themselves without power, it is *necessary* to avoid such sterility of country and to live in very fertile places. Thus, what seemed to be a free choice is restricted as a choice between necessities and decided by the sovereign necessity, the desire of men to command others. Since the most fertile sites will already be occupied by men who have followed their own inclination or Machiavelli's advice, the factual truth of 'choose your site' is 'choose your victim.' At the same time, after seeming to celebrate the marvelous virtue of the builder, Machiavelli remarks that virtue is seen more where choice has less authority.

conventional character of building, Machiavelli uses the word 'build' in all its variants twenty-one times in I, 1. Cf. II, 24, the eighty-fourth chapter, on building 'fortresses,' where 'build' occurs thirteen times.

33 *Discourses,* I, 20

34 Plato, *Laws,* 704d-705c; Aristotle, *Politics,* 1326b27-1327b18, 1330a34-b18; Cicero, *De Republica,* II. 3.5-5.10; Thomas Aquinas, *De Regno,* II, 5. Machiavelli depreciates the importance of the site in *Discourses,* I, 21; II, 3.

In this chapter Machiavelli makes human freedom independent of divine power precisely at the time when most men (not to mention previous writers) have looked for a divine presence – at the beginning of cities; and he calls this freedom 'building' and 'choice.' But out of the first choice he shows the power and virtue of necessity. Machiavelli substitutes necessity for divinity; he shows that since men are independent of divinity because of their necessities, they must decide independently according to those necessities. Men are independent of divinity but not free to build according to their own wishes, least of all in a state of hybristic rebellion against divinity. Men must measure their forces.

Having exposed the truth of 'choosing,' Machiavelli moves to the second way the legislator makes his virtue known, 'building' or 'ordering the laws.' But the character of the laws is determined by the 'choice' of a site; the laws must correct the laziness of the people in the city which has been wise enough to choose a fertile site. The second concern of the legislator is merely the subordinate of the first; the wise city 'should order that the laws constrain to that necessity to which the site does not constrain her ...' The laws should reproduce the constraint of necessity or barrenness; they are a kind of artificial necessity contrived to replace natural necessity. They allow men to take advantage of natural fertility, which otherwise makes men lazy. Without laws, men are unsafe because of their poverty or because of their laziness; with laws, men unlock the bounty of nature or of God. If the desire to command others is a sin, Machiavelli does not say here whether this sin is necessary (forced upon men from outside) or natural (prompted by their own nature); but this cannot be original sin in the Biblical sense of an unforced, voluntary act.[35] Machiavelli wants the government of laws in the Garden of Eden; he wants to combine the two states which the Bible had sundered and which Christianity had separated by the Fall. This combination is nothing mythical or imaginary, for two kingdoms, ancient Egypt by whose laws were produced very excellent men[36] and mod-

---

35 Cf. *Discourses,* I, preface, for Machiavelli's 'natural desire that has been in me always for doing without any respect those things which I believe will bring common benefit to everybody ...'

36 Including Moses?

ern Egypt under the Mamelukes are cited as examples of 'wise states.'

The first concern of the legislator is not the regime – the ordering of the laws by the men who rule – but the site; and the site determines the choice of regime, not particularly by the climate but generally by the need to create artificial necessity. The laws are ordered so as to put pressure on men for the sake of their security. Their security is also the cause of the laws; so the end of the laws, once ordered, is the same as the need which prompts men to make laws. The laws answer the necessity imposed by the desire of men to command others, but they do not rise above that necessity.[37]

Aristotle explained that the reason for the coming-into-being of a polis is not the same as its reason for staying-in-being; men come together to protect life and stay together for the sake of the good life. According to Machiavelli, however, protection is the first and last goal of cities. He implies here what he argues amply elsewhere, that the danger of civilized enemies is as great and as fearful as the pressure of elementary necessities. Every state, however wise or civilized or modern, is liable to be destroyed by 'the Grand Turk.'[38] How could it be otherwise? The solution for insecurity does not attempt more than security; it accommodates – or rather feeds – the desire of men to command others. The 'city' of Rome, in which 'so much virtue was maintained for so many centuries,' grew to 'that empire to which that republic attained.'[39] The Roman republic virtuously attained an empire because it obeyed the need to answer the danger from men who desire to command others. For Machiavelli, 'Rome' means the Roman kingdom, republic and empire (not to mention modern Rome). 'Rome' detracts from the importance of the successive regimes, since all fundamentally had the same end, security.

Machiavelli repeats a story about Alexander the Great and the building of Alexandria to show what he understands by building a city. Alexander, intending to build a city for his own glory, received

37 Lanfranco Mossini, *Necessità e Legge nell'Opera del Machiavelli* (Milan 1962), 70, 260; Kurt Kluxen, *Der Begriff der Necessità im Denken Machiavellis* (Bensberg 1949), 31, 68-71

38 *Discourses*, I, 1; cf. *Florentine Histories*, VI, 37; VIII, 20, 36

39 *Discourses*, I, 1, first sentence; cf. the next to last sentence.

the proposal of a certain Deinocrates,[40] an architect, to build it on Mount Athos in such a way as to give it a 'human form.' Their city would be 'marvelous and rare, and worthy of his [Alexander's?] greatness.' But, having asked the architect what the inhabitants would live on and receiving the reply that the architect had not thought of it, Alexander refused this marvelous project. He decided to 'let that mountain stand' and not to create a city in his own image but to build Alexandria where the inhabitants 'would willingly stay because of the richness of the country and convenience of the sea and the Nile.' The form of a city should not copy the human form, as the city is modelled upon the soul of Plato's *Republic*; for the builder must be free to make his name by serving human necessities instead of finding his glory in seeking the highest human possibilities. If he does so, men will follow him willingly, without imprudent trust in 'the long peace that was born in the world under Octavian.'[41]

When we look at this account of the beginnings of cities as a whole epitomized in the story about Alexander, it must appear fundamentally inadequate. It is also inconsistent with Machiavelli's further thoughts on beginnings in the *Discourses,* and, as will be shown, for a purpose. Machiavelli discusses here what the beginnings of any city whatever *have been,* and what *was* that of Rome. He speaks of beginnings in the past only and uses predominantly ancient examples, referring only to the Sultan and the Grand Turk of modern rulers, and not to them as 'builders.' He does not speak of beginnings that have been made recently or of the beginnings of modern times. Although he had announced his 'new ways and orders' in the preface to the first book, he does not speak here in the first chapter of beginnings that might have to be made now. The new is underplayed in this treatment of beginnings. He mentions the new only three times in

40 On Deinocrates, see esp. Lucian, *pro Imaginibus,* 9; Vitruvius, II, 1-4; Thomas Aquinas, *De Regno,* II, 7. His name means 'terrible ruler'; so Alexander was rejecting the advice of a 'terrible ruler.'

41 Alexandria and Florence are the two cities of unfree origin given in the first chapter, but Machiavelli tells no story about Florence. Cf. *Discourses,* I, 49; *Florentine Histories,* II, 1, 2 on Florence.

reference to or in association with lands newly acquired. The new is what has been acquired, but acquired from the old. The opposition between new and old is not set in view; as we noted, Machiavelli does not make manifest the conflict between 'natives' and 'foreigners' for the choice sites.

This reticence accords with the fact that Machiavelli chooses, in the preface to the first book, to present his new ways and orders as imitating the politics of the ancients. He therefore presents as the obstacle to his enterprise the opinion that the ancients cannot be imitated because the modern world has changed essentially: 'as if heaven, the sun, the elements, men were changed in motion, order and power from that which they were in ancient times.' Machiavelli uses the sameness of moderns and ancients, of new and old, to introduce the possibility of changing the present. With this tactic he can deny that Christianity has made the modern world irrevocably different from the ancient. In silent contrast to Christian political science, he can deny an essential difference between the New Law and the Old Law, and he can imply that the coming of Christ does not hinder, except through belief, the recourse of any prince or republic to ancient examples. Thus, he can begin his attack on what he calls here 'the present religion' for the 'weakness' and 'evil' it brings,[42] without seeming to confront it with his own new ways and orders.

In this first chapter Machiavelli emphasizes not the new vs the old but the old vs the divine. His account of old beginnings brings out the importance of necessity in beginnings, by which he means human as opposed to divine necessities. Alexander, though he built Alexandria for his own glory, built rightly because he built for human glory. His glory would not last if his city did not last, and his city would last, it seems, only if its inhabitants were willing to live there. His glory is in harmony with human necessities, with what men choose in accordance with their necessities, as opposed to the glory that glorifies the human form and seeks the marvelous and the rare. Machiavelli desanctifies the old beginnings. They are not marvelous; they have lasted because of the virtue of the human builder choosing necessity, like Alexander. The old can be explained without reference to the divine.

42 *Discourses,* I, preface. For the understanding of this sentence, see Strauss, *Thoughts on Machiavelli,* 176-7.

The new, however, cannot be explained without reference to the divine, or in Machiavelli's term, to the extraordinary. He does not tell here of the beginnings of cities as they were to men living at the time, but as they seem to us living in the present. That is why his discussion of 'building' and 'choosing a site' seem so notably un-Machiavellian, with almost all of the nastiness, strangeness, and confusion suppressed. He makes the founding of a city seem like the choice of a site by a home buyer in a new suburban development. But having first taught the opposition between the old and the divine, he can proceed to oppose the new to the old. Having established the sovereignty of human necessity over the divine, he can interpret the divine in terms of human necessity. If Machiavelli had discussed religion in the first chapter he could not have demoted it so effectively, and thus could not have reconstructed it, when he does discuss it in the eleventh chapter and thereafter, so aptly to his own prescription. The opposition of the old vs the divine precedes that of the new vs the old in order to prepare it.

One may oppose the new to the old by considering the old when it was new. When the old was new, it was humble and exposed. This much can be inferred from Machiavelli's description of the old beginnings of cities built to escape or anticipate necessity, but of course Machiavelli goes much further in later chapters. He shows that every man was once a man of 'small fortune.' Those who were born to rank or wealth have this same beginning if they look back far enough to the beginning of their rank or wealth. Every man either had a humble beginning in his own lifetime or inherited it from his ancestors who were not born to the purple. In any case, everyone inherits some important things from his city, and all cities had beginnings – that is to say, humble beginnings. All rank depends on rule, and all rule has beginnings of 'small fortune.' Every man who reflects on his beginnings can see that his present place (if he has one) was not given to him without effort. Such reflection dispels the illusion of effortlessness which is the achievement of civilization. One cannot assume the place that he has.

At the same time, reflection on one's beginning reveals the assumption that he must make, which is that every place is occupied. If every reflective man can see that he and his city were once humble in fortune, he can also infer that other men and other cities were then in command. Every man was once a new man, and all who have made their way to power have done so by virtue of the displacement of other men who once held power. They may have made their way by pushing others aside, or their way may have been cleared by natural disaster or divine visitation. Every act of construction presupposes an act of destruction: to act anew is to renovate the old.[43] The Good Book may say that men were originally placed where it was unnecessary to sin, and the good-hearted (who also have *their* place) may accept the consequences of not pushing others aside. But this is merely a comfortable illusion, since the origin of present comforts is not comfortable to examine. Our friendly surroundings were once held by enemies who had to be displaced.[44]

Thus men must acquire their cities, their riches, and their security from others. Their necessity forces them to pursue the new. Machiavelli develops the necessity of security into the necessity of acquiring through the first book of the *Discourses,* so that in the preface to the second book, he is ready to condemn the usual praise of the ancients and to offer a new reason for imitating them. In II, 5 he applies the necessity of the new to religion, showing how men who make new sects are driven to efface every sign of the old. This makes explicit that religion is included in the 'everything' that the founder must make anew, according to I, 26.

Making a new religion: this is the great omission of Machiavelli's first account of the beginnings of cities. He does not speak of religion and he speaks of 'builder' instead of 'founder.' 'Founder' first occurs in the ninth chapter, after a section of chapters, two to eight, on the regime. As we have noted, Machiavelli depreciates the importance of the regime in the first chapter. He does this because he suppresses the opposition between the old and the new, and therefore the difference between the two natural orders of men. When the necessity of acquiring new lands becomes evident, it also appears that some men are more apt and avid in acquiring than most other men. The necessity of acquiring reveals the two 'humours' of 'the people' and 'the great' (I, 4). Whereas Machiavelli had said in the first chapter that 'men' seek to command others, he now shows that men differ in this re-

43 *Discourses,* III, 1, 22
44 *Discourses,* II, 5, 8; III, 1

spect, some desiring to command and others not to be commanded. When acquisition becomes paramount, the regime becomes a problem; the two orders of men, naturally hostile to each other, must be 'managed' by the ruling or princely order. In the first chapter he leaves the impression that laws can reduce discords in a people living at a fertile site by reproducing the necessity of a poor site, but in the following section on the regime he shows that the laws must tolerate discords so that the rulers can manage them. Such management is more difficult than 'building' and must be continuous rather than once for all time. The easy harmony of glory for Alexander and security for Alexandria must be reconsidered when it becomes clear that Alexander and his people have opposed natures and hostile interests.[45]

Machiavelli considers the conventional division of men into natives and foreigners before he considers the natural division into princes and peoples. He conceals at first the difficulty of creating a regime of 'natives' in order to show that men must divide themselves by their own effort. Before they can understand their own nature, they must distinguish themselves from the supernatural; and, in this distinction, the natural differences between men and the human creative power of overcoming them are lost to view. Machiavelli enlisted both the natural and the conventional against the supernatural, and confused them as 'necessity.' After the supernatural has been opposed, the necessity of dividing men into natives and foreigners can be analyzed as recognizing the division in human nature and managing it by human creation or convention.

In this management religion or its like is an indispensable instrument. Religion makes men faithful to the gods, and hence to the men the gods recommend. Founders creating a new regime must have recourse to religion as an indirect and apparently impartial recommendation of themselves, for they cannot offer themselves as rulers openly to the people. Their own nature urges them to arrogant mastery of the people, whose nature prompts them to fear and hatred of this mastery. Men cannot live unless they live together, and they cannot live together if the people see the rulers for what they are. The first

---

45 In *Discourses,* I, 20 Alexander serves as an exemplar of human acquisition in the widest sense, 'acquiring the world.'

necessity of ruling, then, is for the rulers to hide their own nature by means of religion, or in the Machiavellian equivalent, by fraud. Rulers would be as blind as the ruled and would never appreciate this first necessity if they did not see it as a human rather than a divine necessity. That men need religion should be a reproach to their Creator, for if religion were gratitude, it could not be forced upon men. Man's need for religion is thus the cause of his independence, not of dependence. Only when rulers see or sense that men obey themselves in obeying necessity can human necessity appear as the foundation of human freedom.

So Machiavelli gave a first account of the beginnings of cities according to human necessities which omits the first necessity in beginning a city. The first necessity of the beginning (*principio*) is a prince (*principe*) who makes everything anew.[46] As the *arché* is in the architect, Machiavelli finds the *principio* in a human *principe*. The human prince must 'be alone' against God before he can be alone among other men, and he learns the necessity of acquiring from other men by 'acquiring the world' from God. Man's necessity turns out to be this man's necessity, *your* necessity in Machiavelli's familiar address. One cannot speak of 'one's own' always in the third person: your necessity is to be a new prince and make a new beginning.[47]

To indicate that religion made by a founder binds the regime, Machiavelli alternates sections of chapters on founders and religion through the fifty-two chapters remaining in book I after the section on the regime.[48] For a time he separates the founding of the regime

46 Note 'he who has been the beginning,' *Discourses*, I, 1 (I, 127).

47 As Leo Strauss notes, Machiavelli begins thirteen chapters of the *Discourses* with the first person of the personal pronoun; the first of these is I, 2, introducing the thought that the specifically human necessity is the necessity to acquire. Strauss, *Thoughts on Machiavelli*, 312n22. Kluxen's existentialist interpretation (positing *sein eigenes Ich absolut*) goes too far, not because it is bold but because it fails to consider the necessity of acquisition as taking *from,* and hence of religion and rhetoric. Nevertheless, its conventional radicalism is closer to Machiavelli's thought than is conventional blandness; Kluxen, *Der Begriff der Necessità*, 64, 96, 102.

48 See Strauss, *Thoughts on Machiavelli*, 97-106, 312-13, for the plan of the *Discourses*.

from the founding of religion by giving the fame of founding the Roman regime to Romulus and that of founding the Roman religion to Numa. But this separation proves to have been an accident of the opposite characters of Romulus and Numa, the first 'very ferocious and warlike,' the second 'quiet and religious.' Better than either is a king like Ancus, 'gifted by nature in such a way that he could make use of peace and carry on war.'[49] Founding a regime is founding 'new orders' which are, with respect to the old orders, 'extraordinary.' 'And truly there has been no orderer of extraordinary laws in a people who did not have recourse to God ...'[50] Such laws would also be 'foreign' to the people receiving them. Religion communicates what is extraordinary and foreign to the laws, and revives the original fears as they were felt at the beginning.[51] The prince can therefore secure himself and his regime with both the recommendation and the fear of God.

It is the new, the humanly created, rather than the old as related in histories, that is connected to the divine. Wishing to teach princes how to make a new or reordered religion, Machiavelli had to begin by distinguishing his enterprise from 'the present religion.' To do this he made the histories of Titus Livy his Bible and offered his new ways and orders in the rhetorical guise of a commentary on a human book, 'a fragment of an ancient statue.'[52]

9 *Discourses*, I, 9, 10, 11, 19

0 *Discourses*, I, 11. Machiavelli's apology at the beginning of I, 9 was made necessary by the distinction between ordinary and extraordinary which he tried to sustain in I, 2-8, for the founder overcomes it: he makes the ordinary by having recourse to the extraordinary.

1 Cf. *Discourses*, III, 21: Machiavelli, on the way to persuading himself of the truth of Tacitus' maxim in III, 19, suggests parallels between the native prince and the prince who makes himself loved and between the foreign prince and the prince who makes himself feared. But both Hannibal and Scipio were foreigners where they were, respectively, feared and loved; and besides, Machiavelli gives his preference to the methods of Hannibal, the feared enemy of Rome. If it is better for a prince to be feared than loved, it is better for him to be a foreigner or to behave like one. See *The Prince*, 17.

2 *Discourses*, I, preface

SIX

The Concept of *Fortuna*
in Machiavelli

THOMAS FLANAGAN

THE HISTORY OF THE GODDESS FORTUNA[1]

Fortune is only one of a large number of the powers and deities who have been imagined to control human affairs. Within the history of the west, we could distinguish at least the following forces, which have been widely supposed to control our destiny.

Fortune	Fortuna	Tyche
Fate(s)	Fatum(a)	Moirai, Heimarmene
Necessity	Necessitas	Ananke
Providence	Providentia	Pronoia

To separate one from the other is practically impossible, for the lines between all of them were blurred even in antiquity. All of these con-

---

In this paper I have dealt solely with *fortuna* as it is opposed to *virtus*, which is indeed the most common usage in the history of western thought. However *fortuna* or *tyche* has also been contrasted to *natura* or *physis*, in which case the meaning of fortune approaches that of 'accident.' Although I have not treated this topic, it is a theme which should be pursued; for Machiavelli speaks in several places of a relation between *virtù* and *natura,* and hence implicitly of a relation between *natura* and *fortuna.* Cf. the references in A. Parel, 'Machiavelli Minore.'

ceptions, however, refer to different aspects or moments of the fundamental experience that man does not totally control his destiny on the earth. Sometimes we feel that our lives are ruled from without, that we are in the grip of a force which guides our actions; while at other times our doings appear almost as random events, not caused by anything at all. Sometimes we seem to perceive a benevolent plan which shapes our lives, while at other moments there may seem to be no plan at all, or even a malicious one. These and other experiences can be represented in complex and shifting ways by the symbols of fortune, fate, necessity, and providence – singly or in combination.

One set of symbols, those associated with the goddess Fortuna, was particularly important to Machiavelli.[2] Now he did not speak solely of fortune; particularly in his poetic works, he often used other terms. I have found instances where he speaks of providence, the heavens, fate and the fates, the stars, grace, and the times.[3] Of these terms only 'the times' is used rather frequently in Machiavelli's treatises on politics; and when it appears, as I will show below, it is of one piece with the conception of fortune. The other terms are all

2 Most authors who have written on Machiavelli have devoted at least a page or two to *fortuna*, but there is no wholly satisfactory specialized treatment. The three essays cited below are particularly deficient in that they treat Machiavelli's *fortuna* without sufficient reference to its widespread popular usage before, during, and after Machiavelli's era.

Burleigh T. Wilkins, 'Machiavelli on History and Fortune,' *Bucknell Review*, 8 (1959), 225-45; Charles D. Tarlton, 'The Symbolism of Redemption and the Exorcism of Fortune in Machiavelli's *Prince*,' *Review of Politics*, 30 (1968), 332-48; Vincenzo Cioffari, 'The Function of Fortune in Dante, Boccaccio, and Machiavelli,' *Italica* 24 (1947), 1-13

3 The following references are not meant to be complete but merely indicative. The text used is Allan H. Gilbert, ed., *Machiavelli: The Chief Works and Others*, 3 vols (Durham NC 1965).
a / providence: *L'Asino d'Oro*, II; Gilbert, II, 758
b / the heavens: *Discourses*, II, 29; Gilbert, 406-7
c / fate: Letter 137; Gilbert, II, 929
d / the fates: Letter 116; Gilbert, II, 896-7
e / the stars: Letter 116; Gilbert, II, 897
f / grace: 'On Ambition'; Gilbert, II, 739
g / the times: *The Prince*, 25; Gilbert, I, 90

much less frequently employed, and again I have not been able to find occasions where *fortuna* could not just as well have been substituted. On the basis of frequency of occurrence, then, I would conclude that *fortuna* is Machiavelli's major term for designating the uncertainty and dependency of human affairs. The other words appear to be merely literary variations which do not involve a substantial change in meaning. In the following pages, therefore, I will briefly discuss the origin and development of the symbolism of fortune, not to provide a complete history but only to suggest the richness of the tradition upon which Machiavelli drew.[4]

The word *fortuna* is formed adjectivally from the Latin *fors* (luck), which is ultimately derived from the root of *ferre* (to bring). Thus the core of meaning of *fors* is 'that which is brought'; and Fortuna is she who brings it. Similarly the Greek equivalent, Tyche, is derived

On *fortuna* in the classical world, see the relevant articles in J. Hastings, ed., *Encyclopaedia of Religion and Ethics* (New York 1914); and in Pauly-Wissowa, *Real-Encyclopädie der Classischen Altertumswissenschaft*. On the development of the idea after the end of the Roman empire, the recognized authorities are A. Doren, 'Fortuna im Mittelalter und in der Renaissance,' *Vorträge der Bibliothek Warburg* II (1922-3), 71-151; and H.R. Patch, *The Goddess Fortuna in Medieval Literature* (Cambridge, Mass. 1927); 'The Tradition of the Goddess Fortuna in Roman Literature and in the Transitional Period,' *Smith College Studies in Modern Languages* III3 (1922); 'The Tradition of the Goddess Fortuna in Medieval Philosophy and Literature,' ibid., III4 (1922). Two other monographs deal with special questions: Ida Wyss, *Virtus and Fortuna bei Boiardo und Ariost* (Leipzig 1931); Klaus Heitmann, *Fortuna and Virtus – Eine Studie zu Petrarchas Lebensweisheit* (Cologne 1958). Finally there are a number of articles of value: D.C. Allen, 'Renaissance Remedies for Fortune,' *Studies in Philology*, 38 (1941), 188-97; K. Hampe, 'Zur Auffassung der Fortuna im Mittelalter,' *Archiv für Kulturgeschichte*, 17 (1926); Aby Warburg, 'Francesco Sassettis letztwillige Verfügung,' *Kunstwissenschaftliche Beiträge, August Schmarsow gewidmet* (Leipzig 1907); Rexmond C. Cochrane, 'Francis Bacon and the Architect of Fortune,' *Studies in the Renaissance*, 5 (1958). This list omits certain titles by nineteenth-century scholars, but these are easily obtained from the bibliographies in the above works, particularly by Patch, Doren, Heitmann, and Wyss. I have not seen the privately printed monograph of Vincenzo Cioffari, *Fortune and Fate from Democritus to St Thomas Aquinas* (New York 1935).

from a root meaning 'to succeed' or 'to attain.' The basic meaning in both cases is not what we moderns term 'chance,' that is, events which seem to occur randomly. Rather the connotation is that of success, which is brought about by an unseen person or power who works in ways inscrutable to us. Thus there is never a clear distinction between fortune and fate. Both conceptions refer to the order of the gods which can never be fully understood by men. If there is a difference, it is one of emphasis. Fate represents the divine will as something fixed and inflexible, while fortune represents it as elastic, unpredictable, and open to influence by human supplication. According to the authorities, therefore, the worship of Fortuna was not a surrender to chance or randomness in which individual effort was abandoned; it was much more an attempt to propitiate the goddess so that she would smile on an undertaking. Fortuna may be capricious, but her behaviour is not random.

It would be difficult to overestimate the importance of Fortuna in the religious life of ancient Rome. Even before the syncretistic period of the Empire, she was worshipped under a variety of cult names. The fortune of the harvest, the fortune of the sea, the fortune of mothers – whenever life becomes uncertain fortune was worshipped. The symbols denoted success and uncertainty together. She was ordinarily depicted in one of three ways – with a horn of plenty, holding the rudder of a ship, or rotating a ball or a wheel. Always a popular and colourful goddess, fortune's role expanded impressively under the Empire. Pliny the Elder has given us a classic description of how widespread her worship became:

Everywhere in the whole world at every hour by all men's voices fortune alone is invoked and named, alone accused, alone impeached, alone pondered, alone applauded, alone rebuked and visited with reproaches; deemed volatile and indeed by most men blind as well, wayward, inconstant, uncertain, fickle in her favors and favoring the unworthy. To her is debited all that is spent and credited all that is received, she alone fills both pages in the whole of mortals' account; and we are so much at the mercy of chance that chance herself, by whom God is proved uncertain, takes the place of God.[5]

5 Gaius Plinius Secundus, *Natural History* (Loeb Classical Library 1957), II, 22

She became one of those universal deities who gradually replaced the old Roman contingent of gods. Names like Isis-Fortuna, Fortuna Panthea, and Fortuna Populi Romani suggest the wide scope to which her worship attained. She endured to become, as Patch remarks, 'the last of the gods.'[6]

In the higher culture of antiquity – in philosophy, literature, history, and art – fortune occupied a position fully as prominent as in popular worship and superstition. There is no space here to catalogue all the usages; suffice it to say that almost no important writer was free from her influence. In particular it became a part of the conventional wisdom of antiquity to debate the respective contributions to success of *virtus,* or human ability, and *fortuna,* or divine favour. Considerations on the subject were seldom lacking from any work devoted to analyzing human activity. As one writer has put it, 'the contrast between *virtù* and *fortuna* must have been so current in Rome even before the time of Cicero, indeed even so banal, that it could sink to the level of a pedagogical device for rhetorical exercises.'[7]

It is not surprising, then, that Fortuna, both as a popular goddess and a topic of debate for learned men, lived on after the collapse of the Roman Empire. In spite of the polemics of Augustine, who quite logically argued that a notion of fortune is hardly compatible with the Christian faith in an all-wise providence, Fortuna found a secure place in the Christian imagination. In particular, Boethius' work on the *Consolation of Philosophy* provided the mould for much of the speculation on fortune, at least in the early Middle Ages before the recovery of the classics. It is instructive to observe how the image of Fortuna changed as she was adopted by a civilization with a different spirit. In Rome she had been a beguiling figure whose cornucopia was a promise of abundance. *Bona Dea* she was called – the 'good goddess.' But after Boethius she is a much more sombre figure; almost all of her colourful imagery has been lost. Only the wheel remains, which Fortuna grimly turns.[8] Men rise and fall inexorably in the

Patch, 'The Tradition of the Goddess Fortuna in Roman Literature and in the Transitional Period,' 158

Heitmann, *Fortuna and Virtus: Eine Studie zu Petrarcas Lebensweisheit,* 18-19

Doren, 'Fortuna in Mittelalter und in der Renaissance,' 145-51; the article contains an excellent series of reproductions of *fortuna,* as she was variously conceived in the Middle Ages and Renaissance.

medieval conception; there is little if any room for maneuver against her. In this fashion, as a symbol of the transitoriness of earthly glory, Fortuna and the wheel appear throughout Europe during the Middle Ages.

It has been held that the symbolism of Fortuna became particularly widespread during the Renaissance; but this is an oversimplification, since as we have seen, wide interest in the goddess was also present in the medieval era. What began to change in the Renaissance was the spirit in which Fortuna was regarded. After the time of Dante and Petrarch, whose opinions on fortune were still distinctively medieval, she gradually evolved from the grim woman turning her relentless wheel into a much friendlier power who could be a distinct help in human affairs. It is fascinating to see how the symbolism of the wheel was increasingly supplemented by the revived symbols of antiquity, particularly the sailing ship. There are even portraits extant in which Fortuna, although she is still a passenger in the ship, no longer controls the rudder; that is left to the individual himself.[9]

In her revived antique trappings, Fortuna permeated the consciousness of the Renaissance. Just as in antiquity, she was a standard part of literature, philosophy, history and the arts. And, also as in the classical world, she not only appeared in higher culture but in popular life. A complete survey is beyond the scope of this paper, but a few examples will indicate the wide extension of the symbolism of fortune in the era in which Machiavelli grew up. Jacob Burckhardt, for instance, relates the story of a ruler of Bologna who carved the following inscription in Latin on the newly built tower of his palace: 'This monument was built by Giovanni Bentivoglio, the gracious ruler of his land, whose virtue [virtus] and fortune [fortuna] have led to all the good things which a man could want.'[10] Other anecdotes supplied by Burckhardt also demonstrate how the cult of Fortuna extended to the popular festivals. When Alfonso the Great entered Naples in 1443, an important part of the procession was a chariot in which rode a figure of Fortuna. Similarly, when Massimiliano Sforza entered Milan in 1512, Fortuna was the chief figure on the triumphal

---

9 Warburg, 'Francesco Sassettis letztwillige Verfügung'

10 Jacob Burckhardt, *The Civilization of the Renaissance in Italy*, tr. S.G.C. Middlemore (New York 1958), II, 482

arch, elevated over Fama, Speranza, Audacia, and Penitenza.[11] Finally Machiavelli himself, in the *History of Florence,* tells an interesting story about one of the leading citizens of Florence (ca. 1380), Piero degli Albizzi:

> Once when he was giving a banquet to many citizens, somebody ... sent him a silver cup full of sweet meats with a nail hidden among them. When the nail was found and seen by all the guests they interpreted it as a suggestion that he nail fortune's wheel in its present place; since she had brought him to the top of it, it could do nothing else, if it kept turning, than carry him to the bottom.[12]

The preceding paragraphs are far too short to do justice to the history of Fortuna; but they do show how influential she was from antiquity through the Renaissance. Though she appeared in different guises, there was never a time when her presence was not felt in the discussions of intellectuals as well as in the daily doings of popular life.

THE 'SOURCES' OF MACHIAVELLI'S FORTUNA

Even this cursory sketch of the history of Fortuna has important implications for understanding Machiavelli's use of the symbol. In particular, it seems unlikely there is a single 'source' for Machiavelli's ideas on fortune, even though some writers have attempted to discover one. Joseph Mazzeo, for example, has suggested that Machiavelli drew his notion of Fortuna from Polybius.[13] J.H. Whitfield maintains that Machiavelli 'obviously' learned to discuss events in terms of *virtù* and *fortuna* 'from the Latin historians';[14] and he devotes some space to pointing out similarities with Quintus Curtius'

Ibid., I, 417

History of Florence, III, 19; Gilbert, III, 1170-1

Joseph Mazzeo, *Renaissance and Seventeenth-Century Studies* (New York 1964), 154

J.H. Whitfield, *Machiavelli* (New York 1965), 95

life of Alexander the Great, though he does not say explicitly that the latter book should be considered a direct source of Machiavelli's ideas. There are undoubtedly similarities between Machiavelli's *fortuna* and those of Polybius and Quintus Curtius, but to interpret these as evidence that those writers are in a real sense the sources of Machiavelli usage would be an unwarranted exaggeration. For as we have seen, the notions of *virtù* and *fortuna* were the common property of an entire civilization; and Machiavelli would have been exposed to them at every turn, in daily conversation as well as in his study of the classic authors.

We can illustrate the complexity of the problem by referring to the *Discourses,* where Walker has done a thorough job of uncovering the sources which Machiavelli employed in composition. First of all, Machiavelli specifically refers in two places to other authors' notions of Fortuna. In chapter 1 of the second book, where he discusses the role of fortune in the rise of Rome, he mentions Plutarch and Livy as having believed that Rome owed more to fortune than to the ability of her citizens. Machiavelli's interpretation of Plutarch and Livy may be one-sided; we are only interested here in the fact that he was aware of the importance of *fortuna* in their works.[15] The other reference in the *Discourses* is also to Livy. In book II, chapter 29, Machiavelli uses a quotation from Livy as his chapter heading: 'Fortune blinds the intellects of men when she does not wish them to oppose her plans.'[16] Yet, although these are the only passages in the *Discourses* known to me where Machiavelli refers to another author's conception of fortune, it would hardly be safe to conclude that these authors are the only sources. Livy and Plutarch are only two of the seventeen writers[17] whose names or works are explicitly mentioned in the *Discourses*; and of these seventeen, several have contributed notably to the development of the symbolism of Fortuna. Aristotle, Cicero, Quintus Curtius, Sallust, Thucydides, Virgil, and Dante would

15 The reference to Plutarch is to *De fortuna romanorum.* The allusion to Livy cannot be specified; Machiavelli writes only that Livy 'seldom has any Roman make a speech in which he refers to ability without adding fortune.'*Discourses,* II, 1, Gilbert, I, 324

16 Livy, *Histories,* V, 37

17 L.J. Walker, *The Discourses of Niccolò Machiavelli* (London 1950), II, 271

all be mentioned in any reasonably complete account of the history of Fortuna. Polybius, too, whom Machiavelli does not mention by name but whose works (or parts of them) he certainly knew, extensively used the idea of fortune in his writing. Thus even within the pages of the *Discourses*, we can see that Machiavelli drew upon the works of a number of authors who were accustomed to thinking in terms of fortune.

With the exception of Dante, the names above are all of classical writers. Machiavelli was not inclined to cite his contemporaries as authorities, so we do not know exactly whom he read. Yet let us assume for the moment merely that he was familiar with the works of his great Florentine humanistic predecessors: Dante, Petrarch, Boccaccio, Poggio. Here again we find that each of these men was deeply concerned with the impact of fortune on human affairs. To give one final example of another possible 'source': in a letter to Vettori[18] Machiavelli quotes from his Neapolitan contemporary Pontano, who had written a widely circulated tract *De fortuna.* I am not suggesting that the list of sources for Machiavelli's notion of *fortuna* should be extended to include all of these individuals; the point is rather that a definitive list would be rather difficult to compile. Fortune was not only a universal concept in literature and history from antiquity to the Renaissance, but also a widespread part of popular culture. When Machiavelli spoke of *fortuna,* he was using a term which he must have absorbed as a child and which would have come naturally, almost spontaneously to his lips.

MACHIAVELLI'S DOCTRINE OF FORTUNA

The term *fortuna* runs like a refrain throughout Machiavelli's works. Though it might be useful to do a numerical survey of all its uses as Hexter has done for the concept of *lo stato,* I have attempted to establish the meaning of *fortuna* by referring to Machiavelli's major utterances on the subject. Certainly the most famous passage is the twenty-fifth chapter of *The Prince,* where Machiavelli is preparing to exhort the future prince of Italy to action. This chapter is a conveni-

Letter 156, 20 Dec. 1514; Gilbert, II, 960

ent starting point, for it contains in one way or another all the major themes connected with Machiavelli's use of *fortuna*. 'As I am well aware,' this chapter opens, 'many have believed and now believe human affairs so controlled by Fortune and by God that men with their prudence cannot manage them – yes, more, that men have no recourse against the world's variations.'[19] These words express very well what concerned Machiavelli – the riddle of the success or failure of human action. Men attempt 'with their prudence' to carry out some plan, to fulfill some project; but it often appears that their prudence is of no avail against the 'world's variations.' Yet characteristically Machiavelli refuses to endorse the pessimistic opinion that man's strength and cleverness can never prevail against fortune's constant change. 'Thinking on these variations,' he tells us, 'I myself now and then incline in some respects to their belief.'[20] But this is only an occasional inclination, not his real conviction. His true opinion is more complex: 'Fortune may be mistress of one half our actions but ... even she leaves the other half, or almost, under our control.'[21] There follows that famous metaphor, in which Machiavelli tries to illustrate the role which fortune plays in our lives:

> I compare Fortune with one of our destructive rivers which, when it is angry, turns the plains into lakes, throws down the trees and the buildings, takes earth from one spot, puts it in another; everyone flees before the flood; everyone yields to its fury and nowhere can repel it. Yet though such it is, we need not therefore conclude that when the weather is quiet, men cannot take precautions with both embankments and dykes, so that when the waters rise, either they go off by a canal or their fury is neither so wild nor so damaging. The same things happen about Fortune. She shows her power where strength and wisdom do not prepare to resist her, and directs her fury where she knows that no dykes or embankments are ready to hold her. If you consider Italy – the scene of these variations and their first mover – you see that she is a plain without dykes and without any embankment; but

19 Gilbert, I, 89
20 Ibid., 90
21 Ibid.

if she were embanked with adequate strength and wisdom, like Germany, Spain, and France, this flood either would not make the great variations it does or would not come upon us. I think this is all I need to say in general on resisting Fortune.[22]

This I take to be Machiavelli's real opinion of our ability to resist fortune, that there are always precautions we can take which will improve our possibilities of success. It is true that at times Machiavelli sounds a good deal more pessimistic than this. In the *Life of Castruccio Castracani*, for example, he introduces his narrative by remarking on the childhood of many eminent men, whose birth was often marked by marvels and wonders; and then he adds 'I well believe that this comes about because fortune, wishing to show the world that she – and not prudence – makes men great, first shows her forces at a time when prudence can have no share in the matter ...'[23] And again in the *Discourses*, Machiavelli appears to reverse his earlier judgment that the rise of Rome was due more to *virtù* than *fortuna*. He seemingly credits fortune with the power to intervene directly in our affairs to accomplish his goals, regardless of our plans:

Skillfully Fortune does this, since she chooses a man, when she plans to bring to pass great things, who is of so much perception and so much ability that he recognizes the opportunities she puts before him. So in the same way when she intends to bring to pass great failures, she puts there men to promote such failure. And if somebody there is able to oppose her, she either kills him or deprives him of all means for doing anything good.[24]

Yet even in such a pessimistic mood, Machiavelli never counsels us to give up the conduct of our affairs to fortune. Remember the death of Castruccio. After fortune has raised him to glory and then struck him down, he still reflects on what he would have done differently, had he known of his impending death. He would not, he tells his heir, have accumulated so much territory and with it so many ene-

Ibid.
Ibid., II, 534
Discourses, II, 29; Gilbert, I, 407-8

mies. He would have left behind him a smaller but more secure holding. He advises his adopted son, therefore, to pursue the arts of peace
rather than of war. The point of the tale is, I take it, that even in disaster human reason can devise ways of working with fortune and
hence of mitigating the loss. Machiavelli's advice in the *Discourses*
confirms this interpretation. In connection with the passage above,
he tells us:

> I assert, indeed, once more that it is very true, according to what
> we see in all the histories, that men are able to assist Fortune but
> not to thwart her. They can weave her designs but cannot destroy
> them. They ought, then, never to give up as beaten, because, since
> they do not know her purpose and she goes through crooked and
> unknown roads, they can always hope, and hoping is not to give
> up, in whatever fortune and whatever affliction they may be.[25]

Even at the darkest hour, then, Machiavelli counsels never to give
up our aspirations; for we may be able after all to place ourselves in
alignment with her plans. And in fact, in the midst of our uncertainty,
it may be best to pursue an active, aggressive course; for 'Fortune is a
woman and it is necessary, in order to keep her under, to cuff and
maul her.'[26] Yet this element of impetuousness should not be over-
estimated; Machiavelli would never argue that rashness is a virtue.
Boldness may be effective, but only when it is in basic agreement
with Fortune's plans. The core of Machiavelli's teaching on Fortune
I take to be this, that man 'can weave her designs but cannot destroy
them.' This is a theme which Machiavelli has articulated several times
in his writings in almost the same words. To show how uniform Machiavelli's teaching is, it is worth-while to quote the relevant passages
at some length. One very clear statement is found in the twenty-fifth
chapter of *The Prince:*

> any prince who relies exclusively on Fortune falls when she varies.
> I believe also that a prince succeeds who adapts his way of pro-

25 *Discourses*, II, 291; Gilbert, I, 408
26 *The Prince*, 25; Gilbert, I, 92

ceeding to the nature of the times, and conversely one does not succeed whose procedure is out of harmony with the times. In the things that lead them to the end they seek, that is, glory and riches, men act in different ways: one with caution, another impetuously; one by force, the other with skill; one by patience, the other with its contrary; and all of them with these differing methods attain their ends. We find also that of two cautious men, one carries out his purpose, the other does not. Likewise, we find two men with two differing temperaments equally successful, one being cautious and the other impetuous. This results from nothing else than the nature of the times, which is harmonious or not with their procedure.[27]

Equally clear are the comments in book III of the *Discourses,* where Machiavelli discusses the personal factors which enter into success:

Many times I have observed that the cause of the bad and of the good fortune of men is the way in which their method of working fits the times, since in their actions some men proceed with haste, some with heed and caution. Because in both of these methods men cross the proper boundaries, since they cannot follow the true road, in both of them they make errors. Yet a man succeeds in erring less and in having prosperous fortune if time fits his ways, for you always act as Nature inclines you.

We are unable to change for two reasons: one, that we cannot counteract that to which Nature inclines us; the other, that when with one way of doing a man has prospered greatly, he cannot be persuaded that he can profit by doing otherwise. That is why Fortune varies for the same men; she varies the times, but he does not vary his ways.[28]

Again, we find the same sentiments expressed in Machiavelli's letter of early 1513 to Piero Soderini, his patron who had recently been driven from Florence by the Medici. It is significant that this letter, written at a time when Machiavelli himself had sorely suffered the

The Prince, 25; Gilbert, I, 90-1

Discourses, III, 9; Gilbert, I, 452-3

blows of fortune, contains opinions identical to those we have seen above:

> I believe that as Nature has given each man an individual face, so she has given him an individual disposition and an individual imagination. From this it results that each man conducts himself according to his disposition and his imagination. On the other hand, because times vary and affairs are of varied types, one man's desires come out as he had prayed they would; he is fortunate who harmonizes his procedure with his time, but on the contrary he is not fortunate who in his actions is out of harmony with his time and with the type of its affairs. Hence it can well happen that two men working differently come to the same end, because each of them adapts himself to what he encounters, for affairs are of as many types as there are provinces and states. Thus, because times and affairs in general and individually change often, and men do not change their imaginings and their procedures, it happens that a man at one time has good fortune and at another time bad.
>
> And certainly anybody wise enough to understand the times and the types of affairs and to adapt himself to them would have always good fortune, or he would protect himself always from bad, and it would come to be true that the wise man would rule the stars and the fates. But because there never are such wise men, since men in the first place are shortsighted and in the second place cannot command their natures, it follows that Fortune varies and commands men and holds them under her yoke.[29]

All of the passages exhibit the identical teaching. We live in an unpredictable world, and so our actions often do not turn out as we planned. If we were clever enough to understand the times in which we live, and if we were flexible enough to adjust our tactics accordingly, we might always be successful. But this is a practical impossibility; for, as Machiavelli tells us, there never are men so wise nor men with such perfect control over their own character. We act, instead, as nature inclines us. Hence man will never be entirely deliv-

29 Letter 116; Gilbert, II, 896-7

ered from the power of fortune; even plans well laid and brilliantly executed may fail due to unforeseen contingencies. I must disagree with a recent critic who has maintained that for Machiavelli fortune can be 'completely overcome.'[30] It is true that Machiavelli speaks of overcoming fortune; but ordinarily he adds in the same breath that such efforts are eventually bound to fail. Machiavelli in effect promises only that we can increase our chances against Fortune, not that we can eliminate her effects entirely. Where he describes how a man could always have good fortune, this is only to point out the ideal condition which nature will never let us achieve. In Machiavelli one finds, perhaps, a certain enthusiasm for his own ideas, but not a messianic promise that he has the solution to all problems.

The various themes connected with fortune are all woven into Machiavelli's *Capitolo* on the subject. The poem may be divided roughly into three sections. In the first, the author dedicates his lines to the recipient, Giovan Battista Soderini, and then asks that the goddess Fortuna might deign to look favourably on him as well: 'she yet may look on him who has courage to sing of her dominion.' After this plea, Machiavelli begins to describe the dread goddess and to enumerate the things she does to the human race. She 'turns states and kingdoms upside down'; she 'times events as suits her'; and 'Over a palace open on every side she reigns and she deprives no one of entering, but the getting out is not sure.' In general, Fortune presides over our lives and makes it impossible for us to reckon with any assurance of success. Yet as in his prose works, Machiavelli is not content to leave things there. He is driven to seek some way of overcoming bad luck, of making the universe a little more predictable. In this quest he makes a fascinating change in the traditional imagery associated with Fortune. Since the time of Boethius, she had been represented with a single, inexorably turning wheel, on which men could ascend for a while but which would eventually throw them off. Machiavelli, however, writes: 'Within her palace, as many wheels are turning as there are varied ways of climbing to those things which every living man strives to attain.' These many wheels offer new possibilities for outwitting Fortune; for at any one time there is more than one course of action:

0 Charles Tarlton, 'The Symbolism of Redemption and the Exorcism of Fortune in Machiavelli's *Prince*,' *Review of Politics*, 30 (1968), 342

That man most luckily forms his plan, among all the persons in Fortune's palace, who chooses a wheel befitting her wish,

since the inclinations that make you act, so far as they conform with her doings, are the causes of your good and your ill.

Yet you cannot therefore trust yourself to her nor hope to escape her hard bite, her hard blows, violent and cruel,

because while you are whirled about by the rim of a wheel that for the moment is lucky and good, she is wont to reverse its course midcircle.

And since you cannot change your character nor give up the disposition that Heaven endows you with, in the midst of your journey she abandons you.

Therefore, if this he understood and fixed in his mind, a man who could leap from wheel to wheel would always be happy and fortunate,

but because to attain this is denied by the occult force that rules us, our condition changes with her course.

Yet Machiavelli is not deceived by his own remarkable image of the adventurer scrambling from wheel to wheel. *If* we could read Fortune's plan, and *if* we could change our own character and disposition, there might be some hope of keeping up the game indefinitely; but since this is impossible, eventually we will be doomed to fail. This is the same complex teaching that we have found in Machiavelli's other major works: theoretically, continued success might be attainable, if a man could always suit his behaviour to the situation; but it seems to be impossible that any man could be so astute. Hence we must always act in uncertainty. Prudence and audacity will be of assistance in recognizing and seizing the opportunity that offers itself; but in the last analysis, there remains an unpredictability to success and failure that we cannot expect to banish.

FORTUNE AND TRANSCENDENCE

What is the significance of Machiavelli's opinions on fortune? One point needs to be emphasized at the outset: What is most important in Machiavelli's understanding of fortune is precisely that which he never bothered to express in writing. What he left unsaid speaks volumes; for it serves to place his interpretation of fortune in the context of two thousand years of history.

There are, reaching back to antiquity, two great conceptions of fortune, which we might label the immanent and the transcendent. In the immanent conception, the human contest with Fortuna is a closed field of action. It is assumed without question that each man would like to possess the *bona fortunae,* the 'goods of fortune,' however variously they may be imagined – health, wealth, friendship, etc. All men play by fortune's rules, so to speak; they are winners or losers insofar as they achieve those rewards which fortune can bestow. *Virtus* – the ability pertaining to a man – is the counterweight to *fortuna*; a man's own strength and shrewdness can improve his chances in the struggle for the *bona fortunae,* although it can never guarantee success. But it never occurs to the contestant to ask why he should compete for Fortune's favours in the first place. As soon as this question is asked, the spell is broken, and a new conception of Fortune arises. For there is no compelling reason why one has to strive for the prizes which Fortune can distribute. There are other goods, goods of the mind and soul, which do not lie within the power of Fortune to confer or to remove. This insight is at the core of the Socratic teaching that it is better to suffer injustice than to commit it. If a man refrains from evil, he will be happy even if he suffers the worst blows of fortune. In a sense, he can transcend Fortune through refusing to play her game; this is why I have chosen to speak of a transcendental conception.

It is, of course, well known, that the words *virtus* and *arete* became ambiguous during antiquity due to the rise of philosophy. Originally connected with a man's power to achieve something, they later acquired a moral meaning as the perfection of the soul. It is perhaps less well known that, as I have pointed out above, the connotations of *fortuna* developed in precisely the same way, from immanence to transcendence. Hence there is no universal doctrine of antiquity concerning *virtus* and *fortuna,* but rather two distinct conceptions. When we read in Livy that 'fortune favours the bold,' we are confronted with the mood of immanence, where fortune's rewards appear worth seeking. Yet when we read in the *Consolation of Philosophy* that all fortune is good fortune because it can never rob the soul of virtue, the concern is with transcendence over fortune by directing one's attention to the divine good.

As far as the evidence of written documents is concerned, the immanent conception of fortune practically perished during the Middle Ages. It is unlikely that all men gave up their hopes of success in this world; but those who expressed themselves in writing were more concerned about the world to come. The solution of Boethius, which is really the method of transcendence developed by classical philosophy, persisted; but there was also developed a more distinctively Christian formulation of the problem. According to Boethius, all fortune was good because it could not touch the virtue of the inner man; but this notion still leaves logical problems for the Christian. Why does evil happen? The answer of a consistent faith is to see in the perturbations of fortune the workings of divine providence. Bad fortune is not only something to be transcended; it is part of God's plan to lead us to perfection. This identification of *fortuna* with providence is the solution adopted by Dante in the famous seventh canto of the *Inferno*.[31] It is also the attitude indicated by an interesting seal found in Hungary, on which the design consists of a wheel with the head of Christ in the centre. Around the outside is the inscription *Et Deus in rota:*[32] 'God in the wheel.' The implication is clear: in the centre of our shifting fortunes, we can find the divine plan of salvation.

It is informative to compare this thirteenth-century representation of Fortune's wheel with Machiavelli's image of the multiple wheels. In less than three hundred years the transcendent response to fortune has given way to the immanent – Machiavelli's adventurer, who skips from wheel to wheel, never stops to consider what the purpose of his striving is. His plans and desires are confined within the rules prescribed by Fortuna. He will achieve success if he can stay in harmony with her plans, that is, by selecting the correct wheel; if not, he is

31 Cf. also Chaucer's *Balade of Fortune*, II, 65-8:
   Lo, th'execucion of the magestee
   That al purveyeth of his rightwisnesse,
   That same thing 'Fortune' clepen ye,
   Ye blinde bestes, ful of lewednesse!
32 Doren, 'Fortuna im Mittelalter und in der Renaissance,' 147, contains an illustration.

doomed to failure. Nowhere in this imagery is there the slightest hint that bad fortune is not able to harm the soul, or that ill luck might be part of an overall design to lead man to redemption. Machiavelli does not even attack these considerations of transcendence; they are simply foreign to him, and he does not bother to mention them.

Throughout Machiavelli's works we find the triumph of the immanent conception of Fortuna. She is always the opponent, success is always the goal. Previously this had not always been so. In the thirteenth century, it was necessary to consider not only the means of achieving success but also the possible ill effect on the soul. Petrarch's famous discourse on fortune, for example, is entitled *De Remediis utriusque fortunae*: 'Remedies for both kinds of fortune.' The book is written in the form of two conversations; in the first, Reason debates with Joy, in the second with Sorrow. The point of both dialogues is the same, namely that both joy over success and sorrow over failure are immanent, transitory emotions. The correct response to both is to turn to God. Reason quotes with approval the advice of Lactantius: 'They that know God, are not only safe from incursions of Devyls, but also ... are not tyed by destinie.'[33] This is the epitome of the medieval transcendence over fortune – liberation from both good and bad luck. In comparison, it is worthwhile to read what Machiavelli says about the proper response to good fortune; for his words clearly illustrate the gap that separates his view from the medieval one. In the third book of the *Discourses,* Machiavelli comments on the words of Camillus who was once made dictator of Rome and then fell into disfavour: 'As for me, the dictatorship did not exalt my spirits nor exile depress them.'[34] Machiavelli continues:

From this we learn that great men are always in every sort of fortune just the same; if that varies, now raising them now putting them down, they do not vary, but always keep their courage firm and so closely united with their way of life that we easily see that Fortune does not have power over a single one of them. Quite different is the conduct of weak men, because they grow vain and

33 Petrarch, *Phisicke against Fortune, as well Prosperous as Adverse,* tr. Thomas Twyne (London 1579), 14
34 Livy, *Histories,* II, 7

are made drunk with good fortune, assigning all their prosperity to an ability which they have not displayed at any time. As a result, they become unbearable and hateful to all around them. From this situation, then, issues some sudden change in their lot, and when they look that in the face, they fall at once into the other defect and become despicable and abject. Consequently princes of that sort, when in adversity, think more about running away than about defending themselves, since, having used good fortune badly, they are unprepared for any defense.[35]

In his own way, Machiavelli is suggesting that there is a danger attached to good fortune; but his interpretation is totally immanent. Good fortune may be bad for a weak man because he will become insolent and not take sufficient precautions for the future. Hence a lucky success may lead directly to a later downfall. But there is no implication here that success in itself is a questionable thing; it is only dangerous if it does not perpetuate itself. The ultimate standard of judgment is thus clearly the *bona fortunae*; no transcendent considerations are present at all. The 'remedy' for good and bad fortune is not to turn to God but to use success wisely so that it will not slip from one's grasp.

If the response to success is to strive for still more, the loss of the transcendent dimension is equally visible in the reaction to failure. Here again, Machiavelli does not seek consolation in thoughts of eternity. He offers rather a type of resigned stoicism which accepts what cannot be altered but which does not turn from earthly to other-worldly considerations. Witness his own case. After his fall from his position, after his imprisonment and sufferings, Machiavelli can do nothing but salvage a little pride in the fortitude with which he endured his unhappiness. 'As to turning my face to resist Fortune,' he wrote to Vettori shortly after his release from prison, 'I want you to get this pleasure from my distresses, namely that I have borne them so bravely that I love myself for it and feel that I am stronger than you believed.'[36] He must have had the same unhappy experiences in mind when he wrote in *The Ass of Gold*:

35 *Discourses*, III, 31; Gilbert, I, 498
36 Letter 119; Gilbert, II, 899

Ma perche il pianto a l'uom fu sempre brutto,
sie debbe al volto della sua fortuna
voltare il viso di lacrime asciutto.

'But because weeping has always been shameful to a man, he
should turn to the blows of Fortune a face unstained with tears.'[37]

Similar considerations apply to Machiavelli's humorous little poem
Dell'occasione ('On Opportunity'). In it the poet meets Opportunity,
who explains to him how hard she is to catch: her hair falls forward
over her face, so she cannot be recognized, while in back she is bald,
so she cannot be seized while she runs. The poet asks her who her
companion is, and she replies that it is Penitence; and 'whoever does
not know how to capture me will get her.'[38] In this dialogue there is
no hint that Penitence refers to anything other than simple regret at
having let opportunity slip by. There is no suggestion at all of the
medieval repentance which guides the soul to thoughts of immortal-
ity. Admittedly one should not make too much of this one short
poem; Machiavelli consciously modelled it on an epigram of Auso-
nius, and the thought expressed is his. Yet Machiavelli felt the poem
worth imitating, so he probably found nothing amiss in the contents.
Furthermore, this is not an isolated instance; it is only one of a series
of cases where Machiavelli speaks of fortune and kindred themes
without ever mentioning that transcendence over fortune is at least
a conceivable option. Such repeated silence forces us to conclude
that such possibilities of transcendence must have been absent from
Machiavelli's mind when he used the symbolism of fortune.

This analysis of Machiavelli's use of *fortuna* is largely independent
of the vexed question of his religious convictions. I have only suggested that when he spoke of *fortuna,* he did so exclusively in an immanent context. This does not mean that in other situations Machiavelli did not reflect on the transitory nature of the *bona fortunae.* If,
for example, we take the 'Exhortation to Penitence' at face value, its
implication is that we should become conscious of our entanglements

7 *The Ass of Gold,* III, 11.85-7; Gilbert, II, 757
8 L.18: 'chi non sa prender me, costei ritiene.' Machiavelli, *Opere* (Milano 1965),
VIII, 325. The poem is not contained in the Gilbert edition.

in the world 'And repent and understand clearly/that as much as pleases the world is a short dream.'[39] Yet regardless of how genuine Machiavelli's emotions of penitence were, it is clear that, in this case, he did not choose to express them with the symbolism of *fortuna*. We also find a similar situation in the *Capitolo* 'On Ambition.' Here Machiavelli gives us a very powerful description of the bad effects of ambition:

> Pass over Siena's fraternal contests; turn your eyes, Luigi, to this region, upon these people thunderstruck and bewildered,
>
> you will see how Ambition results in two kinds of action: one party robs and the other weeps for its wealth ravaged and scattered.
>
> Let him turn his eyes here who wishes to behold the sorrows of others, and let him consider if ever before now the sun has looked upon such savagery.
>
> A man is weeping for his father dead and a woman for her husband; another man, beaten and naked, you see driven in sadness from his own dwelling.
>
> Oh how many times, when the father has held his son tight in his arms, a single thrust has pierced the breasts of them both![40]

It is significant that this moving description is quite divorced from any reference to fortune. Though Machiavelli is capable of pity, he does not express it with references to fortune. Where *fortuna* does appear in the poem, it is toward the end, where the frame of reference has shifted considerably – Machiavelli has concluded that ambition can never be exorcised from the heart, and that therefore the only remedy is to bring it under control through forceful government. It is at this point, when musing on the difficulty of creating a government which can curb ambition, that he remarks that 'in the world most men let themselves be mastered by fortune' (11.176-7). Thus we must conclude that, even though Machiavelli was conscious at times of the desire for transcendence over the limitation of politics,

39 Petrarch, Sonnet 1; quoted by Machiavelli at the end of the 'Exhortation to Penitence,' Gilbert, I, 174

40 Gilbert, II, 738; 11.124-38

this desire was expressed in other ways than by the symbolism of *fortuna.*

Although, as I shall point out in the next section, there are certain inconsistencies in Machiavelli's use of *fortuna,* there is this one regularity, that the dimension of transcendence over the struggle with fortune is never present. In this respect, Machiavelli represents the culmination of two centuries of development since Dante and Petrarch. In this period, as I have remarked, the immanent conception of fortune modelled on that of antiquity had increasingly appeared alongside the other-worldly, medieval notion. The result was the extraordinary confusion in the identity of *fortuna* which many historians have perceived in the Renaissance. Chabod, for example, writes that:

"Fortune" is very hard to define – At one moment in conformity with the Christian adaptation of the ancient concept, it appears in the guise of an *ancilla Dei* – At another it resumes its ancient character of a blind, uncontrollable fate.[41]

Felix Gilbert has observed the same phenomenon in his study of the protocols of the Florentine *pratiche*:

Thus to the Florentine Fortuna had preserved many of the characteristics of a pagan goddess ... Yet at the same time this pagan goddess exerts her power in a Christian world and has to be integrated in it ... thus it is not possible clearly to distinguish between what is done by God and what is done by Fortuna.[42]

With Machiavelli, however, this tension between the differing ideas of fortune is resolved in favour of the immanent conception. Although Machiavelli occasionally refers to God instead of fortune, these tend to be stylized references which do not exhibit any deep feeling.[43]

41 Federico Chabod, *Machiavelli and the Renaissance,* tr. David Moore (New York 1965), 189
42 Felix Gilbert, *Machiavelli and Guicciardini* (Princeton NJ 1965), 41
43 E.g., in the *History of Florence,* VII, 21, Machiavelli speaks of certain citizens 'conducting themselves as though God and Fortune had given them the city to be plundered.' Gilbert, III, 1364. In the *Second Decennale* he writes of the

They are not joined to any profound reflections on the transitoriness of earthly pursuits. In all the cases where Machiavelli speaks at any length about Fortune and with any great emotion, his frame of reference is clearly the closed world of immanent political action, where all men by definition strive for the *bona fortunae*.

THE PLACE OF FORTUNE IN MACHIAVELLI'S THOUGHT

Students of Machiavelli have differed widely in assessing the role of *fortuna* in his thought. One position, advanced by several eminent scholars, is that generally speaking, *fortuna* represents the breakdown of reason in Machiavelli's thinking. Where he could not go any farther in explaining a phenomenon, he would attribute it in quasi-superstitious fashion to the workings of fortune. Burd, for example, says with respect to fortune that 'whenever Machiavelli – and Guicciardini too – were taken off the lines familiar to them, their natural acumen appears to desert them and they share the superstition of the age.'[44] Burd implies, although without adducing any weighty textual evidence, that Machiavelli's notion of fortune was astrological in character. Ernst Cassirer seems to have come to similar conclusions, although he grants Machiavelli perhaps a bit more rationality. In *The Myth of the State*, he writes that Machiavelli knew that even the best political advice was sometimes ineffective.

> His logical and rational method deserted him at this point. He had to admit that human things are not governed by reason, and that, therefore, they are not entirely describable in terms of reason. We must have recourse to another – to a half-mythical power. "Fortune" seems to be the ruler of things.[45]

tribulations of Italy 'by divine wisdom foreordained.' Gilbert, III, 1457. In *The Prince*, ch.11, he declares that ecclesiastical principalities are 'maintained by God,' Gilbert, I, 44. This last statement I would interpret ironically; the first two appear to be stylized references only.

44 Burd, *Il Principe* (1891), 355
45 Ernst Cassirer, *The Myth of the State* (New Haven 1963), 157

By and large, Chabod also shares this opinion, that *fortuna* is at least half-mythical. He declares that Machiavelli sometimes regarded *fortuna* 'as the force and logic of history,' but more often 'as a mysterious, transcendent grouping of events, whose incoherence is unintelligible to the human mind.'[46]

An almost antithetical interpretation has, however, been developed by Leonardo Olschki. According to Olschki, Machiavelli produced in *The Prince* a 'new science' of man and society in much the same way as Galileo created a new science of matter. The fundamental concepts of this science were *fortuna* and *virtù*. Whatever may be the connotations of *fortuna* in Machiavelli's literary works, in *The Prince*

fortune is neither a goddess nor a personification, neither an allegory nor a metaphor, as it has been in poetry, in Machiavelli's own Capitolo on Fortune, or in moral philosophy ... it is ... an abstract and secular concept ... In other words: fortune represents the passive condition of political success in conquests or internal administration. *Virtù* is its active counterpart.[47]

Thus fortune and virtue are 'technical terms of a rational system of political thought';[48] they are the building blocks of a scientific analysis of political behaviour. It would be hard to imagine a position more contrary to that of Burd, Cassirer, and Chabod, who see in *fortuna* not an advance in rational thought but a survival of a pre-logical description of the world.

I find it impossible to accept the full burden of Olschki's argument. It is not enough that scientific concepts be abstract and general, so that they can refer to a multitude of phenomena. They must also be relatable in such a way that the result is a testable proposition. In other words, there must be associated with the pure concepts operational definitions which permit empirical verification. In this respect Machiavelli's notions of *fortuna* and *virtù* are utterly deficient. He gives no rules, either explicit or implicit, by which each can be defined. In practice, therefore, their use is tautological. If a man's at-

46 Federico Chabod, *Machiavelli and the Renaissance*, 69-70
47 Leonardo Olschki, *Machiavelli the Scientist* (Berkeley 1945), 37-8
48 Ibid., 39

tempts, like those of Cesare Borgia, fail in spite of impressive efforts, the result must be due to the malice of fortune. The logical problem involved is rather similar to that of the modern dilemma of environment and heredity. The concepts appear to be reasonable, and yet the lack of unimpeachable operational definitions makes it impossible ever to decide between them.

Yet even if Olschki's controversial thesis cannot be accepted entirely, it suggests the problem facing Machiavelli's reader. The term *fortuna* is used so often and in so many different connections that it is easy for confusion to arise over its precise meaning. I suggest, furthermore, that there is good reason for this confusion and for the disagreement between Olschki and other students of Machiavelli. There is in fact a fundamental ambiguity in Machiavelli's *fortuna* which makes it appear to be now a mythical image, now a rational concept. Without ever acknowledging that he is speaking of two different things, Machiavelli employs *fortuna* to designate not only the unexpected occurrence of an unique and contingent event, but also the whole constellation of social forces in which the event transpires. This is a problem of which the modern development of statistical theory has made social scientists acutely aware. It is becoming obvious that one can describe the macro-structure of society (or at least certain aspects of it) in terms of probability, but that this yields no information about the occurrence of a single event. To give an example, one can make estimates of social mobility within a class system, and thus make predictions about the levels to which certain percentages of a social stratum will probably rise; but this does not enable us to say anything about a specific individual. With respect to the behaviour of the system, his behaviour must be taken as random or fortuitous.

Similar epistemological questions arise not only in statistical models but also in the genetic explanations of the historian. One can trace the antecedents of a social event, and suggest why it 'had to happen'; but it is impossible to explain why it happened on a particular day and involved the people it did. At this point the historian usually points to the role of personality or the individual; but this is a thinly disguised appeal to the principle of chance, which merely transfers the problem to the psychologist.

I would argue, then, that it is perfectly in accord with the common principles of modern social science to distinguish between the macro-level of causation and the micro-level of fortuitousness. Now this is a distinction which Machiavelli did not draw. Obviously he cannot be blamed for not doing so; it is only in this century that we have become aware of the critical and ineradicable role of chance in scientific explanation. But even though we can hardly reproach Machiavelli for not being aware of the difficulty, the fact remains that his failure to do so renders his conception of *fortuna* ambiguous and mystified. For under *fortuna* he includes not only the truly fortuitous and contingent single event, but also the entire context in which such events occur; and while the individual event must remain mysterious, the large-scale constellation of social forces is in principle explicable.

It is noteworthy that when Machiavelli is speaking of *fortuna* in this second sense, he frequently substitutes the totally secularized concept of 'the times' (*i tempi*). This happens in several of his most important discussions of fortune. Yet it would not be accurate to state that he replaces *fortuna* with *i tempi*. It is rather the case that he uses the two terms interchangeably at certain points. Although the germ of the notion is there in his work, he is not ready to say with Montesquieu that:

> it is not fortune who governs the world, as we see from the history of the Romans. There are general causes, moral or physical, which operate in every monarchy, raise it, maintain it, or overthrow it; all that occurs is subject to these causes; and if a particular cause, like the accidental result of a battle, has ruined a state, there was a general cause which made the downfall of this state ensue from a single battle. In a word, the principal movement draws with it all the particular occurrences.[49]

It is only with the benefit of hindsight that we can say that Machiavelli's use of *fortuna* to describe large-scale constellations of circumstances is a mystification.

Yet even though Machiavelli was not conscious of epistemological problems in the fashion of modern investigators, he was an extraordinarily acute student of politics. Hence, when he uses *fortuna* to describe a potentially intelligible concatenation of factors, this does not

---

49 Montesquieu, *Considerations on the Greatness and Decadence of the Romans* (1734), cited in J.B. Bury, *The Idea of Progress* (London 1920), 145-6

remain a total mystification. We can see at work the analytical powers of a man whose credo it was that it is well to reason upon all things. Thus even though *fortuna* is fundamentally a symbol of a power or force which is beyond fathoming, Machiavelli's conception of it contains a striking amount of rationalism.

The first point to consider is his relation to astrology. The Renaissance was indeed a superstitious era, even more so than the Middle Ages, now that certain of the restraints of the orthodox faith in divine Reason had been weakened. Most men believed in omens and magic of some type, and Machiavelli was no exception, if we are to take at face value *Discourses*, I, 56: 'Before great events occur in a city or a region, there are signs that presage them or men who predict them.' And yet I must disagree with Burd that Machiavelli's notion of *fortuna* is an astrological one. On the contrary, wherever Machiavelli attributes events to the workings of fortune, astrology and superstition of any sort are noticeably absent. Although it seems true that he believed in the existence of omens, Machiavelli did not use astrology as an operating approach to political analysis. Instead he preferred to work out rational explanations based on personal motives or impersonal forces. Hence, in spite of the chapter on omens in the *Discourses*, what is remarkable in Machiavelli's use of *fortuna* is precisely the absence of superstitious associations. I would conclude that *Discourses*, I, 56 is due to Machiavelli's desire to write a complete treatise, taking into account the day's conventional wisdom; that chapter most decidedly does not represent his typical approach to politics.

If occult forces do not play any noteworthy role in Machiavelli's thinking on politics, neither does the more respectable practice of prayer. In *L'Asino d'Oro* he specifically rules out divine favour or intervention in favour of reliance on more immediate means of action:

> To believe that without effort on your part God fights for you, while you are idle and on your knees, has ruined many kingdoms and many states.

> But there should be no one with so small a brain that he will believe that, if his house is falling, God will save it without any other prop, because he will die beneath that ruin.[50]

50 *The Ass of Gold*, V; Gilbert, II, 764

Characteristically, Machiavelli adds that prayer is of some value – because it promotes 'union and good order' among those participating, and on the solidarity of the group 'rests good and happy fortune'! He could hardly say more clearly that man must rely on his own efforts if he is to achieve his goals, and that he cannot expect any supernatural benefits. It is highly instructive, too, to look more closely at the one time when Machiavelli appears to say that God intervenes in human affairs. In the eleventh chapter of *The Prince,* he takes up the topic of ecclesiastical principalities, only to say that it would be presumptuous of him to discuss them, since they are 'set on high and maintained by God.'[51] Yet how much credence can be placed in such an assertion, when Machiavelli is discussing the papal states in a book dedicated to win the favour of a close relative of the pope? Furthermore, immediately after humbly refusing to discuss the politics of the papacy, Machiavelli starts a new sentence with 'nevertheless' and goes on to deliver a number of comments about the success of the papacy under Alexander VI and Julius II. I, for one, would seriously question whether Machiavelli thought the papal states were particularly protected by God in their political dealings.[52]

Yet just as we cannot ignore the rationalistic elements in Machiavelli's conception of fortune, so we cannot wish away the very real irrational components. This is the truth contained in Cassirer's dictum that Machiavelli's *fortuna* is 'half-mythical.' Particularly when he is referring to the unique and contingent event, he does so in words which suggest that fortune possesses consciousness, personality, and intention.

I am not referring so much to obvious literary devices, such as that in the twenty-fifth chapter of *The Prince,* where Machiavelli refers to Fortuna as a woman who has to be handled with authority, as to other places where he seems to say in a straightforward way that Fortuna consciously plans our lot. In the *Discourses,* for example, he quotes with approval Livy's saying that 'Fortune thus blinds the minds of men when she does not wish them to resist her power,' and then continues in a similar vein:

1 Gilbert, I, 44
2 I am afraid that the assumption of Father Walker that these words of Machiavelli were sincerely meant and demonstrate his religious faith, is a piece of wishful thinking. Cf. Walker, *Discourses,* I, 80

Skillfully Fortune does this, since she chooses a man, when she plans to bring to pass great things, who is of so much perception and so much ability that he recognizes the opportunities she puts before him. So in the same way when she intends to bring to pass great failures, she puts there men to promote such failure. And if somebody there is able to oppose her, she either kills him or deprives him of all means for doing anything good.[53]

The rest of the paragraph is an impressive enumeration of the things which Fortuna accomplishes when she is in the mood. Similarly the whole story of Castruccio Castracani is meant to illustrate how Fortune intervenes in human affairs because she wishes 'to show the world that she – and not prudence – makes men great.'[54] There is perhaps a tendency for modern readers to skip lightly over passages like these or to rationalize them as pieces of allegory. Yet they occur so frequently in Machiavelli's works that we should be careful not to underrate their importance. It is safer to assume that, even if Machiavelli did not think of Fortuna as a specific woman in a specific place, he must have conceived of her in a way we would today call mythical, which does not strictly differentiate abstract concepts from the human emotions bound up with them.

It would be convenient if one could say that Machiavelli had two distinct conceptions of *fortuna,* a rational one referring to large social causes and synonymous with *i tempi,* and a non-rational one referring to the fortuitous crystallization of these causes in a single event. But matters are not so simple. Machiavelli himself was not aware of the distinction we have made. He did not distinguish between that which is unknown, but potentially intelligible, and that which is on principle unknowable. The most that can be done is to draw the distinction in hindsight and to suggest that it grows naturally out of Machiavelli's use of *fortuna* and *i tempi,* even if it did not occur to Machiavelli himself.

53 *Discourses,* II, 29; Gilbert, I, 407-8
54 Gilbert, II, 534

SEVEN

In Search of Machiavellian *Virtù*

JOHN PLAMENATZ

The most vilified of political thinkers is also the one of whom it has been said that he 'concentrated all his real and supreme values in what he called *virtù*.'[1] There is nothing here to be surprised at; for those who have been shocked by Machiavelli have been so, not only by his seeming to justify murder, cruelty, and treachery, but by his way of speaking about virtue.

Machiavelli is no longer shocking, and it is widely agreed that those who were shocked by him in the past misunderstood him. But he is still a subject of controversy. In particular, there are differences of opinion about what he called *virtù*. These differences are, I think, less about what is to be understood by the term, what qualities it refers to, than about the place of *virtù* in Machiavelli's political thought generally and his conception of man. Some ninety years ago Villari said that Machiavelli 'always used the word *virtue* in the sense of courage and energy both for good and evil. To Christian virtue in its more general meaning, he rather applied the term *goodness,* and felt much less admiration for it than for the pagan virtue that was always fruitful of glory.'[2] Later scholars, though they have qualified this ver-

---

1 F. Meinecke, *Machiavellism: The Doctrine of Raison d'Etat and Its Place in Modern History,* tr. Douglas Scott (London & New Haven 1957), 31

2 P. Villari, *Life and Times of Machiavelli,* tr. Linda Villari, 4 vols (London, n.d.), II, 92

dict, have not disagreed with it substantially – though they have some-times believed that they were doing so. It is not true that Machiavelli always used the word *virtù* in this general sense, or in narrower senses that fall within its scope. He sometimes used it in quite other senses. It has been questioned whether he admired *virtù* more than he did goodness, and it is doubtful whether what he understood by goodness (*bontà*) has much that is peculiarly Christian about it. Still, though writers since Villari's time have gone further than he did in distin-guishing the various senses that Machiavelli gave to *virtù*, they have not seriously challenged his account of it. They have tried rather to improve on it.

No one has gone further than Meinecke in treating the idea of *virtù* as the key to understanding Machiavelli's conceptions of man and of the state. Meinecke distinguishes two important senses in which Ma-chiavelli uses the term. Sometimes he has in mind what is nowadays called *civic virtue,* and sometimes something altogether more rare and excellent – a virtue peculiar to rulers and leaders of men, and es-pecially to founders of states and religions. This second virtue, to dis-tinguish it from the first, we might call *heroic* – though Meinecke does not give it that name. Heroic and civic virtue are not mutually exclusive; indeed, they are closely related in the sense that each sus-tains the other or gives scope to it, but they are different.

If, among Machiavelli's twentieth-century interpreters, Meinecke makes the most of *virtù*, Professor Whitfield seems to make the least. 'There is,' he says, 'no doctrine of *virtù* in Machiavelli. If there were it would be easy to discover in his works, but Machiavelli was not given to such theorizing, and he himself would be the first to be sur-prised at the stir the word has caused.'[3] Whitfield, in his English way, felt perhaps a certain impatience with other scholars 'theorizing' about a writer who, in his eyes, has the merit of not being 'given to theorizing.'

Professor Whitfield is right; there is no doctrine of *virtù* in Machia-velli. Machiavelli does not define the word, even in the most general way, let alone distinguish different senses in which he uses it. Nor is it part of a systematic theory about man and the state, for Machia-velli has no such theory. There is no more a doctrine of *virtù* in Ma-

3 J.H. Whitfield, *Machiavelli* (Blackwell 1947), 95

chiavelli than there is a doctrine of *vertu* in the plays of Corneille. Still, what each expresses by the word is worth, and has received, close scrutiny; for this scrutiny is one way, and a good way, of getting at how they think and feel about man.

Neither Meinecke, who says that Machiavelli 'concentrates his real and supreme values in *virtù*,' nor Whitfield, who denies that he has a doctrine of it, disagrees with Villari that part of what Machiavelli understands by *virtù* is energy or strength of will. No moderately attentive reader of *The Prince* and the *Discourses* can help but notice that Machiavelli finds *virtù* both in the Roman citizen devoted to the republic and in such men as Romulus, Lycurgus, Moses, and Numa Pompilius, the 'founders' of states or religions. Though Machiavelli does not define either the virtue of the citizen or that of the maker or restorer of a state or religion, though he does not point to the differences between them, there can really be no doubting that he does not attribute the same range of qualities to the citizen and to the heroic creator or preserver of what brings order to men.

Thus, though there is no doctrine of *virtù* in Machiavelli, there is no denying that he uses the word in related and yet different senses, and that the attempt to explain how they differ and how they are connected with his other ideas about man, the human condition and the state, is an attempt to interpret what can properly be called a philosophy. Because a writer produces no systematic theory, it does not follow that he has nothing that deserves to be called philosophy – for his ideas may be coherent and may have implicit in them a comprehensive attitude or way of looking at the human condition, either at all times and everywhere or within broad limits of time and territory. Of course, there are inconsistencies and obscurities in Machiavelli; but then there are also in the much more systematic Hobbes, who loved to define and to distinguish. And it may be that Machiavelli was not the less consistent and lucid of the two.

Though Machiavelli did not 'theorize' about *virtù*, Whitfield does so for some thirteen pages and to good purpose. Machiavelli, he says, sometimes contrasts *virtù* with *viltà*, and at least once with *ozio*, but more often with *fortuna*.[4] Now, *viltà* is cowardice, or faint-heartedness, and sometimes baseness or meanness, and *ozio* is idleness. So

4 Ibid., 97

that Whitfield agrees with Villari that *virtù* is, first and foremost, courage and energy; for courage is the opposite of cowardice, and energy of idleness. And though courage and energy are not properly the *opposites* of fortune, they can be *opposed* to it. Machiavelli speaks of fortune, sometimes, as if it were a person, as if it had purposes of its own, benevolent or malevolent, and at other times as if it were opportunity that a man may take or not take; and he speaks of it also as whatever in human affairs is unforeseen and must be faced when it comes. He speaks of it as sailors, in the old sailing days, spoke of the sea, as if it were both friend and enemy, propitious and threatening, itself unconquerable but the occasion of human defeats and victories. Fortune is what man is 'up against'; and *virtù* is opposed to it in the sense that it makes the best of it, either by taking advantage of what it brings or by bearing up under it. Here again *virtù* is courage and energy, and something more besides; it is fortitude, or courage in adversity, and also intelligence and resourcefulness, the ability to recognize how you are placed and to act in time and effectively. There is nothing that Whitfield says or implies about *virtù* to which either Villari or Meinecke need disagree.

This is not to suggest that he only repeats what they, who wrote before he did, said. For example, he shows how close Machiavelli stands to other writers, earlier or later, who never, as he did, shocked posterity. He quotes from Cicero's *De Officiis* (II, X, 320): 'For they [men] do not despise everyone of whom they think ill. They think ill of those who are wicked, slanderous, fraudulent, ready to commit injustices, without indeed despising them. Wherefore, as I said, those are despised who, as the saying goes, are of no use either to themselves or others, in whom there is no exertion, no care for anything.'[5] This is good, and to the point. At least since Villari's time, Machiavelli's 'pagan' idea of *virtù* has been contrasted with the 'Christian' idea of *bontà*. Yet even the best of Christians does not despise all that he blames; he does not despise, any more than Machiavelli did, courage and energy, fortitude and resourcefulness – even in the wicked, even when he blames what they could not have done had they not had these qualities. Actions that require *virtù*, though sometimes evil, are never despicable. Cicero said it, or rather implied it, long before Machiavelli did.

5 Ibid., 100

Excellent, too, and to the point, are Whitfield's quotations from La Rochefoucauld: 'Weakness is more opposed to virtue than is vice,' or 'No one deserves the name of good unless he has strength and boldness enough to be wicked – all other goodness is most often a form of idleness or of impotence of the will,' or 'There are evil heroes as well as good ones.'[6] The virtue that La Rochefoucauld speaks of is not Machiavelli's *virtù*, but the two ideas have a good deal in common. Where there is virtue,·for La Rochefoucauld as for Machiavelli, there is strength of will. But Professor Whitfield goes too far when he suggests that what passes uncondemned in Cicero and La Rochefoucauld (and in others) is found shocking in Machiavelli. The Frenchman never said, and Whitfield does not show that the Roman did either, that actions ordinarily held to be wicked are justified when they are committed for the founding or preserving of the state. This doctrine – whatever is to be said for or against it – is not to be found in La Rochefoucauld and is not implied by the passage that Whitfield quotes from Cicero. But it is to be found in Machiavelli or at least it has seemed so to those who have accused him of condoning wickedness. To quote from some of the great 'moralists' to make clearer what Machiavelli meant by *virtù* is an excellent idea but to use the quotations to suggest that he is no more open than they are to the accusation that he justifies immorality is to misuse them.

I have touched briefly on the views of three writers, Villari, Meinecke, and Whitfield, who have all in their different ways thrown light upon what Machiavelli meant by *virtù*. They do not all three say the same things. Neither Villari nor Whitfield distinguishes, as Meinecke does, *civic* from what might (for want of a better word) be called *heroic* virtue. Indeed, Meinecke himself does not go far in making this distinction; he rather suggests that it ought to be made than puts himself to the trouble of making it, for he does not explain in detail how the two sorts of virtue differ. He goes no further in this direction than to say: 'it [*virtù*] therefore embraced the civic virtues and those of the ruling class; it embraced a readiness to devote oneself to the common good, as well as the wisdom, energy and ambition of the great founders and rulers of states.'[7] But 'common good'

6 Ibid., 100-1. Whitfield quotes from La Rochefoucauld in French, but I give these quotations, as all others in this article, in English.

7 Meinecke, *Machiavellism*, 32

is a vague term, and the founder and the ruler may be as ready as the ordinary citizen to promote it. Civic virtue is perhaps better described as a readiness to perform the duties of one's office or role in the state than as devotion to a common good. The citizen, and not only the ruler, needs 'energy' if he is to be a good citizen, and even some measure of wisdom. As for ambition, I doubt, for reasons that I shall give later, whether it is to be included in Machiavellian *virtù*.

We may regret that Meinecke did not explain more adequately and fully the difference between these two kinds of 'virtue,' but we cannot deny that they differ considerably and are closely related, and that both are important in the thought of Machiavelli. Nor can we go far in disagreeing with Meinecke's account of what they consist in, for he says too little about them to allow us to do that. He neither repeats what Villari said nor contradicts him, and is not contradicted by Whitfield. Where he goes wrong – so at least it seems to me – is not so much in his meagre account of what Machiavelli meant by *virtù*; it is rather in some of the conclusions he draws from it. The distinction he makes between *civic* and what I have called *heroic* virtue is one that needs to be made, though it ought to be made more clearly than he makes it. But to say, as he does, that 'the ethical sphere of his (Machiavelli's) *virtù* lay in juxtaposition to the usual moral sphere like a kind of world on its own'[8] which was, for Machiavelli, a 'higher world' is to misinterpret Machiavelli, attributing to him beliefs and attitudes which there is no good reason to believe were his. And it is just as misleading to say that 'the development and creation of *virtù* was for Machiavelli the ideal, and completely self-evident, purpose of the state.'[9] There are no better scholars in the world than the Germans. Yet the weight of German scholarship sometimes lies heavy on what it studies, pushing it out of shape. How it does so in this case I shall try to show later. But first let us look at some examples of how Machiavelli speaks of *virtù* in the two most often read of his books, *The Prince* and the *Discourses*.

If we read only English translations of Machiavelli, we are hard put to it to discover what he meant by *virtù*. For his translators, more often than not, do not render *virtù* by 'virtue.' They have an excel-

8 Ibid., 33
9 Ibid., 34

lent excuse for not doing so; for *virtù*, as Machiavelli uses it, often does not mean what 'virtue' means in the English of our day. So they render *virtù* by some other word, such as valour, ability, merit, courage, or genius, or by some combination of words. Take for example the nineteenth chapter of the first book of the *Discourses,* which in most editions, both Italian and English, is from two to three pages long. In it Machiavelli speaks of *virtù* ten times; Detmold, in one of the most widely used of English translations, renders *virtù* by 'virtue' only twice, and on both occasions adds the word 'valour,' presumably in the hope of coming closer to the original; while Allan Gilbert, the most recent and perhaps the most accurate of Machiavelli's translators into English, abstains altogether from the word 'virtue' in his version of this chapter.[10] On all ten occasions he renders *virtù* by ability, leaving it to the reader to judge from the context what kind of ability is in question. Detmold renders *virtù* by 'character,' 'virtue and valour,' 'vigour and ability,' 'genius and courage,' 'good qualities and courage,' 'great abilities and courage,' 'military ability,' 'merits.' If we take only this chapter, Gilbert is the more prudent translator of the two, and also the more faithful to the original. Yet *virtù*, as Machiavelli uses the word, has not quite the same meaning, or range of meanings, as the broader and more colourless English word 'ability.' Which is not to suggest that Gilbert was wrong to prefer it to the more varied expressions to which Detmold resorted.

In the third chapter of *The Prince,* Machiavelli praises the Romans for their foresight. He says of them that 'seeing their troubles far ahead, [they] always provided against them, and never let them continue in order to avoid war, because they knew that such a war is not averted but is deferred to the other's advantage ... Nor did they approve what all day is in the mouths of the wise men of our age: to profit from the help of time; but they did profit from that of their own vigor [*virtù*] and prudence.'[11] Here *virtù* is associated with prudence. The Romans looked far ahead, taking resolute and timely ac-

10 For Detmold's rendering see his translation of the *Discourses* in the Modern Library College edition of *The Prince* and the *Discourses,* 172-4; for Gilbert's see *Machiavelli: The Chief Works and Others,* tr. Allan H. Gilbert, I, 244-5.

11 Gilbert, *Chief Works,* I, 17. I shall quote only from Allan Gilbert's translation of Machiavelli, putting the word *virtù* or other Italian words or phrases in brackets next to Gilbert's renderings of them.

tion. What, according to Machiavelli, do the wise – the falsely-wise – mean by 'the help of time'? They mean that we can see only a little way ahead, and that therefore difficult decisions are best left untaken. This is the excuse of the pusillanimous. True, we cannot be sure of the future, but we must look ahead as far as we can, seeing what is to be done for the best, and doing it in good time. With the old Romans, at least in the eyes of Machiavelli, foresight, energy, and courage went naturally together.

In the sixth chapter of *The Prince*, speaking of men who have become rulers, Machiavelli says: 'they had from Fortune nothing more than opportunity, which gave them matter into which they could introduce whatever form they chose; and without opportunity, their strength of will [*la virtù dello animo loro*] would have been wasted, and without such strength, the opportunity would have been useless';[12] and then, a little further on, he continues: 'Their opportunities then made these men prosper, since their surpassing abilities [*la eccelenza virtù loro*] enabled them to recognize their opportunities. As a result, their countries were exalted and became very prosperous.'[13] Here *virtù* consists, in the first place, of strength of will or mind, and in the second, of insight. The possessor of *virtù* sees his chance to mould something to his own design, not some inert or physical thing, but something human, some community or some aspect of communal life; he has imagination and intelligence enough to see what can be done, to see what is invisible to others, and strength of purpose enough to do it. He is strong, bold, and of good judgment, to his own great advantage and to the advantage of his people or community.

This is not to say that, in the opinion of Machiavelli, these qualities fail to qualify as *virtù* unless their possessor actually gets what he wants for himself or his people. Courage, energy, and intelligence do not cease to be what they are when they fail of their purpose. Small men have small purposes and are often successful, but their success is no evidence of *virtù* in them, and great men – who are great because their courage, energy, and intelligence are out of the ordinary – sometimes fail. One of the meanings that Machiavelli gives to *virtù* is

12 Ibid., 25
13 Ibid., 26

the capacity to form large and difficult purposes, and to act resourcefully and resolutely in pursuit of them. *Virtù,* in this (the heroic)
sense, is imagination and resilience as well as courage and intelligence.
There is no scope for it except where there are difficulties, where
there are risks to be taken; and where risks are taken, there is a
chance of failure. Machiavelli's feelings towards the most notorious,
and (in some eyes) the most oddly chosen, of his heroes varied considerably. There was a time when he came close to despising Cesare
Borgia – not because Borgia failed of his purpose but because he lost
his nerve and his dignity when things went against him.

Villari is right when he says that Machiavellian *virtù* is 'fruitful of
glory.' The actions it inspires are of the kind that bring fame or reputation: fame where *virtù* is heroic and reputation where it is civic. But
it is a mistake to include, as Meinecke does, ambition among the
qualities that make up *virtù.* I have found no example of Machiavelli
using the word in such a way as to suggest that ambition is itself a
part of *virtù.* True, he thought well of ambition, and was himself ambitious. The desire for glory promotes *virtù*; it is the strongest of the
forces that move men to display it, especially the heroic kind. And
even the citizen who displays only civic *virtù* is concerned for his
good name; and this concern, though it is not what is ordinarily called ambition, is akin to it. But to hold that ambition is a prime mover
of *virtù* is still not to treat ambition as a part of *virtù.*

In some of the most discussed pages he wrote, in the eighth chapter of *The Prince,* Machiavelli denies that a really wicked man who
achieves a great ambition can be said to be virtuous, even though he
displays great strength of mind and courage. This denial has been
called half-hearted, and is certainly ambiguous. Speaking of Agathocles, a potter's son who by ruthless means became tyrant of Syracuse,
Machiavelli says: 'It cannot, however, be called virtue [*virtù*] to kill
one's fellow-citizens, to betray friends, to be without fidelity, without mercy, without religion; such proceedings enable one to gain
sovereignty but not fame. If we consider Agathocles' ability [*se si
considerassi la virtù di Agatocle*] in entering into and getting out of
dangers, and his greatness of mind in enduring and overcoming adver-
sities, we cannot see why he should be judged inferior to any of the
most excellent generals [*a qualunque eccelentissimo capitano*]. Nevertheless, his outrageous cruelty and inhumanity ... do not permit

him to be honoured among the noblest men [*che sia infra li eccelentissimi uomini celebrato*].'[14] The translator, in a footnote to the passage I have quoted, suggests that the first *virtù* means moral excellence, and the second, the kind attributed to Agathocles, courage and prudence. This, no doubt, is why he renders only the first as 'virtue.'

Now, the other great 'captains' – for example, Romulus or Cesare Borgia – to whom Machiavelli attributes *virtù* were not morally excellent. Or at least, he was not pointing to their moral excellence when he spoke of their *virtù*. He was pointing to much the same qualities in them as he found in Agathocles – to their courage, energy, fortitude, and ability to see and to seize opportunities. These qualities are, of course, compatible with moral excellence just as they are with cruelty, murder, and perfidy. They are qualities that men, wherever they recognize them for what they are, are disposed to admire. It is not peculiar to Machiavelli that he admired them. They are also, so Machiavelli tells us (and surely he is right?), qualities that men are the readier to recognize and to admire, the better they like, or the more they come to accept, their effects. That is why the crimes of the man of heroic *virtù* are so often excused when his achievement is recognized, and why he is admired in spite of them. He is not admired for being murderous, perfidious, and cruel. For the cowardly, the irresolute, and the stupid, and those who lose their heads in the face of danger or unexpected difficulties, may also kill, betray, and be cruel. He is admired for the largeness and boldness of his purpose, for his resolution, courage, and skill in carrying it out, for daring to do what has to be done to achieve it. Yet there are limits to this admiration; it is sometimes given grudgingly or even withheld from someone of whom it cannot be denied that he possesses these rare qualities. Not because he lacks moral excellence; for the others, the honoured, the *celebrati*, may do so too. Borgia, as Machiavelli describes him, is not less selfish than Agathocles. But because his purpose, when achieved – no matter what his motives in pursuing it – is not accepted by others, is not found good by them or does not attract their sympathy, or else because, in pursuing it, he commits unnecessary crimes. If he is wantonly cruel or treacherous, or if his purpose or achievement is unintelligible to others or awakens no response in them, then his

14 Ibid., 36

qualities are not admired or perhaps even recognized, or are so grudgingly, even though they are of a kind ordinarily much admired. *Virtù*,
wherever it is recognized, is apt to be admired because it consists of
qualities that most men understand and wish they had. Why then was
it not admired in Agathocles? Why the reluctance to admit that he
had it? Was it because he lacked moral excellence? Or because he was
entirely selfish? I doubt whether Machiavelli had such reasons as these
in mind when he wrote the eighth chapter of *The Prince*. Not that he
cared nothing for moral excellence or unselfishness. But these things,
I suggest, seemed irrelevant to him when he was asking how it came
about that Agathocles was less admired than other men of no greater
strength of purpose, resourcefulness and courage than himself.

The *virtù* that Machiavelli speaks of in *The Prince* is for the most
part not civic but heroic. In the *Discourses* he has more to say about
the *virtù* of the citizen, and what he says there allows us to draw
some conclusions about how the two kinds of *virtù* are connected.
In the eleventh chapter of book I he says: 'Kingdoms depending on
the vigor [*virtù*] of one man alone are not very lasting because that
vigor departs with the life of that man ... It is not, then, the salvation
of a republic or kingdom to have a prince who will rule prudently
while he lives but to have one who will so organize it that even after
he dies it can be maintained.'[15] And in the first chapter of the same
book he says: 'Those who read in what way the city of Rome began,
and by what lawgivers and how she was organized, will not marvel
that so much vigor was kept up in that city for so many centuries
[*che tanta virtù si sia per più secoli mantenuta in quella città*] and
that finally it made possible the dominant position to which that republic rose.'[16]

The *virtù* 'of one man alone' is the *virtù* of the ruler or of the
founder of a state or religion, whereas the *virtù* that survived in Rome
for centuries was widespread among the citizens. Clearly, there are
here two kinds of *virtù* in question; they may have something in
common but they also differ. If a state is to be well organized or reformed, it must have a founder or restorer who has the first and rarer
kind of *virtù*. But, unless it is well organized or reformed, its citizens

15 Ibid., 226
16 Ibid., 192

are unlikely for long to have much of the second kind, the kind that many can share. So much is, I think, clearly implied by Machiavelli in these and other chapters of the *Discourses,* even though he never distinguishes between two kinds of *virtù.*

Speaking in the *Discourses* (book I, chapter 4) of the dissensions between patricians and plebeians in the Roman republic, he says that a republic cannot 'in any way be called unregulated [*inordinata*] where there are so many instances of honorable conduct [*dove sieno tanti esempli di virtù*] ; for these good instances have their origin in good education; good education in good laws; good laws in those dissensions that many thoughtlessly condemn. For anyone who will properly examine their outcome will not find that they produce any exile or violence damaging to the common good, but laws and institutions conducive to public liberty.'[17] The examples of *virtù* are examples of devotion to the republic and respect for her laws, of civic virtue, and we are told that they abounded in Rome, not only in spite of dissensions, but indeed – though indirectly, no doubt – because of them. Dissension sometimes enhances respect for law, and therefore civic virtue, since this respect is part of that virtue; and sometimes has the opposite effect. In the *History of Florence* (book III, chapter 1), Machiavelli enquires why discord between the nobles and the people strengthened the republic in ancient Rome and weakened it in Florence. It was, he thinks, because the Roman people, unlike the Florentines, were moderate and content to share power with the nobles. Thus 'through the people's victories the city of Rome became more excellent [*virtuosa*] ... and ... as she increased in excellence [*virtù*] , increased in power.' Whereas in Florence, the nobles, deprived of office by the people, when they tried to regain it 'were forced in their conduct, their spirit, and their way of living not merely to be like the men of the people [*popolani*] but to seem so ... [so much so that] the ability in arms [*virtù dell'armi*] and the boldness of spirit [*generosità di animo*] possessed by the nobility were destroyed, and these qualities could not be rekindled in the people,

17 Ibid., 203 – I do not know why Gilbert has translated *esempli* by *instances* rather than *examples,* for Machiavelli is speaking here of conduct which he thinks is exemplary.

where they did not exist, so that Florence grew always weaker and more despicable.'[18]

It would seem, then, that even civic virtue is, or may be, aristocratic in origin, and later acquired by the people from the nobles, provided that the people are moderate. The *virtù* of the citizen is more than just respect for the laws and institutions, and more than courage and devotion to the community; it is also a kind of wisdom or self-restraint which it would be misleading to call *prudence,* as that word is now used in English.

The *virtù* of the citizen does not consist of all the qualities in him that help to make the state strong; it consists only of qualities that he exhibits when he acts as a citizen. The Romans, at least in the days of the republic, were (so thought Machiavelli) a religious people, and Rome was the stronger for their being so. Yet being religious is no part of *virtù*, as Machiavelli conceives of it. For religion sustains both goodness (*bontà*), or what might be called private morals, and civic virtue. We are told in the *Discourses* (I, 55) that: 'Where this goodness [*bontà*] does not exist, nothing good can be expected, as nothing good can be expected in regions that in our time are evidently corrupt, as is Italy above all, though in such corruption France and Spain have their share. If in those countries fewer disorders appear than we see daily in Italy, the cause is not so much the goodness of the people – which for the most part no longer exists – as that they have a king who keeps them united, not merely through his ability [*virtù*] but also through the still unruined organization of these kingdoms. In Germany this goodness and this religion are still important among the people. These qualities enable many republics to exist there in freedom and to observe their laws so well that nobody outside or inside the cities dares to try to master them.'[19] It is the *virtù* of its citizens that makes a state formidable, and this *virtù* is sustained by religion and good morals. It is sustained also by good laws and institutions, for if a state were not well organized (*ordinata*) *virtù* could not survive for long inside it. Thus good laws and civic virtue support one another, and both are supported by religion and morals.

8 Ibid., III, 1141
9 Ibid., I, 307

The well-ordered state is not – so Machiavelli implies – the slow work of time, the undesigned effect of human endeavour that men learn to value as they come to appreciate its benefits. It is the achievement of one, or of at most a few, clear-sighted and bold men who see further and dare more than other men do. These men, the founders and restorers of states and religion, possess a *virtù* far rarer than that of the ordinary citizen, even at his Roman best. They have greater foresight and insight, more firmness of purpose, more ruthlessness (*ferocia*), and a courage that most men – even the brave – lack. They can set aside scruples to achieve some large aim. They may not be good men, but it is good that there should be such men; for if there were not, there would exist no well-ordered states, and therefore little scope for either the more ordinary virtue of the citizen or for the goodness that Machiavelli always praises except when it endangers the state. This goodness, which he attributes to the old Roman and to the German of his own day, is not quite goodness as the Christian understands it, or as many who are not Christians have understood it, whether in our times or in others. He says so little about it that we cannot be sure quite what it consists of. He says much less about it than about *virtù* – which does not in the least mean that he holds it of little account. On the contrary; for he tells us that no community can do without it – can for long have either internal security or be formidable to other communities. All this he tells us, though he also tells us that sometimes it takes a man willing to set this goodness aside to establish or to save a community.

If we do Machiavelli the simple justice of attributing to him only opinions that he expressed or clearly implied, we must not even say that he valued goodness, as distinct from *virtù*, merely for its political effects. We must say only that he had more to say about its political effects than about its nature – which is perhaps not surprising in a historian and a writer on politics.

It is a pity that Meinecke should say that, for Machiavelli, the 'ethical sphere of *virtù*' is 'higher' than the 'usual moral sphere' because it is 'the vital source of the state,' or that 'the development and creation of *virtù* is for him the 'self-evident purpose of the state.'[20] In

20 Meinecke, *Machiavellism*, 33-4

spite of this and other attempts to make a German philosopher of him, Machiavelli remains obstinately an Italian of the Renaissance.

Certainly, he tells us that it takes a man of rare *virtù* to found, pre- serve, or restore a state, and that such a man, to achieve his purpose, may have to do what is ordinarily condemned as an atrocious crime. But to say this is not to imply that there is an 'ethical sphere' higher than ordinary morality. Nothing that Machiavelli says about *virtù*, so far as I can see, justifies Meinecke's attributing this belief to him. No doubt, Machiavelli does imply that there is a sphere of action in which ordinary moral rules do not always apply. He implies also that, unless the men who act in this sphere disregard these rules when they have to, the other sphere, in which the rules do always apply, cannot be established or preserved. That, more or less, is his position as it is usually, and no doubt correctly, interpreted.[21] There are two spheres, and they are, as Meinecke says, 'juxtaposed' – for neither can exist without the other. In a world without scope for heroic virtue, there would be no scope for civic virtue either. Though Machiavelli does not say this in so many words, it is a fair inference from what he does say, especially in the *Discourses*. But it is not a fair inference that he considered one of these spheres 'higher' than the other.

Indeed, we might well ask, higher in what sense? For Meinecke does not tell us. He points to nothing in Machiavelli's argument that could justify our concluding that, in his eyes, one sphere – the one that allows of 'necessary crimes' – is higher (or for that matter lower) than the other. The belief imputed to him by Meinecke follows from noth- ing he said. Among the many respectable defenders of Machiavelli quoted by Lord Acton in his introduction to Burd's edition of *The Prince* is Fichte, the champion of another kind of virtue. 'Questions of political power are never,' says Fichte, 'least of all among a cor- rupt people, to be solved by moral means, so that it is stupid [*unver- ständig*] to cry down *The Prince*. Machiavelli had a ruler to describe and not a monk.'[22] Must we say, then, that Fichte also believed in a

---

1 The sociologist might argue that, even in the case of the most ordinary of mor- tals, life consists of several interdependent spheres, and that rules that apply to one sphere often do not apply to another.

2 *Il Principe*, ed. L. Arthur Burd (Oxford 1891), xxxvii. Surely, Fichte ought not to have said that such questions are *never* solved by moral means. Machia-

'politico-ethical' sphere *higher* than the sphere of ordinary morality? Or if we refuse to say so, must we then conclude that he wrote these sentences in a moment of aberration?

There is no warrant, either, for saying that, for Machiavelli, 'the development and creation of *virtù*' is 'the self-evident purpose of the state.' Nowhere does he speak of any such purpose. There is to be found in his writings no conception of a good or a best life for man, and therefore no attempt to justify the state on the ground that it makes possible that kind of life. What is the *virtù* that Meinecke has in mind when he attributes this belief to Machiavelli? Is it what he calls civic virtue? Or is it the *virtù* that he says is of a higher order, the kind that I have called heroic? On the face of it, it would seem to make better sense to treat civic virtue, rather than the other, as the purpose of the state; for it is the virtue that flourishes in the state. It can exist only in a political community; and so we can speak of it without absurdity as an end to which the political community, the state, is a means. We need not speak of it in this way, not even if, following Aristotle, we speak of the state as a means to 'the good life'; for our conception of that life may include much more than civic virtue. Still, we can so speak of it. But how does the state stand to the *virtù* which is – as Meinecke interprets Machiavelli – of a higher order? This is the *virtù* that establishes or restores the state, and so the state is its product. How then can this *virtù* be the purpose or end of the state? Does the worth of the state consist above all in the fact that the making and preserving of it are occasions for certain kinds of excellence? Is the state to be valued wholly – or at least primarily – as a work of art? Or rather (which is not quite the same thing) as an effect of *virtù*; of rare courage, strength of mind, insight and foresight?

There is no shred of evidence that Machiavelli thought of *virtù*, whether civic or heroic or both together, as the end of the state. On the contrary, there is evidence in plenty that he valued the *virtù* of the ruler or leader largely because it establishes or preserves the state. Only the creation or preservation of the state excuses actions that would otherwise be inexcusable. In the *Discourses* (I, 10) he says:

velli did not say it. How these German philosophers, even the best of them, exaggerate!

'those men are infamous and detestable who have been destroyers of religions, squanderers of kingdoms and republics, enemies of virtue [*delle virtù*],[23] of letters, and of every art that brings gain and honor to the human race ... And no one will ever be so foolish or so wise, so bad or so good, that ... he will not praise what is to be praised and blame what is to be blamed.'[24] If the 'purpose' of the state were only to give occasion for displays of *virtù*, this purpose might sometimes be achieved in destroying it and not in establishing or restoring it; for the business of destruction can require as much *virtù*, especially of the heroic kind that Meinecke says is the higher in the Machiavellian scale, as the business of construction: as much and as rare courage, tenacity of purpose, foresight and skill. It all depends on what is being destroyed or created. Though it takes a Titian to paint a picture by Titian but not to destroy one, it may take a Caesar to destroy a Roman republic.

Though Machiavelli never enquires what is the purpose of the state, he does in the *Discourses* (I, 3) say that the lawgiver must assume that all men are evil. He then quotes the saying 'that hunger and poverty make men industrious, and the laws make them good.'[25] But in the next sentence he qualifies what he has said by suggesting that where there is a good custom, there is no need of law. In the idiom of a later age, we can attribute to him the belief that good laws and good customs make men good – that is to say, disposed so to behave that they do not harm but benefit others and themselves. If he had been asked what the state should do for men, he would probably have answered that it should give them security, and perhaps have added that it should dispose them to goodness. It is much more likely, I suggest, that he would have given this answer to a question he never put to himself than the answer that Meinecke attributes to him.

It is also misleading to say, as Villari does, that Machiavelli 'like the ancients ... sacrifices the individual to the state, but in his opinion the

---

3 As Professor Whitfield points out, Machiavelli seldom uses *virtù* in the plural; when he does so, he has in mind, not the *virtù* discussed in this article, but good or evil qualities more generally. See Whitfield, *Machiavelli*, 98.

4 Gilbert, *Chief Works*, I, 220

5 Ibid., 201

state is indifferent to every activity save the political and the military, and is solely engaged in guarding the security of its own existence and increasing its own strength.'[26] For this, too, is to assume that Machiavelli raised questions he did not raise, and gave or implied certain answers to them. No doubt, he admired the Romans for their willingness to make great sacrifices for the republic. But he never enquired what the citizens should be willing to do for the political community he belongs to. He made no attempt, as later writers were to do, to define the limits of the duty of the individual to the state, or to argue that there are no limits. If we take the political writers most concerned for the individual, his rights and aspirations – such liberals as Constant, Humboldt, and the younger Mill – we do not find them denying that the citizen ought to be called upon to risk his life for the state, or to make other great sacrifices for it. They do, of course, define the obligations of the state to its citizens, and they argue or imply that citizens have a moral right, under certain circumstances, to disobey or resist their rulers. That is why we call them liberals. They do what Machiavelli never attempted. But that does not give us the right to conclude that Machiavelli, who addressed his mind to quite other problems, took up a position opposed to theirs. If to sacrifice the individual to the state is to approve his risking his life in defence of it, then most liberals sacrifice him; and if it is to deny that he ever has the right to resist his rulers, then Machiavelli does not sacrifice him. To say that he does or does not is equally misleading; for it is to suggest that he answers a question that he never even puts to himself.

The writers who speak of him in this way are perhaps moved to do so by what he says about *virtù*. Since the questions of deepest concern to him in both *The Prince* and the *Discourses* relate to the state and its establishment and preservation, it is only to be expected that he should attend particularly to the qualities which he believes men must possess if the state is to be well-ordered and strong. These are the qualities that make up what he calls *virtù*. He admires them, or some of them, very much, even when they are manifest in what he thinks are necessary 'crimes.' He expresses much louder admiration for these qualities than he does for goodness as distinct from *virtù*. But then they are more directly relevant to the questions he puts and tries to answer. There is no warrant for saying that he looks upon *virtù* as higher than goodness, or thinks of it as the purpose of the state, or that he sacrifices the individual to the state – whatever that may mean.

Chabod says that Machiavelli's absorbing passion is for politics, and that he takes little interest in anything else. This is substantially true; for Machiavelli, though he speaks of other things, especially in his plays and letters, speaks of them much as he does of politics. As, for example, when he speaks of love – or, rather, of the pursuit of women. Here too there is something definite to be attained, and the pursuer must be resourceful, skilful, and bold if he is to attain it. Love, as Machiavelli speaks of it, is an activity less absorbing, less admirable, less fruitful of glory, than government and war, but in several respects it is similar. It is a game, perhaps, a distraction, and yet is not unlike the serious business from which it distracts. I speak, of course, not of any theory about love to be found in Machiavelli's writings, nor of his treatment of women, but only of an attitude to love revealed in his two plays and some of his letters.

'The truth,' says Chabod, 'is that Machiavelli leaves the moral ideal intact and he does so because it does not concern him.'[27] Perhaps it would be better to say that it does not concern him directly; for, as we have seen, he holds that a community cannot be well ordered for long, nor formidable to others, unless its members are honest and good – unless, like the old Romans and the Germans of his day, they have *bontà* and not merely *virtù*. And *bontà* has more of morality about it than has *virtù*. But Machiavelli has little to say about it, and has nowhere a word of sympathy for the troubled conscience. As Chabod puts it, 'he is ignorant, not only of the eternal and the transcendent, but also of the moral doubt and the tormenting anxiety that beset a conscience turned in upon itself.'[28]

Ridolfi expresses a different opinion, and speaks of 'the intimate religious foundation of his conscience which breathes from all his works.'[29] It seems to have breathed for few besides Ridolfi. By all

Federico Chabod, *Machiavelli and the Renaissance,* tr. D. Moore (London 1958), 142

Ibid., 93

Roberto Ridolfi, *The Life of Niccolò Machiavelli,* tr. Cecil Grayson (London 1963), 253

means, let us take care how we speak of Machiavelli. Let us not say that he was without religion or that he was untroubled by conscience, or – as some have said – that his *Exhortation to Penitence* was not a moment of piety in his life but a 'frivolous joke.' Chabod, taken literally may well be wrong; Machiavelli was perhaps not 'ignorant of the eternal and transcendent' and was almost certainly (being intelligent, sensitive, and self-critical) often a prey to moral doubt and anxiety. No man reveals all that is in him in the writings he leaves behind him. But the fact remains that Machiavelli has much to say about *virtù* and little about moral goodness, and that *virtù*, as he speaks of it, has nothing to do with conscience. Machiavelli was not entirely a political animal; no man ever is. Yet the spirit that 'breathes from all his works' is political.

Not only because he writes mostly about politics and war but also – and above all – because the image of man that his writings project is, in a broad sense of the word, political. He seems to admire above all the man who knows what he wants and who acts resolutely and intelligently to get it. Such a man need not be engaged in politics or war; he need not be a ruler or a general, a citizen or a soldier. He can be anything, if only he has definite aims making large demands on him, and has strength of mind and ability enough to meet them. Machiavelli never said that the qualities he so much admired are displayed only in politics and war, and we are not to conclude that he thought so. Yet they are displayed largely in these two spheres, and they are the spheres in which he took the deepest interest. The man who knows what he wants and acts resolutely to get it must often, especially if he has some large and difficult aim, use others for his purposes. He need not always do so (he may be an artist) but often he must. He is a wielder of power and influence. So the sphere of *virtù*, though it is wider than just politics and war, is nevertheless in a broad sense political. It consists above all of activities in which men work together, or against one another, or make use of each other, in the pursuit of definite aims.

It consists of only a part of life. Now, in general, it is no criticism of a man to say that he is concerned with only a part of life. If he makes his theme clear to his readers and leaves nothing important out of account, they have no cause of complaint. The economist studies only a part of human behaviour, and when he makes assumptions about the motives, aims, and capacities of men, presumably makes only such as he thinks are relevant to his purpose. Nobody is moved to say of Ricardo that he is ignorant of the eternal and the transcendent, or of moral doubt and anxiety. And if anyone did say it, we should think it beside the point. But when Chabod says it of Machiavelli, we think it a point worth making, whether we agree with him or not. We think this, not because Machiavelli's subject is politics and not economics, but because of the way he writes about it, the quality of his interest in it. He does not go about his business as Ricardo does about his; he does not attempt a systematic explanation of just one sphere of human activity, making only such assumptions about men's aims and capacities as he thinks necessary to his limited purpose. Unsystematic though he is, limited though his interests are, he makes large and bold statements about man, so that his readers get the impression that he claims to be taking the measure of their species. And the impression is not mistaken.

Machiavelli is a great writer whose moods and feelings infect his readers. What he admires is indeed admirable, and also rare. Firmness of purpose, presence of mind, resourcefulness, the ability to see more clearly and further than others, fortitude in adversity: these qualities and the others that make up *virtù* are everywhere exalted. It is through them, above all, that man makes his presence felt in the world, and in them that he takes pride. *Virtù* is opposed to *fortuna*, to chance, to the unforeseen, to the external and the hostile. Machiavelli appeals to sentiments that are strong in most men – to men without religion as much as those with it. To display *virtù* is not to do God's will, nor is it to behave morally; it is to make your will and your person count for something in the eyes of other men and your own. Which is not to say that *virtù* cannot be displayed in the service of God or in acting morally. Machiavelli, who in some moods despised Savonarola, in others admired him; he admired him for what he had of *virtù* (courage, a strong will, and fortitude) and despised him for what he lacked (understanding and foresight).

There is a perverse streak in Machiavelli. He likes to make himself out worse than he is. He likes at times to shock his contemporaries, and he has shocked posterity to the threshold of our own 'unshockable' age. Yet his 'phiiosophy' is not so much immoral as it is defective. For, unlike the 'political scientist' of today, he does present us with something that deserves to be called a philosophy: with reflections upon what is essentially human about man. He has a philosophy in the sense that Montaigne – who is even less systematic than he is – has one.

If we conceive of man as Machiavelli describes him we miss a great deal that is distinctively human about him. We forget that he is a contemplative being and a problem to himself, that he is as much frustrated as inspired by his imagination, that many of his purposes – no matter how exalted and powerful he is – are half-formed and change imperceptibly. Above all, we forget that much that makes life seem valuable to him comes of his uncertainties and hesitations, his doubts and anxieties, his sense that there is more to him than he is aware of, his not quite knowing what he is moving towards even though he is to some extent self-propelled. Those who do not know what they want and are not resolute in trying to get it are not necessarily poor in spirit. Men are not always allies or enemies, masters or servants, in the pursuit of definite aims; they are also involved with one another, and with the groups and communities they belong to, in ways that are comforting or hurtful, exciting or depressing, and yet unrelated to such aims. These sides of life are just as much specifically human, setting man apart from the other animals, enriching his imagination, sharpening his intelligence, deepening his emotions, as the formation and pursuit of clear and realistic aims.

Machiavelli did not deny this; he merely took no account of it. If he had neglected it because it was not relevant to his purpose, there would be no objecting to him on that score. If he had been what we today call a political scientist, it would be absurd to complain that he had too political a conception of man. But he was not a political scientist in that sense; he did not aim at explaining systematically a limited but important sphere of human activity. True, he wrote very largely (though unsystematically) about politics; but in the course of doing so he indulged in reflections about man that suggest that man is pre-eminently political in the sense that what he values most in his own species are rare qualities finding their largest scope in politics and war, or in activities similar to them. It may be true that man admires these qualities as much as any, but it is not true that they, more than others, give savour to his life. Machiavelli did not say they do but he wrote as if he thought they did. He made altogether too much of *virtù,* especially the heroic kind.

EIGHT

Machiavelli *Minore*

ANTHONY PAREL

Machiavelli writes in the epistle dedicatory of the *Discourses* that that book contains all that he has to say on the subject of politics: 'in it I have set out all I know and all I have learned in the course of my long experience and steady reading in the affairs of the world.' A similar statement is also made in the epistle dedicatory of *The Prince*, written about five years earlier than the *Discourses*:

> I have found among my treasures nothing I hold dearer or value
> so high as my understanding of great men's actions, gained in
> lengthy experience with recent matters and my continual read-
> ing of ancient ones. My observations – which with close attention
> I have for a long time thought over and considered, and recently
> have collected in a little volume – I send to Your Magnificence.

These statements raise the general question of the relationship of *The Prince* and the *Discourses,* or, more generally, of his major works to his minor works. If the former contains all that he knows on the subject of politics, what is the political relevance of the latter?

No doubt *The Prince* and the *Discourses* form a class by themselves. Of all Machiavelli's writings, they alone follow a conscious method of political analysis. Compared with them even the *History of Flo-*

rence and *The Art of War,* though counted as his major works,[1] are of secondary importance. However, every student of Machiavelli's political theory must sometimes wonder what the relevance of the rest of his writings is to his political theory. To put the question slightly differently, what is the relation between his major and his minor works?

This question, it seems, can be best answered at two levels – first, at the level of the general norm that should govern the relationship between the two classes of writings; and secondly, at the level of detailed study of each of the minor works, or groups of minor works. What follows below is only a preliminary investigation into the problem of their relationship. A definitive study of it will require much greater research than is possible at the moment.

As for the general norm that should govern the relationship between the two classes of writings, the epistles dedicatory cited above hint at a partial answer. There Machiavelli speaks of the two sources of his political theory, namely experience and history. The experience to which he refers is obviously that gained as a civil servant of the government of Florence; to be precise, as the second secretary of the second chancery from 1498 to 1512. As his famous letter of 10 December 1513 to Vettori attests, it was during those fifteen years that he studied the art of statecraft.[2] 'Studying' included, of course, putting in writing his observations and impressions, often in the form of reports or recommendations sent to his government. These writings,

1 For a discussion of the relationship between Machiavelli's major works, see Leslie Walker, *The Discourses of Niccolò Machiavelli*, 2 vols (London & New Haven 1950), I, 53-60.
2 Machiavelli to Francesco Vettori, 10 Dec. 1513, Allan H. Gilbert, *Machiavelli: The Chief Works and Others*, 3 vols (Durham, NC 1965), II, 927-32; Franco Gaeta, *Opere*, VI (Milan 1961), letter 140
3 For the Italian text of all the legations and commissions, see Niccolò Machiavelli, *Opere* (hereafter *Opere*), ed. Sergio Bertelli (Milan 1964), III-V. Of the forty-three legations and commissions included in these volumes, thirty-six were written between 1498 and 1511.

generally referred to as *legazioni* and *commissarie*,[3] make up three volumes, which in turn constitute nearly one-third of all his writings. They tell us exactly what Machiavelli's practical experiences in the art of statecraft had been. He himself informs us that during those fifteen years he had not been, as he puts it, 'sleeping or playing' but honestly and seriously gathering data out of which one day he would draw his political conclusions.[4] In other words, the legations and commissions form an important part of a carefully gathered body of materials out of which emerge *The Prince* and the *Discourses*.

To the same period before 1512 also belong the majority of what have been described as *scritti politici minori*[5] and nearly half of Machiavelli's letters.[6] In these writings, too, one can trace the origin and development of some of the important ideas of Machiavelli, ideas which find mature expression in *The Prince* and the *Discourses*.[7] Without going into detail we may conclude that, as a rule, the writings which pre-date his fall from official life (1512) constitute an important part of the empirical foundations of his political theory.

So much for minor writings which pre-date *The Prince* and the *Discourses*. There are also minor works which were written concurrently with these major works, or which followed them. Among these are

4 'and through this thing [*The Prince*] if it were read, they [the Medicis] would see that for fifteen years while I have been studying the art of the state, I have not slept or been playing ...' Gilbert, II, 930
5 Minor political writings of this period are found in Gaeta, *Opere*, II, 1-216. Only a few have been translated into English. See Gilbert, I, 101-20; III, 1436-9.
6 Gaeta, *Opere*, VI. Of the 239 letters included in this volume as many as 116 were written before 1511. For the English translation (incomplete, but substantial) see Gilbert, II, 883-1012.
7 A good example is Machiavelli's doctrine on the importance of the army to government, that is, the importance of military virtues to the virtues of citizenship. Long before military virtues were expressed in *The Prince*, the *Discourses*, and *The Art of War*, they were expressed in such discourses as 'Words to be spoken on the law for appropriating money, after giving a little introduction and excuse' (1503), Gilbert, III, 1438ff.; 'L'ordinanza fiorentina'; 'Provisioni della republica di Firenze per instituire il magistrato de'nove ufficiali dell'Ordinanza e Milizia, dette da Niccolò Machiavelli' (1506), Gaeta, *Opere*, II, 77-131.

his literary works and the remainder of the discourses and letters, written between 1512 and 1527.

The letters undoubtedly throw additional light on Machiavelli's practical experiences in political matters. In this respect, they complement the legations and commissions. These letters reveal the portrait of the complete man. Without them our knowledge of the major works would be incomplete, as the letter of 10 December 1513 to Vettori shows, in regard to *The Prince.*

As for the legations and minor discourses which post-date *The Prince* and the *Discourses,* the general norm is that they too shed fresh light on certain aspects of Machiavelli's thought. As two of this type of minor writings will be discussed in some detail below, we need not say more on this category here.

It is his literary works,[8] however, that deserve our special attention. For they bring to light more clearly than other writings an important

8 For the complete Italian collection of the literary works, see Gaeta, *Opere,* VIII, 'Il teatro e tutti gli scritti letterari,' Gaeta (1965). For an English translation of a substantial number of these works see Gilbert, II, 735-1022; also J.R. Hale, *The Literary Works of Machiavelli* (London 1961). Hale's introduction is valuable. He argues that Machiavelli's literary works should be considered as 'autonomous works of art.' This obviously goes against my thesis here supported by the authors cited in notes 8-11 below. Hale goes on to say that if the literary works are treated autonomously they would increase

'an understanding of the didactic works in a far profounder sense than through supplying of reflexions of thought about politics, human nature and fate. His politics have lived because they too are works of art, and, in their less flexible way, were subject to the same creative, shaping pressures as were his literary works. The way in which a thing is said is part of its meaning, and in assessing the judgements of a writer on politics, and considering his arguments, his emphases, and his use of evidence – if that man was also the greatest dramatist of his age, would it not be prudent to keep that fact in mind?'

As autonomous works of art, Machiavelli's literary works, except *Mandragola* and *Belfagor,* would not stand the test of time. Here Ridolfi's statement may be recalled: 'Machiavelli was more a poet when he wrote in prose than when he wrote in verse ...' R. Ridolfi, *The Life of Machiavelli* (London & Chicago 1962), 82; see also ibid., 167-8, where Ridolfi justifies Ariosto's omission of Machiavelli from a list of contemporary poets in his *Orlando Furioso.*

aspect of Machiavelli's genius. They formally reveal Machiavelli the artist, the poet, the writer who uses literary imagination as a vehicle of political truth. The conveying of truth through imagination means that, for Machiavelli, reason and science are not the exclusive media of valid political communication. He balances rational and scientific truths against truths intuitively and imaginatively seen. For politics affect the whole man, and Machiavelli is fully aware of this. There is, in short, a mixture of reason and imagination, science and advocacy, in Machiavelli: and the literary writings bear full testimony to this mixture.

Hence it is not surprising that more and more scholars have begun to attach great importance to the 'duality' of his genius, and to interpret his political theory, especially his moral doctrines, from that perspective. Thus Ridolfi writes:

He was and remains a politician, an artist, a poet, who besides his scientific reasoning power felt the sudden and varied impulses of artists and poets: and if one cannot cast doubt on the fundamental coherence and logic of his thought, in order to understand what has been and still is called the enigma of Machiavelli, we must take account of those impulses and of his nature full of contrast and variety.[9]

Croce also believes that a 'poetic vision' was always alive in Machiavelli, and that it illuminated his politics.[10] Similarly Luigi Russo admonishes us against the danger of speaking of Machiavelli's 'thought' and his 'art' as if they were mutually independent realities. He suggests that we must rather speak of the 'arte-pensiero' of Machiavelli.[11] Renaudet expresses a similar idea when he states that in Machiavelli's genius there was the union of 'vérité' and 'poésie' expressing itself on the one hand in 'hard positive intelligence,' and on the other 'in the imaginations of a visionary.'[12]

The literary works also remind us of the influence of poets on Machiavelli. In discussing him, most political theorists have been so long

9 Ridolfi, *Life of Machiavelli*, 252
10 Croce, *Philosophy, Poetry, History* (London 1966), 983
11 Luigi Russo, *Machiavelli* (Bari 1957), 98-9
12 A. Renaudet, *Machiavel*, 2nd ed. (Paris 1956), 175, 241

under the spell of Livy, Cicero, Tacitus, and others that they seem to forget that Machiavelli was influenced also by Dante, Petrarch, Ovid, Tibullus. This disregard is all the more inexcusable since Machiavelli openly admits his indebtedness to this class of writers.[13] Admittedly, the influence on him of poets is less than that of historians and political theorists, but not much less as to justify the neglect of the former's influence. Dante[14] and Petrarch,[15] in particular, deserve special mention. They fed Machiavelli's imagination. His patriotism, his *italianità* – in short, the element of advocacy in his writings – to a great extent was owed to them.

13 Describing his daily routine during the months he was writing *The Prince,* he writes to Vettori (in the letter already cited): 'Leaving the grove, I go to a spring, and thence to my aviary. I have a book in my pocket, either Dante or Petrarch, or one of the lesser poets, such as Tibullus, Ovid and the like.' Gilbert, II, 928

14 Dante's influence on Machiavelli cannot be exaggerated. The latter's 'long study and great affection' for *The Divine Comedy* are shown in the imitation of style, as well as in the use of expressions, forms, and verses taken from Dante. Ridolfi, *Life of Machiavelli,* 82. It should not be forgotten that for reducing his impressions and scattered information in *The Prince* into a 'scientific' form, it is Dante's authority that Machiavelli cites. Letter of Machiavelli to Vettori, 10 Dec. 1513. For other direct references to Dante, see *Discourses,* I, chs.11, 51; *History of Florence,* bk.II, chs.18, 24; *Discorso o dialogo interno alla nostra lingua (A Dialogue on Language,* in Hale, *Literary Works of Machiavelli,* 175-91); Letters 120, 139, 199, and 200 (Gilbert, II). For indirect references to Dante, see *The Prince,* ch.15; *The Ass of Gold,* ch.2, ll.22ff.; *Life of Castruccio Castracani, Epigram on Soderini,* and *Carnival Songs.* For an extensive survey of political influences on Machiavelli see Walker, II, 271-306. It is typical of the traditional attitude towards Machiavelli that even so thorough a scholar as Walker stops short of giving sufficient attention to Machiavelli's literary sources.

15 Petrarch's influence on Machiavelli is second only to that of Dante. It is striking that *The Prince* ends with a quotation from Petrarch (Canzone 16, 13-16). It is as if Machiavelli adopts Petrarch's longing for Italian unity.

Similarly, *The Exhortation to Penitence* also ends with a quotation from Petrarch's *Sonnet,* I: 'Repent and know clearly that what pleases the world is but a brief dream.' For other direct references to Petrarch, see Machiavelli's Letters 127 and 137, Gilbert, II; *History of Florence,* VI, ch.29.

Hence, the literary writings may not be dismissed as mere occasional diversions,[16] fit only for the attention of the literary critic. They must be treated as tools for the understanding of the major works. In the final analysis they have the tendency to soften the harshness of judgment on human nature that one finds in *The Prince* and the *Discourses*. They show that Machiavelli's political theory comprehended not only philosophy and empirical data, but also imagination and intuition.

It follows that, for those who would reduce, or pretend to reduce politics to an exact science, Machiavelli will remain a permanent stumbling block. The intuitive and the imaginative parts defy systematization. For this reason his literary works lie outside the scope of his 'new method' but not outside his political vision. Here T.S. Eliot's observation on Machiavelli seems appropriate:

No account of Machiavelli's views can be more than fragmentary. For though he is constructive he is not a system builder; and his thoughts can be repeated but not summarized. It is perhaps a character of his amazing exactness of vision and statement that he should have no "system"; for a system almost inevitably requires slight distortions and omissions, and Machiavelli would distort and omit nothing.[17]

Political theorists naturally squirm at the suggestion that there are in Machiavelli's philosophy more things than what political theory, narrowly conceived, dreams of. If one would look at politics only from the narrow perspective of a particular method of political analysis this squeamishness is perhaps inevitable. It only goes to show the limitations that result from imposing a particular method, to the exclusion of other methods, for the study of politics. Whatever the ad-

16 Gaeta argues that the element of 'occasionalità' is not absent from some of the major works, especially *The Prince*, because but for the fall from power in 1512 Machiavelli would perhaps have never written it. On the other hand, 'occasionalità' is only *apparent* in the case of certain minor works, since they too spring from the same inspiration which produced the major works. *Opere*, VIII, 'nota introduttiva,' ix

17 T.S. Eliot, 'Niccolò Machiavelli,' in *For Lancelot Andrewes: Essays on Style and Order* (London n.d.), 58-9

vantage of particular methods, one may not ignore political truths merely because they are expressed through the literary medium. For as Stendhal writes, 'Politics in a work of literature is like a pistol-shot in the middle of a concert, something loud and vulgar, and yet a thing to which it is not possible to refuse one's attention.'[18] Political ideas in Machiavelli's literary writings cannot easily be systematized. Nevertheless, they throw much light on our understanding of his political thought.

Turning now to the second level of analysis of the minor writings, I have taken the following selected minor works for detailed study: *The Exhortation to Penitence*, the tercets on *Ingratitude* and *Ambition*, *Mandragola*, *The Ass of Gold*, the *Discourse on Remodeling the Government of Florence*, and *A Pastoral*.

The Exhortation to Penitence

The Exhortation to Penitence, which was first called also *Discorso morale*, has remained a continual source of embarrassment to most Machiavelli scholars. Its piety and theology do not accord with their own preconceived notions of Machiavelli, his amoralism and his historical image. Even Villari could think of it only as a 'veiled irony,' and Croce as a 'frivolous joke.'[19] Brucculeri argues that a sermonet by the improvised preacher does not suffice to restore a solid and balanced view on morality and religion, and that a tree must be judged not by its leaves but by its fruit ('dal frutto si conosce l'albero non dalle foglie').[20] The prejudice is so great that an impassioned evaluation of the *Exhortation* has so far remained most difficult.[21]

The exact date of the *Exhortation* is not known. According to Ridolfi, the handwriting of the autograph manuscript suggests that

---

18 Quoted in Irving Howe, *Politics and the Novel* (London 1961), 15

19 Ridolfi, *Life of Machiavelli*, 328

20 A. Brucculeri, 'Machiavelli e il suo pensiero politico e religioso,' *Civilta Cattolica*, 2434 (1951), 427.

21 The first major exception is Ridolfi, *Life of Machiavelli*, 242, 253-4, 328.

it was written in the last years of Machiavelli's life.[22] In 1495 Machiavelli had become a member of a lay religious order, the Company of
Piety. And Allan Gilbert speculates that the *Exhortation* might have
been a sermon preached to the members of this order.[23]

The essential point of the *Exhortation* is that it puts in correct perspective Machiavelli's view of man and mortality. It clearly and formally subscribes to the Christian doctrines of creation, original sin,
redemption, grace, repentance, and salvation through good works.
Evil in man and society is finally traceable to the orthodox doctrine
of original sin. The world of politics has a theological explanation.
Machiavelli's description of human nature as found in *The Prince* is
a description of human nature without grace efficaciously operative
in it. T.S. Eliot drives home the point when he writes:

> The world of human motives which he [Machiavelli] depicts is
> true – that is to say, it is humanity without the addition of super-
> human Grace. It is therefore tolerable only to persons who have
> also a definite religious belief; to the effort of the last three cen-
> turies to supply religious belief by belief in Humanity the creed
> of Machiavelli is insupportable. ... What Machiavelli did not see
> about human nature is the myth of human goodness for which
> liberal thought replaces the belief in Divine Grace.[24]

According to the *Exhortation,* the original sin of man is 'ingratitude' towards God. Man is God's creature. Life is God's gift. There
is a moral law that ought to govern the relationship between God and
man, between the benefactor and the beneficiary; the law of gratitude. Man ought to show this gratitude by living according to his teleology, which is the glorification of God and the attainment of man's
own happiness through the proper use of his faculties of body and
mind.

> So every object is created for the glory and good of man, and
> man is alone in being created for the good and glory of God, who

---

22 Ibid., 328
23 Gilbert, I, 70
24 Eliot, 'Niccolò Machiavelli,' 63-4

gave him speech that he might praise him, gave him sight, turned not to the ground as for the other animals but turned to the sky, in order that he might always see it, gave him hands in order that he might build temples, offer sacrifices in His honor, gave him reason and intellect in order that he might consider and understand the greatness of God.[25]

But man deviates from the path of this primordial moral law. Historical and social man often acts contrary to the ultimate purpose of his life:

That tongue made to glorify God blasphemes him; that mouth, through which he must be fed, he makes into a sewer and a way for satisfying the appetite and the belly with luxurious and excessive food; those thoughts about God he changes into thoughts about the world; that desire to preserve the human species turns into lust and many other dissipations.[26]

The outcome of this disorientation of man's teleology is that he becomes less than man, half man and half beast, the political consequences of which are fully dealt with in *The Prince*:

Thus with these brutish deeds man changes himself from a rational animal into a brute animal. Man changes, therefore, by practising this ingratitude to God, from angel to devil, from master to servant, from man to beast.[27]

Ingratitude to God has a moral relationship with all the social vices:

All the sins of men, which, though they are many and in many ways are committed, nonetheless for the most part can be divided into two groups: one is to be ungrateful to God [*essere ingrato a Dio*], the second is to be unfriendly to one's neighbour [*essere inimico al prosimo*].[28]

25 Gilbert, II, 172
26 Ibid.
27 Ibid., 172-3
28 Ibid., 172

The first sin necessarily leads to the second: 'Whoever, then, lacks it [grace] must necessarily be unfriendly [*inimico*] to his neighbour.'[29] Of the two sins, the first is more fundamental.[30]

In the *Exhortation,* Machiavelli mentions specifically usury, slander, and deception as the most common sins practised by man against his neighbour. Elsewhere he speaks of ambition and ingratitude to men: two of his *capitoli* are entitled *Ingratitude* and *Ambition*.[31]

Both *Ingratitude* and *Ambition* are described (using almost biblical phraseology) as having mysterious origins. Thus *Ingratitude:*

When stars, when the heavens were indignant at human pride, for man's abasement, Ingratitude then was born in the world ... in the breasts of princes and kings she lives. There as in her chief abode she makes her nest; from thence she anoints the hearts of all other men with the poison of her treachery.[32]

And the origin of *Ambition* is described as follows:

Hardly had God made the stars, the heavens, the light, the elements, and man – master over so many things of beauty – and had quelled the pride of angels, and from Paradise had banished Adam with his wife for their tasting the apple, when (after the birth of Cain and Abel, as with their father and by their labor they were living happy in their poor dwelling) a hidden power which sustains itself in the heaven ... to man's being by no means friendly – to deprive us of peace and to set us at war, to take away from us all quiet and all good, sent two Furies to dwell on the Earth.[33]

29 Ibid., 173
30 Ibid.
31 *Tercets on Ambition,* probably written in 1509, Gilbert, II, 735-40. *Tercets on Ingratitude,* written probably from 1507 to 15, Gilbert, II, 740-5
32 Gilbert, II, 740. On the importance that Machiavelli attaches to ingratitude, see *Discourses,* I, chs.28-32.
33 *Tercets on Ambition,* Gilbert, II, 735-6. Although Machiavelli speaks of ambition and avarice in equal terms, it is clear that in Machiavelli's mind ambition is the more general vice and avarice, usury, like desire for self-glory, etc., particular species of it. For some references to ambition in *The Prince,* see such

The pursuit of political aims are often frustrated by Ingratitude: she holds 'three cruel arrows anointed with poison':

> The first of the three that comes from her quiver makes a man merely bear witness that he has received a benefit; without according any return he confesses it;

> And the second, which she next takes out, makes a man forget the favour he receives; yet doing the giver no injury, he merely denies it;

> The last makes a man never remember or return a favour, and to the extent of his power he rends and bites his benefactor ...

> Never does Ingratitude perish: never is she destroyed; a thousand times she rises up, if once she dies, because her father and her mother are immortal.[34]

Scipio Africanus, Miltiades, Aristotle, Phocion, Themistocles, Julius Caesar, Ahmed Pasha – Machiavelli mentions them by name – all perished because of Ingratitude. Machiavelli's conclusion is that in the art of politics trust and benevolence are harmful: 'the prince you have made then fears your taking what you have bestowed and does not keep faith or compact with you, because more powerful is his dread of you than the obligations incurred.'[35] There is only one prudent lesson to be learned from this reflection on Ingratitude: 'let everyone flee from courts and governments, for there is no road that takes a man faster to weeping over what he longed for, when once he has gained it.'[36]

chs. as 3, 4, 7, 9, 11, 12, 18, 19; *Discourses,* I, 37, 42, 52; II, 21, 22; III, 2, 11, 24. For a fuller list of references from the *Discourses,* see Walker's index, Walker, *Discourses of Niccolò Machiavelli,* II, 346. The centrality of ambition as a key to the explanation of man's social vices cannot be doubted. Machiavelli seems to have been so impressed with its ubiquity that even when he quotes St Paul's peroration on charity (1 Cor. 13:13) he somehow manages to include ambition as a sin against charity as well. St Paul's list of such sins does not include ambition. See *The Exhortation to Penitence.*

34 Gilbert, II, 741
35 Ibid., 742-3
36 Ibid.

Ambition is equally disruptive of political calculations. In the poem on *Ambition*, Machiavelli describes the vice of political ambition as an extension of selfishness, which seeks personal glory as distinct from the glory of the *patria*. Reduced to a general principle ambition destroys the common good of the state. Machiavelli sees three manifestations of ambition. First, it is seen as the cause of political instability, 'variations in earthly things':

That which more than anything else throws kingdoms down from the highest hills is this: that the powerful with their power are never sated. From this it results that they are discontented who have lost, and hatred is stirred up to ruin the conquerors; whence it comes about that one rises and the other dies; and the one who has risen is ever tortured with new ambition and with fear. This appetite destroys our states; and the greater wonder is that all recognize this transgression, but no one flees from it.[37]

Secondly, ambition is the reason for the political ruin of Italy. Cowardice and bad government had been joined with ambition, and 'every sort of distress, every kind of ruin, every other ill' has overtaken Italy.[38] Thirdly, ambition can yield some positive results if it is joined with 'judgement and sound intellect,' 'method and vigor' (*virtù armata*). *Virtù*, if it is available, can transform egocentric ambition into patriotism:

When through her own nature a country lives unbridled, and then, by accident, is organized and established under good laws, Ambition uses against foreign peoples that violence which neither the law nor the king permits her to use at home (wherefore homeborn trouble almost ceases); yet she is sure to keep disturbing the sheepfolds of others, wherever that violence of hers has planted its banner.[39]

What stands out in all this – in his reflections on ingratitude towards God, ingratitude practised by men among men, on unregulated

37 *The Ass of Gold,* Gilbert, II, 762. The idea is repeated in *Ambition,* ibid., 736.
38 Gilbert, II, 737
39 Ibid.

ambition – is Machiavelli's moralistic attitude. Men are condemned as evil. Machiavelli sees no human solution to these vices. The only effective solutions are repentance and grace. 'Penitence therefore is the only means for annulling all the ills, all the sins of men ...'[40] King David, St Peter, St Francis, and St Jerome are the models of good behaviour here, in contrast to Machiavelli's political heroes, Moses, Romulus, Cesare Borgia, and others.[41] The world of grace and the world of *virtù* stand apart. Though there is a theological explanation of political corruption, there is no theological remedy for it. Sin is a moral cause of political decay, but grace is not an efficient cause of political regeneration. Machiavelli understood this distinction. Political ills required remedies other than spiritual remedies: they required good laws and good arms, good customs and good education. Instead of piety was required prudence: 'there should be no one with so small a brain that he will believe if his house is falling, that God will save it without any other prop, because he will die beneath that ruin.'[42] Or as Machiavelli puts it elsewhere, 'the heavens do not wish or are not able to support a city that is determined to fall in any case.'[43]

He is not suggesting here anything unheard of in medieval theology. The latter clearly recognized the distinction between God's efficient causality as the first cause, and the causality of creatures, as secondary causes. God did not replace his creatures in the sphere of their activities. Thus it was not strange that the spheres of Caesar and God were clearly demarcated. What Machiavelli does is to uphold this distinction honestly and to deduce the conclusions that logically follow from it.

Political corruption and regeneration are consequences of human action. God does not intervene in these human activities. Theology may explain why men are selfishly ambitious, ungrateful, usurious, deceptive, slanderous; but in the political sphere theology offers no direct solutions. Grace can produce spiritual regeneration in individuals; it cannot bring about political regeneration. In this sense politics is an

40 *Exhortation,* Gilbert, I, 171

41 Ibid., 174

42 *The Ass of Gold,* Gilbert, II, 763-4

43 *Words on Appropriating Money,* Gilbert, III, 1443

autonomous type of activity. The transcendence of religion does not permit grace to be an efficient cause of political regeneration, but religion as an immanent force in society can reinforce political *virtù*.

The *Exhortation* indicates clearly that Machiavelli appreciated the transcendental elements of religion, and that he understood that they could not be used as tools of politics. Nor were the armed prophets his only heroes. The saints too were heroes, though not in the sphere of political excellence. The *Exhortation* does not so much show that Machiavelli became disillusioned with politics as that he realized that there is a world which lies beyond politics. As Ridolfi points out, it shows that Machiavelli has arrived at the supreme knowledge contained in the Petrarchan lines with which it closes:

> cognoscere chiaramente
> che quanto piace al mondo e breve sogno.
> [to know clearly that what pleases the world is but a brief dream] [44]

In the final analysis, that is, in terms of man's final destiny, political excellence does not represent his highest glory. At best, politics is a salvaging operation, putting together the broken pieces of human capabilities, capabilities shattered by sin against God and man. Man's final destiny can only be attained by repentance and grace.

Mandragola. THE WORLD WITHOUT VIRTU

In view of the importance of *virtù* to Machiavelli's political thought it is useful to look into Machiavelli's conception of a world without it, which in my opinion is depicted in *Mandragola*.[45] 'Not to know Mandragola,' claims Allan Gilbert, 'is not to know *The Prince*.'[46] And Villari writes: 'Mandragola is the comedy of a society of which *The Prince* is the tragedy.'[47]

44 Ridolfi, *Life of Machiavelli*, 242
45 Written in 1518, Ridolfi, *Life of Machiavelli*, 170; Gaeta, *Opere*, VIII, xii
46 Gilbert, II, 775
47 Villari, *Life and Times of Machiavelli*, II, 349

The plot is familiar. Callimaco, a Florentine youth, just returned from a long stay in France, falls in love with a married Florentine woman, Lucrezia. The play centres on the story of her successful seduction. Nicia, her husband, is a rich but stupid lawyer. He has no children but desperately longs for some. Callimaco, on the advice of a friend, Ligurio, poses as a doctor. The doctor prescribes a potion of mandrake (hence the play's name) which will remove Lucrezia's sterility. There is one catch, however: whoever first sleeps with Lucrezia after she has taken the potion will die. Callimaco, disguised as a stranger, volunteers to 'risk' his life and to sleep with Lucrezia. In this adventure he is helped by Lucrezia's mother; Ligurio, a villainous parasite; Fra Timoteo, the confessor; Nicia's stupidity; and Lucrezia's own gullibility. Callimaco obtains his end; even more, he manages to receive a standing invitation to continue as the 'family friend.'

Various interpretations have been given to the political significance of the play. Sumberg and Parronchini see allegory in it: marriage and family imitate political life; they create a small society; Callimaco is the father of new Italy. Nicia alternately stands for Lorenzo and Soderini, both incapable rulers. This interpretation is made all the more plausible by the fact that Lorenzo's wife was in fact sterile, and Nicia happens to be the name of an incapable Athenian general in the Peloponnesian War.[48] However, purely allegorical interpretation is generally rejected by critical scholars. Luigi Russo sees the play as 'etico-realistica,' and having universal significance.[49] For Croce the world portrayed in *Mandragola* is not that of a cynic but of a pessimist: not of a cynic 'perchè egli ha l'anelito all bontà e all purezza' but of a pessimist, 'perchè egli non vede nella realtà spiraglio alcuno per il quale possa penetrare quella bontà e purezza.' Self-love and utility (specifically, pleasure and avarice) prevent higher morality from exercising any influence on the characters.[50] Ridolfi holds that the purpose of the play, if it had a purpose, was to make men think, not laugh.[51] Veiled in the art is the political doctrine of *verità effettuale*. Alberto Moravia takes a slightly different stand. *Mandragola* for him

48 Thucydides, *The Peloponnesian War*, bk.VII, ch.23
49 Russo, *Machiavelli*, 42
50 Ibid., 102
51 Ridolfi, *Life of Machiavelli*, 173

reflects a deeply tired spirit as regards private values, religion and moral conscience. *The Prince*, and the other political works, are a magnificently successful attempt to whip this spirit into life by means of the only passion that still stirred in it: political passion.[52]

The spirit is exhausted, but Machiavelli thinks (erroneously, according to Moravia) that he can revive it by military and political techniques. 'Only religious forces could have acted as the real means of revival. Machiavelli did not recognize this.' This is the reason why 'in *Mandragola* we have the expression or image of a man worn out as regards ethical values yet unable to recognize his exhaustion.'[53] The ethical atrophy is something which Villari also notes as the extraordinary feature of the play: the 'appalling absence of conscience in all the characters, their horrible freedom from moral responsibility, and the manner in which they pass from good to evil without seeming to be aware of any change.'[54] Briefly, *Mandragola* is a foil to *The Prince*. In *The Prince*, we have the emphasis on *virtù* as the basis of *verità effettuale*, whereas in *Mandragola* the emphasis is on *fraude, inganno* and *ingegno*.

Both works are action-oriented and like De Sanctis, I see no contradiction between the playwright and the political theorist. The basis of Machiavelli's approach is unchanged. As De Sanctis reminds us, imagination still remains subordinate to the real world as shown by experience and observation, though it is not eliminated from it.[55] For

under the frivolous surface are hidden the profoundest complexities of the inner life, and the action is propelled by spiritual forces as inevitably as fate. It is enough to know the character to guess the end. The world is a consequence and its premises are in the spirit of the character, in the forces that move it. Whoever can calculate these forces will win. Chance, the supernatural, the

52 Alberto Moravia, *Man as an End*, tr. Bernard Wall (London 1965), 95
53 Ibid., 104
54 Villari, *Life and Times of Machiavelli*, II, 348
55 Francesco De Sanctis, *History of Italian Literature*, II (New York 1931, 1959), 545

marvellous, are all discredited, and are replaced by character. So Machiavelli the artist is the same, after all, as Machiavelli the politician, and Machiavelli the historian.[56]

The prologue of the play indicates the reason for the moral enervation, for the appalling freedom from conscience, the absence of *virtù*: 'the present age is degenerate compared to the ancient *virtù*' ['per tutto traligna da l'antica virtù et secol presente'].[57] A world in which pleasure and profit – forms of self-love – become the sovereign concern and from which honour and valour are absent, life becomes more easily calculable: fraud can succeed, and there is no need for violence. Every character in the play practises fraud in one form or another, except, of course, Nicia. But then he falls a victim of it – being too stupid even to practise it. There is no trace of heroism in the play. It represents an over-civilized society, one overtaken by '*ozio*' in the triad *virtù-tranquillità-ozio*.

The two most interesting characters are Timoteo and Callimaco.[58] Timoteo is the epitome of what was wrong with Italian Christianity –

---

56 Ibid., 582
57 For Machiavelli's ideas on the Roman *virtù* of the past and on the corruption of the present Italian states, and on the need to 'imitate' the past, see the *Discourses* generally, e.g., I, pref., 39; III, 43.
58 Hale is alone, I think, in thinking Ligurio to be the prototype of a Machiavellian figure,

'the play's taut spring, forcing all the wheels to rotate until the alarm is over and the lady is won ... who by insinuation and aside, now by direct assault, shakes Fortune into submission – obeying rules for the man of action preached by Machiavelli elsewhere.' (*Machiavelli and Renaissance Italy*, 186)

If Machiavelli preached anything, surely it was not *virtù* without honour; Machiavelli himself characterized Ligurio as a 'parasite' who lives on the margin of society. Such a view, one is certain, was never Machiavelli's conception of the new prince. Similarly, Mazzeo sees in *Mandragola* 'the model of what a perfect diplomatic solution would be, a solution which would be painfully realistic yet one in which all sides would get what they want.' *Renaissance Studies*, XXXI, 3 (Apr. 1962), 279. I doubt if it is fair either to diplomats or

a corrupting religion cannot co-exist with a healthy state. The former was the fundamental cause of Italian decadence. 'We Italians [then] owe to the Church of Rome and to her priests our having become irreligious and bad.'[59] This indictment of the church is fair if Timoteo is an authentic representative of the corrupt church of an Alexander VI or a Julius II.

The friar's fundamental sin was avarice.[60] As a religious superior the only fault that he finds in his fellow monks is that they are not as avaricious as himself.

> How many times I have told these friars to keep her clean! And then they are puzzled if worship falls off. I remember when there were five hundred images here, and today there're not twenty. We're to blame, because we haven't known how to keep up her reputation. We used to go in procession before her every evening after compline and have lauds sung for her every Saturday. We were always making vows to her then, so that folks would see new images before her; in confession we all the time encouraged men and women to make vows to her. Now none of these things is done, and then we are puzzled if business gets slack. Oh, how few brains these friars of mine have![61]

His interest in his penitents also is governed by profit. The church is 'where my stock-in-trade fetch a higher price.'[62] He understands women perfectly. They are the 'most liberal givers' as well as the 'most vexing': 'he who deals with them gets profit and vexation together,'[63] and Timoteo is prepared for any amount of vexation for the sake of profit. He knows that women can ultimately be bamboozled precisely

to Machiavelli to say that fraud is the basis of success in diplomacy, or that there is any such thing as a 'perfect diplomatic solution.' *Mandragola* is rather the picture of a corrupt society which will be overrun by foreigners or given over to internal dissentions, chiefly because of lack of *virtù*.

59 *Discourses*, I, 12
60 Although there is a suggestion of sexual immorality in Clizia, II, 3
61 *Mandragola*, act V, sc.1
62 Ibid., sc.3
63 Ibid., act III, sc.4

because they are good.[64] So he is prepared to persuade a pregnant convent girl to commit abortion ('to keep up the reputation of the nunnery, the girl and the relatives') but with the appearance of virtue, namely for 'God and charity.' As for Lucrezia, her original position was that even if she were 'the only woman left in the world and the human race had to begin from me' she would not consent to adultery.[65] But Timoteo's theology and his sacramental power not only overcome her reluctance but also render the outcome enjoyable. Timoteo's argument is simple: 'the end justifies the means':

> Where a good is certain and an evil uncertain, you ought never to give up the good for fear of the evil. Here you have a certain good, that you will become pregnant, again a soul for the Lord. The uncertain evil is that the man who lies with you after you have taken the medicine may die; yet there are also those who don't die. But because the matter is uncertain, it is not a good thing for Messere Nicia to run this risk. As to the action, the notion that it's a sin is a fairy story, because the will is what sins, not the body, and what would make it a sin would be your husband's displeasure, but you will be pleasing to him; or if you should take pleasure in it, but you will get displeasure from it. Besides, one's purpose must be considered in everything; your purpose is to fill a seat in paradise, to please your husband. [el fine si ha a riguardare in tutte le cose][66]

Callimaco's leading passion is pleasure. The end to which this leads him is difficult and dishonourable, but, given his *inganno*, practicable. 'Nothing is ever so hopeless that there isn't some means that lets one hope for it, and even though it's poor and weak, still a man's resolve and eagerness [la voglia e il desiderio] to carry the affair

64 Ibid., sc.9
65 Ibid., sc.10
66 Ibid., sc.11. Compare this with the famous 'si guarda al fine' of *The Prince*, ch.18. Also compare Lucrezia's fate in the light of *The Prince*, ch.15: 'A man who wishes to make a profession of goodness in everything must necessarily come to grief among so many who are not good.'

through keep it from seeming so.'[67] Callimaco knows what he wants: he knows the circumstances and how to take advantage of them. He knows the leading passions of those most helpful to him: both Ligurio and Timoteo are susceptible to temptations of money. He uses his *inganno*: 'When a thing's to a man's advantage, you can believe, if you take him into your confidence, that he'll give you honest service.'[68] It is not necessary for success in one's undertaking to have the same interests as those with whom one deals. So long as one knows the point of compatibility and incompatibility with others, one can always hope for success. Prudence is the practical knowledge of this situation. To this extent Callimaco displays prudence. He attains his object. But that does not make him glorious; he is a sort of bloodless and enervated Agathocles.[69] Callimaco represents, I think, success without honour. One may agree with Mossini that throughout the play there is a tacit contraposition of the heroic idea of *virtù* found elsewhere in Machiavelli's writings and the characters portrayed in the play.[70] Callimaco and Timoteo are good examples of men in whom self-love manages to direct all the forces of their soul to the sovereign passion that dominates them: profit or pleasure.

The play portrays another aspect of Machiavelli's concept of religion, one which is in sharp contrast to that portrayed in the *Exhortation*. There Christianity was presented in its pure, transcendental form, as a means of man's personal salvation. In the *Mandragola*, on the other hand, we are suddenly made to realize what the corruption of Christianity can mean to society. A corrupt form of Christianity is far worse even than Roman paganism. Paganism, to its credit, promoted the cultivation of *virtù* by means of appeal to miracles, ceremonies and pageants.[71] But a corrupt Christianity can procure neither

67 *Mandragola*, act I, sc.1

68 Ibid.

69 See *The Prince*, ch.8.

70 Lanfranco Mossini, *Necessità e Legge Nell'Opera del Machiavelli* (Milano 1962), 111-12

71 Machiavelli's ideas on the political uses of miracles and oracles (*Discourses*, I, 12ff.) should be read in conjunction with his ideas on the relation between God and human action as inferred from *The Ass of Gold, Life of Castruccio Castracani*, Gilbert, II, 555, and *Mandragola*.

salvation nor *virtù*. Timoteo's religion is worse than empty formalism:[72] it is a cancerous growth on society, slowly destroying even the natural sense of honesty of those who pretend to profess it.

That Machiavelli considered this loss of natural religious sentiment a great loss to Italian politics is beyond doubt. 'How can those who feel contempt for God respect men?' he laments in *The Art of War*. 'What sort of good form, then, can be stamped upon this matter?'[73] Political redemption of Italy is impossible because the Italian church, more accurately the papal states, stands in the way; and the corrupt religious example of the clergy has robbed the people of '*antica virtù*.' *Virtù* has been replaced by *inganno*. An over-civilized people living in a state of *ozio*, with *virtù* extinguished, come to depend more and more on cleverness and strategems. Machiavelli scorns the 'common belief' of the contemporary Italian princes

> that a prince need only to think of a sharp reply in his study, to write a fine letter, to show quickness and cleverness in quotable sayings and replies, to know how to spin a fraud, to be adorned with gems and gold, to sleep and eat with greater splendour than others, to be surrounded with wanton pleasures, to deal with subjects avariciously and proudly, to decay in laziness, to give positions in army by favour, to despise anybody who showed them any praiseworthy course, and to expect their words to be taken as the responses of oracles.[74]

Mandragola presents an artistic portrait of this society without heroic and civic *virtù*. Religious corruption, in its own way, is responsible for the tendency toward political corruption.[75] The story of *Mand-*

---

72 'I said matins, read a life of the Holy Fathers, went into church and lit a lamp that had gone out, changed the veil of the Madonna who works miracles.' *Mandragola*, V, 1

73 *The Art of War*, bk.VII, Gilbert, II, 723

74 Ibid., 724

75 Compare the Machiavellian notion of the relation of religion to *virtù* to Ibn Khaldun's (1332-1406) notion of *asabiya* to religion. *Asabiya* (group feeling), inseparable from human beings, renders one group superior to another. Its increase or decrease in a group determines the political rise or decline of that group. The tendency towards luxury diminishes *asabiya*, while simple disci-

ragola, as Villari has noted, begins and ends within the walls of the church,[76] as if the church is symbolic of the Italian church. Machiavelli was certain that Italy would 'raise up dead things' more easily in poetry, in painting, and in sculpture than in politics.[77] As for political renovation, Italy was in an impossible position – it had lost its ancient *virtù*, and one major prop of ancient *virtù* – the ancient religion – was replaced by a corrupting version of Christianity. The secular prince, even if he was to be found, would still find it difficult to 'raise up' the ancient *virtù* until there was a reform of religion. *Mandragola* convincingly argues that such a reform was necessary.[78]

The Ass of Gold. NATURALISM IN MACHIAVELLI

The idea of nature (*natura*) like that of matter and form (*materia* and *forma*) is a relic from medieval scholastic terminology that we find in Machiavellian writings. By *natura* Machiavelli means human

pline (to Khaldun's way of thinking, the virtues of bedouin life) and a puritan style of life increase it. For more on *asabiya* see Khaldun's *The Muqaddimah,* translated into English (3 vols) by Franz Rosenthal. When *asabiya* combined with the 'supernatural' religion of Islam, as was the case in the first century of Islam, the Arabs became an irresistible force in history. In the case of Machiavelli, *virtù* is seen as more vigorous when joined with the 'natural' religion of the pagans than the 'supernatural' Christian religion. With this difference apart, there is a strong similarity between Machiavelli and Khaldun in that the tendency to luxury destroys *asabiya* as well as *virtù*.

76 Villari, *Life and Times of Machiavelli,* II, 349
77 *The Art of War,* bk.VII, Gilbert, II, 726
78 Though for Machiavelli the reform of religion was essential to the reform of society and to political renovation, the purpose of the religious reform was that it would lead to the 'imitation' of ancient *virtù.* The decline of Italy, Machiavelli tells us in the *Discourses,* is due more to the 'lack of a proper appreciation of history,' meaning Roman history, than to 'the weak state to which the religion of today has brought the world' or to 'the evil wrought in many provinces and cities of Christendom by ambition conjoined with idleness.' *Discourses,* I, pref. What Machiavelli expected from religious reform was the restoration of *antica virtù.* A religious reform that aimed only at spiritual purification would not, I think, have satisfied his political theory.

nature as distinct from the ambiguous Renaissance meaning of human nature as well as the goddess Nature. Nature is the principle of human action. It is also a standard of human action. Thus, he who follows nature cannot be rebuked.[79] At the same time Machiavelli believes that human nature is somehow defective, that it cannot always do what it ought to do. 'Men cannot command their natures.'[80] Ambition and avarice cancel the bounties of Nature.[81] Discipline is therefore necessary for the success of any human action: 'discipline can make up where Nature is lacking.'[82] For the achievement of success, man requires the favours of *fortuna* and *i tempi* as well as discipline and prudence.

In *The Ass of Gold* (1517) Machiavelli expands on the theme of man's natural deficiencies and the need for political discipline. Here human nature is contrasted with animal nature. Animals with their instinctive *virtù* pursue their ends more predictably and successfully than men with their half-man, half-beast nature. Reason and will, though in themselves superior to instinct, are of little avail to the political man because undesirable passions such as ingratitude and ambition prompt him to act against his rational nature.

In *The Ass of Gold* (it ends abruptly with the eighth chapter) the author, disguised as an ass, wanders into the netherworld of Circe. There he is met by one of Circe's lieutenants who, like Beatrice, conducts him through the various regions of the kingdom and introduces him to its animal inhabitants. These animals, of course, were men in their earthly life. They were turned into animals by Circe in accordance with the political merits or demerits of their previous existence. Machiavelli's use of symbolism must be noted. Human kingdoms are symbolized by the kingdom of Circe. The political man is but half man, or rather he is but an animal in disguise. Machiavelli finds out that many whom he had regarded on earth as Fabiuses and Catos

---

79 Machiavelli to Vettori, Gilbert, II, 961
80 Cf. Croce: 'Machiavelli's longing is for an unattainable society of good and pure men ...' *Philosophy, Poetry, History: An Anthology of Essays by Benedetto Croce*, tr. and ed. by Cecil Sprigge (London 1966), 656. See also Machiavelli to Soderini, Gilbert, II, 897.
81 *The Ass of Gold*, Gilbert, II, 772
82 *Ambition*, Gilbert, II, 737

turned out to be rams and sheep.[83] The cat that he meets in the land of Circe is being continually mocked by other animals because, although prudent and of good breeding, it nevertheless lost its prey due to too much patience. Similarly, the lion had his claws cut and teeth pulled through his own counsels, the ox is without his horn, and the bloodhound is without his eyesight. Machiavelli gives many more examples of defective animals. They symbolize the ways in which man falls short of discipline. Circe's animals are inferior to the animals of the natural animal kingdom. The latter have no defects, no imbalances in their natures because they are 'closer friends to Nature' and obey Nature. They practise prudence without instruction; and, as for their *virtù*, it rivals even that of the ancient Romans![84]

In contrast, man always desires 'that which Nature cannot supply';[85] he is led by self-love; 'So much your self-love deceives you that you do not believe there is any good apart from human existence and its worth.'[86] In man, Nature's bounty is cancelled by ambition and avarice. In short, 'No animal can be found that has a frailer life and has for living a stronger desire, more disordered fear and greater madness' than man.[87] Even the pig in Circe's kingdom is happier than man on earth: 'in this mud I live more happily,' the pig informs Machiavelli, 'here without anxiety I bathe and roll myself.'[88]

These reflections seem to place the political man in a dilemma. He must follow his own nature, which he must constantly remake, discipline, and direct. The will must be freed from ingratitude and ambition; it must be transformed by patriotism. The re-creation of man is an indispensable part of the political process. The political man must so discipline himself as to have a balance between his desires and his actions.[89] Only on this condition can he win the favours of

---

83 *The Ass of Gold*, Gilbert, II, 769

84 Ibid., 771-2

85 Ibid.

86 Ibid. I do not know why Gilbert translates 'umana essensa' by human existence.

87 Ibid.

88 Ibid.

89 Thus Machiavelli praises even a relatively obscure figure like Hiero of Syracuse because in him all qualities were in perfect balance and he lacked nothing. *The Prince*, ch.6

Fortuna and take advantage of *i tempi*. The curious irony is that in *The Ass of Gold* Machiavelli makes use of brute animals to teach man this salutary political lesson.

A Pastoral: The Ideal Ruler; A Discourse on Remodeling the Government of Florence

The philosopher of *verità effettuale* was also an imaginative writer who could express his real longings through poetry. *A Pastoral: The Ideal Ruler*, written between 1513 and 1519 and dedicated to Lorenzo de Medici, is a good illustration of Machiavelli's poetry. In this poem the ruler (a 'counterpart to the Prince')[90] is portrayed, not as a disciple of Chiron, but as a gift of the gods, not of one god, but of many.

'In you I see all the virtues[91] brought together; nor does it seem a marvel, because in shaping you not one god only took part in so great a work.'[92] There is no trace of evil or fraud in this ruler. His role is seen as both guiding his 'flock' and keeping them happy in the 'sheepfold'[93] and acting as a mediator between God and man. 'Heaven was striving to show its virtue [*virtù*] when it gave us a man so surpassing, to make us partake its beauties.'[94]

If *A Pastoral* portrays the idealized version of the prince, the *Discursus*[95] portrays the idealized version of the republic. Tommasini

---

90 Gilbert, I, 97

91 *Ogni virtù*, in the singular, indicating one total reality or synthesis of all virtuous qualities

92 *A Pastoral*, Gilbert, I, 98-9. The gods mentioned are Jove, Vulcan, Venus, Mars, Mercury, Juno, and Saturn.

93 The idea of the ruler as pastor, the subjects as flock, and the kingdom as sheepfold occurs also in *The Ass of Gold*.

94 *A Pastoral*, Gilbert, I, 98. The 'divine' aspect of politics is also repeated in *A Discourse on Remodeling the Government of Florence*.

95 Gilbert, I, 97-116. Ridolfi thinks that *Discursus florentinarum rerum post mortem iunioris Laurentii Medices* is the correct title of this work. Gilbert apparently has adopted what Ridolfi calls the spurious title, 'Discorso sopra il riformare lo stato di Firenze ad instanza di papa Leone X.'

viewed it as 'il supremo epilogo de Discorsi,'[96] and Leslie Walker observes that it shows 'how Machiavelli would have applied the principles laid down in his *Discourses*.'[97] Its value does not lie in the practical suggestions which Machiavelli made, and which were never accepted by Pope Leo X,[98] but rather in its theoretical assumptions. These are, first, that all ruling must take into account the nature of the people to be ruled; it requires the conscious recognition of the broad outlines of the aspirations and ambitions of the ruled. As for Florence, its inhabitants naturally loved freedom and equality; it was therefore unwise to impose a princedom on them, princedoms being more suitable for those who do not love equality and liberty. Only a republic could correspond to the nature of Florentines.

Secondly, good government requires that the people have a share in it. Their share must correspond to their ambitions and socio-economic conditions. One of the relatively few times that Machiavelli mentions socio-economic factors in his political analysis is found in the *Discursus*. 'Those who organize a republic ought to provide for the three different sorts of men who exist in all cities, namely the most important [*primi*], those in the middle [*mezzani*] and the lowest [*ultimi*, called also *il universale*].' By sharing interests, ambition becomes harmonized. This is a better way of dealing with ambition than to let it produce civil strife. The harmonizing role is not played by the leader, but, ideally, by institutions

> that can by themselves stand firm. And they will always stand firm when everybody has had a hand in them, when everybody knows what he needs to do and in whom he can trust, and no class of citizen, either through fear for itself or through ambition, will need to desire revolution.[99]

96 Cited in Carmelo Caristia, *Il Pensiero Politico di Niccolò Machiavelli*, 2nd ed. (Naples 1951), 93

97 Walker, *Discourses of Niccolò Machiavelli*, I, 471

98 The Pope's purpose appears to have been simply to quiet 'the hottest lovers of liberty by throwing a sop to their hopes and illusions.' Villari, *Life and Times of Machiavelli*, II, 279

99 *A Discourse*, Gilbert, I, 115

How unfair historians have been to Machiavelli! Here we find him ex-pounding that 'needs' and 'trust' can harmonize in 'institutions,' that 'fear' and 'ambition' need not necessarily lead to revolutions; in short, that that organization of politics is best in which power is shared. And power becomes legitimized in the process of its being shared.[100]

Thirdly, the ideal objective of a ruler ought to be subordinating individual interests to the *bene commune*. Machiavelli sees in the attainment of this ideal of politics the highest fulfilment of man's nature. 'No greater gift, then, does Heaven give to a man, nor can Heaven show him a more glorious road than this' (namely, to govern by institutions and to be thanked for it by the people).[101]

The exhortation to Pope Leo X on which the *Discursus* ends, en-couraging him to aim at this highest human glory, may well be com-pared to the *Exhortation to Penitence*. If the latter reveals Machia-velli's spiritual idealism, the former reveals his political idealism. It places Aristotle and Plato in a better light than the preface to the *Discourses*, I and *The Prince*, chapter 15 would suggest. Although, unlike Solon and Lycurgus, Aristotle and Plato did not found cities, they still acted honourably by writing about politics. Even if the practice of politics is the most glorious activity for a man, a theory of it is not irrelevant; in fact, for some men, political theorizing may be their only way to fame.

I believe the greatest honor possible for men to have is that will-ingly given them by their native cities; I believe the greatest good

100 Compare *Discourses*, I, 11: 'It is not, then, the salvation of a republic or a king-dom to have a prince who will rule prudently while he lives, but to have one who will so organize it that even after he dies it can be maintained.' Also, com-pare *Discourses*, I, 17. There Machiavelli argues that longevity and health of republics will depend not only on able leaders but also on the *virtù* of the peo-ple (matter). However great the achievements of the hero, if the matter is cor-rupt, the reform will not outlast his lifetime, unless 'extra-legal' means are used.
101 Note the almost Ciceronian note of his rhetoric: 'neque enim est ulla res, in qua proprius ad deorum numen virtus accedat humana, quam civitatis aut con-dere novas aut conservare iam conditas.' 'For there is really no other occupa-tion in which human virtue approaches more closely the august function [*numen*] of the gods than that of founding new states or preserving those al-ready in existence.' *De Republica*, I, 7, Loeb Classics trans.

to be done and the most pleasing to God is that which one does to one's native city [*patria*] . Besides this, no man is so much exalted by any act of his as are those men who have by laws and institutions remodelled [*reformato*] republics and kingdoms; these are, after those who have been gods, the first to be praised. And because they have been few who have had opportunity to do it, and very few of those who have understood how to do it, small is the number who have done it. And so much has this glory been esteemed by men seeking for nothing other than glory that when unable to form a republic in reality, they have done it in writing, Aristotle, Plato, and many others, who have wished to show the world that if they have not founded a free government [*un vivere civile*] , as did Solon and Lycurgus, they have failed not through their ignorance but through their impotence for putting it into practice.[102]

CONCLUSION

The secondary writings contribute much to demolish the image of misunderstanding about Machiavelli. Only sheer prejudice can prevent scholars from balancing his political theory, founded on reason and experience, against truths seen by him in the light of faith, imagination, and intuition. Despite his claims in the epistles dedicatory of *The Prince* and the *Discourses* that he had put all that he knows into those books, the fact remains that he did not. He put into them only those elements in his thought which fit his scientific method; the other elements are found scattered elsewhere in his writings lacking a methodological nexus.

Machiavelli's acceptance of original sin and grace makes his world view closer to that of Augustine and Dante than to that of Livy or Polybius. Just as the *Inferno* and the *Purgatorio* cannot be interpreted correctly except in the light of the *Paradiso,* so Machiavelli's cyclic view of history, his theory of corruption and regeneration, his strictures upon human nature, Christianity, and political morality, cannot be finally evaluated except in the light of his concept of original sin and grace.

Although original sin may explain political amoralism, grace will not cure political corruption. On this point Machiavelli's stand is radically opposed to the theologian's. The latter sees in grace not only a means to spiritual salvation, but also a remedy for social and political regeneration. This interpretation, according to Machiavelli, is not verified by facts. He sees in grace a purely spiritual power which leads man only to his heavenly glory.

Machiavelli believes that man must pursue the task of political and social regeneration on a purely human basis. The man who aspires to *virtù* must be content to work with a 'fallen' human nature. His task is truly heroic because he has to reform and discipline this nature. Compared to heavenly glory, to which man is called by grace, the pursuit of terrestrial glory is but a short dream. However much Machiavelli might seem to esteem the ancient, pagan ideal of *virtus humana*, it undergoes a subtle Dantesque transformation in his hands because it is put in perspective by *gratia divina*.

The enigma of Machiavelli remains. But I would say that this enigma is more a matter of method and system than of truth. Only when we seek to reduce all the elements of his thought to a system does Machiavelli appear to be enigmatic. He clearly understood the interplay of moral aspirations and practical necessities, the longing for redemption and the actual experience of sinfulness. These are not matters of enigma, but of experience. Even though Machiavelli does not place them in a coherent philosophic or theological system, or even in his scientific method there can be no doubt that Machiavelli *minore* subjects the apparently conscience-free man of Machiavelli *maggiore* to a rigorous examination of conscience.

NINE

The Relevance of Machiavelli
to Contemporary World Politics

ANTHONY D'AMATO

THE DIFFERENCES

No matter how well Machiavelli understood and expressed the machinations of city-state politics in his day, his writings are at best an im-
perfect model of contemporary world politics.* There are of course
aspects in Machiavelli's model analogous to the present world, as well
as features that are irrelevant (fortresses, moats, weaponry). If one
could say with assurance which aspects of Machiavelli's writings are
directly analogous to current politics, then one might learn something from his discussions of alliances, the reliability of auxiliary
troops, the calling in of external assistance for one's own internal
political problems, and other such insights. But the fact is that one
must thoroughly understand contemporary world politics before it is
possible to say with assurance which aspects of Machiavelli's model
are relevant. In that case, there is not much further need for Machiavelli's model; it would only be of interest to those who feel the need
of praising (or criticizing) Machiavelli.

To an extent, of course, this is true of any theory – that to know
whether the theory applies we have to construct another theory.
Nevertheless, the theoretical construction of a model of world politics may help us gain insights into the real world to the extent that

*See introduction, pp. 26-8 (ed.).

we have confidence in the correspondence of the features of the model to reality as we know it.

Machiavelli's model of city-state politics 500 years ago does not give us the degree of confidence necessary for our acceptance of his trains of thought or his conclusions. This is not because the number of his actors was small (five important Italian city-states plus France, Switzerland, Spain, and Turkey) compared to the 120 nations today, but rather because of the fact that airborne nuclear weapons were introduced in 1945 rendering nations permeable and summarily destructible. The mere presence of these weapons in the hands of two superpowers necessarily distorts all other world power interrelationships. Local wars today may look like the kinds of wars Machiavelli talked about, in varying degrees of resemblance, but this is only because the major powers allow the wars to proceed as they do. In a broader sense, we must ascribe to nuclear weaponry the fact that local wars since 1945 have indeed remained local. The 'powder keg' of the Middle East would several times by now have erupted into World War III were it not for the deterrence exercised by the two nuclear superpowers. It is also hard to imagine that Vietnam or Korea could be the scenes of multipower participations within small geographical limits except for our knowledge that vast nuclear destructibility lurks in the background exercising, so far, a sobering and controlling effect.

Even the concepts of power and military force have changed dramatically since 1945. Although writers such as Morgenthau, Thompson, and Kennan have articulated their neo-Machiavellian notions of power politics largely since 1945, their own images had been cast firmly in pre-1945 reality. What they have said about the primacy of military power and forcible containment has had slight correspondence with the reality of the post-World War II era. In fact, military power has not been an important factor either for national security or for aggrandizement for most nations in the past quarter century. Boundary lines in Europe have remained almost precisely where they were in 1945 (including the troublesome and widely considered 'unstable' situation in divided Berlin in a divided Germany). Both the Federal Republic of Germany and Japan have increased their national 'power' and GNP from the ashes of 1945 to positions today exceeding their own pre-1939 inventories; this increase has been accomplished without war and without even the feeling that either nation is heading toward war or attempting to provoke one. Perhaps the most dramatic example of the lack of utility of military force is the American experience in Vietnam. The United States first threatened massive bombing of North Vietnam and then, when the threats produced little if any change in the attitudes of Hanoi, actually carried out the threat, dumping more tonnage into that tiny land than all the combatants used in all of World War II. The actual bombing had, if anything, even less effect upon North Vietnam than the threat of bombing. The story with respect to ground troops is even less impressive. By American statistics, which probably are inflated with respect to enemy dead, it costs the United States well over one million dollars to kill a single Viet Cong. Had the United States instead simply given that much money or purchasing power to the Viet Cong, the war would probably have ended a long time ago, with many lives saved.

Military power has become a peculiar concept because of the existence of nuclear weapons. It seems absurd for the United States to use expensive conventional weapons in Vietnam when the United States is overstockpiled with nuclear weapons. This absurdity is not lost on the Vietnamese (nor on the Koreans before them). Anything short of nuclear extinction is not a credible threat, nor is the threat of nuclear extinction itself (as Secretary of State Dulles learned in 1954 when he called it 'massive retaliation'). But if the terms 'force' and 'power' actually have different meanings and connotations today due to the existence of the ultimate weapons, then Machiavelli's use of those terms is not isomorphic with respect to our present theories of world politics. His model, in short, contains basic linguistic divergences as well as empirical differences.

THE SIMILARITIES

Machiavelli's relevance to contemporary world politics lies in a different dimension: that of the psychology of human behaviour. Despite the atomic bomb, we have a high degree of confidence in the sameness of man today with the human model analyzed by Machiavelli. Although 'nature has given each man an individual face,' Mach-

212 The Political Calculus

iavelli wrote to Piero Soderini, 'men do not change their imaginings and procedures.'[1] This theme forms a cornerstone of the *Discourses*. It is worthwhile to study history, because history affords a basis for prediction. 'The affairs of the world ... are carried on by men, who have and always have had the same passions,' and therefore it is not surprising that 'of necessity the same results appear.'[2]

Before taking up the constancies of human nature in Machiavelli's writings that are of immediate relevance to present-day world politics, let us consider briefly his theoretical-linguistic method.

Both for literary effect, and to exude an air of having comprehended all possibilities, Machiavelli typically uses words in paired opposites. For example, speaking of the qualities which bring 'blame or praise' to princes, he says in part:

> one is considered a giver, one grasping; one cruel, one merciful; one a promise-breaker, the other truthful; one effeminate and cowardly, the other bold and spirited; one kindly, the other proud; one lascivious, the other chaste; one reliable, the other tricky; one hard, the other tolerant; one serious, the other like-minded; one religious, the other unbelieving; and the like.[3]

We know today, in light of psychology and psycholinguistics, that human nature cannot so readily be polarized for descriptive purposes, that indeed what seems to be a 'negation' for purposes of Aristotelian logic[4] is really a cluster of personality factors.[5] These factors are not necessarily antithetical; on a spectrum of personality traits they would not necessarily be at opposite ends. For example, from the Stoics through the Utilitarians, 'pleasure' was the opposite of 'pain,' yet today we know that De Sade was closer to the truth in describing the transmogrification of pleasure and pain in his fictional descrip-

---

1 Letter to Soderini, no. 116; in Allan Gilbert, *Machiavelli: The Chief Works and Others* (Durham, NC 1965 [hereinafter cited as Gilbert]), II, 895, 896-7

2 *Discourses,* III, 43, Gilbert, I, 521

3 *The Prince,* 25, Gilbert, I, 58

4 Cf. Alfred Korzybski, *Science and Sanity,* 4th ed. (Lakeville, Conn. 1958), 7-15.

5 See D'Amato, 'Psychological Constructs in Foreign Policy Prediction,' 11 *Journal of Conflict Resolution* 294 (1967).

tions of masochism and flagellation. Secondly, if we consider 'love' and 'hate,' we hardly have to pause in this post-Freudian era to recognize that 'love-hate' itself describes a state of mind, a true Hegelian synthesis of an intense feeling (which itself might be contrasted with the emergent psychological thesis of the 'apathetic personality').

Machiavelli himself transcended the jejune confinements of logical negation; although he used antinomies for pedagogic and advocatory purposes, he was too astute a student of human nature to be straitjacketed by them. The best proof of this is his constant use of case studies drawn from history or experience. His ever-ready examples do not merely illustrate his verbal generalities; rather they substantively enrich the content of his theory. We are all familiar with theorists (such as Talcott Parsons) who remain so long on the abstract verbal level that the more we read of them the more their constructs appear to be flying off into irrelevant space. Words, after all, are very vague abstractions with different connotations for each reader; the writer who remains on the abstract level may mean all things to every reader and not one consistent thing to more than one of them. How much more meaningful is the still-life verbal painting of a real event! The concrete example cuts between the vague edges or words and adds new meaning and content to them.

Moreover, Machiavelli abandoned his own antinomies after the literary effect of the moment was produced. His own verbal theories explode the capsulated negations by introducing new concepts which triangularize the logical relations. For instance, 'prudence,' 'force,' and 'fraud' are used by Machiavelli as in a triangular relationship to each other; no one is necessarily the opposite of one alone of the others.[6] The same may be said for 'fear,' 'greed,' and 'hate,'[7] and among Machiavelli's most fundamental concepts a triangular relationship exists as to 'virtù,' 'fortuna,' and 'necessità.' Nor are the triangles equilateral; 'fear,' for example, is stronger than 'greed,' as Machiavelli writes in the *History of Florence*,[8] and in the *Discourses* he writes that force without fraud is not enough to enable a man of humble

6 *Words on Appropriating Money*, Gilbert, III, 1439. The same point is implicit in Machiavelli's discussion of the lion and the fox. *The Prince*, 18, Gilbert, I, 65

7 *The Prince*, 7, Gilbert, I, 34; id. 17, Gilbert, I, 62; *Discourses*, III, 21; Gilbert, I, 477

8 Bk.V, Gilbert, III, 1250

fortune to come to a high rank but fraud without force would be enough.[9]

This linguistic method already has introduced some of Machiavelli's substantive discernments of human motivation. Let us now look in greater detail at the notion of rewards and punishments that Machiavelli, as the first political scientist, held so basic to his entire theory.

Politics, reduced to its lowest common denominator, is the science or art of getting somebody else to do what you want him to do. International politics, accordingly, is the study of inter-nation influence. Nations are composed of men, and men have a remarkably constant nature. Men, like animals, will react to rewards and punishments – persuasion, or the appeal to man's reason, is simply the Machiavellian art of making clear what those rewards and punishments will be. But what, precisely, is a 'punishment' and what is a 'reward'? In the first place, and most crucially, they are not the opposites of each other. Machiavelli points out in the *Discourses* that new rewards do not erase old punishments of the same magnitude.[10] Men of high rank (such as the Pope) remember old injuries more than new benefits, as Cesare Borgia learned to his great sorrow.[11] Nor should rewards and punishment be handled in the same manner. Penalties should be given all at once, but benefits should be spread out gradually over time.[12] Secondly, rewards and punishments complement each other; without the one, the other loses efficacy. The Romans learned the important lesson, according to Machiavelli, that if penalties are to be given for wicked deeds then a system of rewards for good deeds must be set up and maintained.[13] On the other hand, a reward once given is final; it should confer no lasting immunity to punishment. If a man who had previously been rewarded commits an

9 Bk.II, 13, Gilbert, I, 357

10 Id. III, 4, Gilbert, I, 426: 'Every ruler can be reminded that never have new benefits erased old injuries; and so much the less in so far as the new benefit is less than the injury.' The words 'so much the less' imply that present benefits do not erase equivalent past injuries.

11 *The Prince*, 7, Gilbert, I, 34. See also Letter to Vettori, no. 128, Gilbert, II, 903, 908.

12 *The Prince*, 8, Gilbert, I, 38; *Discourses*, I, 45, Gilbert, I, 289

13 Id., I, 24, Gilbert, I, 251

evil deed, Machiavelli writes that he should be punished 'without regard to his good deeds.'[14] Lastly, future deprivations have a greater influence on behaviour than anticipated rewards. It was through fear of the threatened loss of Florentine support, according to Machiavelli, that made the King of Naples keep his pact with Florence in 1480.[15] Earlier, in 1429, a past benefit (being freed from prison) was not remembered by a certain Messer Jacopo as compared to a 'danger' that he and his fellow Florentines were in.[16] It is a clear Machiavellian maxim that 'threats are more dangerous than deeds';[17] put differently, fear, 'as always happens,' is a 'stronger' emotion than greed or the hope of gain.[18]

That rewards and punishments are not opposite to one another is a theory recently emerging from behavioural psychology. In his brilliant study of *The Explanation of Behaviour*, Professor Taylor demonstrates a basic difference between avoidance behaviour (fear) and reinforcement conditioned behaviour (rewards). A rat in a maze may make a correct response to shock on the first trial, or a totally different but also correct response on the second trial:

> For instance, a rat may escape from shock administered in the path of a maze by running quickly ahead. On the next trial, he will stop and refuse to enter the path.[19]

This is clearly not 'learned behaviour' as in the case of a series of rewards that condition, or teach, a rat to perform complex maneuvers. Moreover, it is very difficult to extinguish avoidance behaviour; the fear of the maze remains even though there is no longer any shock.[20] This behaviour is to be contrasted with the comparative ease of extinguishing learned behaviour when the reward is taken away. In short, recent experimental psychology substantiates Machiavelli's insights into this aspect of human nature.

4 Ibid.
5 *History of Florence*, VIII, 22, Gilbert, III, 1413
6 Id., IV, 18, Gilbert, III, 1208
7 *Discourses*, III, 6, Gilbert, I, 429
8 *History of Florence*, V, 13, Gilbert, III, 1250
9 Charles Taylor, *The Explanation of Behaviour* (London 1965), 254
0 Id., 257

216 The Political Calculus

On the international level, as has been suggested, we are moving out of the era of the efficacy of force and the threat of force. Nevertheless, nations will continue to attempt to influence other nations. We may infer from Machiavelli's analysis that rewards and punishments are not the opposites of one another – but rather can overlap – the existence of four categories: punishment, non-punishment, reward, and non-reward. If we have a non-punishment international situation, maneuverability will be effected by the control of rewards and non-rewards. For a non-reward to have any effect upon a nation, there must be a flow of rewards as well (recall Machiavelli's statement that penalties will not work without benefits). It is very likely that international 'rewards' in this new era will be economic: the goal of the 'good life' in material terms is no less appealing to the politically awakened masses in the world today than it was to Machiavelli's fellow Florentine citizens. We may therefore look for international political manipulation to be expressed primarily in terms of trade and aid.

The point to be remembered, however, is that unless a nation sets up a pattern of expectation of conferred rewards, the 'threat' of halting those rewards will be meaningless. The United States, for example, has given countries in Latin America considerable help in the form of foreign aid, and as a result has enjoyed the full political support of the Latin American bloc in the United Nations. However, the United States has recently cut back sharply on its foreign aid program, and as a result we may expect the countries of Latin America to challenge the United States in the United Nations and to cause trouble to American interests (fishing, mining, oil, and so forth) within Latin America. Since the United States is cutting its foreign aid appropriations because of domestic political pressures as translated by Congress and a Republican president, it is clear that there is no hope for an increase in aid to Latin America if the latter were to change its divergent course and begin doing what American capitalists would like. Thus the United States, having set up at considerable expense a reward stream in the form of foreign aid to Latin America, is probably going to lose its influence there because, as a democratic and slow-moving government, it lacks the ability to reverse its course and restore the stream of aid. The Soviet Union, by contrast, threatened to reduce its aid to Czechoslovakia but did not actually cut off that aid, and as a result Czechoslovakian policies more favourable to the Soviet Union were accepted by the people of Czechoslovakia. A more serious threat to the eastern bloc than Czechoslovakia's political reforms of 1968 has been the recent policy of Rumania of constructing steel, rubber, and glass factories within the essentially agricultural economy of Rumania. Although these plants are economically inefficient for Rumania – the country would make more money sticking to agriculture – eventually they will remove a powerful inducement to Soviet co-operation, for Rumania will not be dependent upon the Soviet Union for steel and capital goods.

THE LEGAL FACTOR

Apart from *The Art of War*, Machiavelli placed much less emphasis on power and force than his subsequent interpreters have imagined. He was, after all, a diplomat, not a general. Military force to him was largely 'given' – if you had it, or were willing to pay for it, you could make use of it; if you did not have as much of it as you thought you needed, then recourse must be had to diplomacy. Machiavelli's *Legations* contain advice for better armies, for citizen armies, for more attention to military matters; as in *The Art of War*, Machiavelli here was addressing himself to Florentines. But his *work* was directed at non-Florentines; the skills of diplomacy, which he practised and later analyzed, were premised upon securing advantage to Florence *non-militarily*. Machiavelli would have had little worth as a diplomat for Florence or as a writer for subsequent generations if the major part of his message was an exhortation to increase military strength and the use of force. It can be as futile to tell a statesman to get a larger army as it is for an investment adviser to tell a prospective client to get more money before he invests; the prince as well as the client are interested in the best utilization of the resources they presently have. Machiavelli well knew this, and thus his writings explore at length tactics short of the use of force.

One such tactic, perhaps far more important in the nuclear age where the boundaries between permissible international acts and those which might contain escalatory consequences have to be more sharply drawn than in Machiavelli's day, is the resort to the claim of legality. Machiavelli did not have too much to say about the concept of law, but what he did say is extremely suggestive and important. What he said about law was, after all, said in the very 'realistic' and law-disparaging context of his times.

Before dealing directly with Machiavelli's notion of law, let us consider briefly what that term has meant to most writers since his time. The emergent nation-state in the writings of Hobbes and the theory of the legislative sovereign in Bodin combined to lay the groundwork for a positivist concept of law that achieved its apotheosis in the lectures of John Austin. Austin claimed that law was the command by the sovereign within a state, a command that carried with it a threat of punishment if the addressee did not obey. In a basic sense this is a might-makes-right (or at least 'legal right') theory; the sovereign lawmaker within a state fashions, at his pleasure, laws that carry with them the threat of punishment at the hands of the state. The positivist theory has had great appeal in England and in the United States, as well as in the Soviet Union, and its current most articulate proponent, Professor Hart, claims that we need to trace laws to a sovereign or quasi-sovereign within a state (he uses a process called 'rules of recognition') in order to identify them as laws. He also, incidentally, draws a sharp line between law and morality as if to underline the fact that if might makes legal right it does not make moral right.

With positivism in the ascendency, the outlook for 'international law' was bleak. Austin quite consistently refused to regard 'international law' as law; he called it 'positive morality.' In the absence of a supreme international sovereign which could punish nations for disobeying its commands, there could be no international law 'properly so-called.' Positivists since Austin have made some feeble attempts to restore the title of international law, the most important one probably that of Professor Hart.[21] But since positivism is so firmly grounded in a command-backed-by-sanction theory, it is unlikely that international law would have much respect among positivists (save, perhaps, for the concession made by Soviet jurists and others to treaties – laws binding upon nations because of their actual con-

---

21 See Anthony D'Amato, 'The Neo-Positivist Concept of International Law,' 59 *American Journal of International Law* 321 (1965).

sent – though this concession does not explain why a nation cannot subsequently change its mind).

The verbal theory of positivism, downgrading international law, co-incided nicely with the era of force in international politics where law, particularly in the twentieth century, has appeared to many observers to be a delusion insofar as restraining nations is concerned.[22] However, as the utility of force drops off sharply, it will more and more appear that nations, most of the time at any rate,[23] are obeying international law.[24] This custom of obeying law will in turn reinforce further obedience and make it difficult, or at least costly, for a nation to depart from the law. But what kind of 'law' is it that they will obey? It is certainly not 'law' as defined by the positivists, but after all if the positivist definition does not accord with reality then that hardly matters. Let us see what Machiavelli would have called it.

Machiavelli's concept of 'law' is realistically stripped of all medieval notions of something apart from, and higher than, man. In the medieval view, 'law' somehow 'exists,' and magistrates or princes 'find' or 'discover' it when they 'apply' it to cases they are called upon to judge. To Machiavelli, laws are man-made, sometimes out of whole cloth when a state is founded.[25] Although it is prudent for a founding prince to continue many of the old laws that the people were accustomed to,[26] he clearly has the power to change all of them. Moreover, a prince has the power to violate the laws; Machiavelli furnishes many examples of this.[27] But there we come upon a crucial point. While the prince may depart from, or violate, laws that even he has made in the first place, there is no suggestion in Machiavelli

---

22 For a recent sharply analytical statement of this basic position see Stanley Hoffman, 'International Law and the Control of Force,' in Karl W. Deutsch and Stanley Hoffman, eds., *The Relevance of International Law* (Cambridge, Mass. 1968), 21-46.

23 See Louis Henkin, *How Nations Behave* (New York 1968).

24 This is not surprising; states after all are the creators as well as the subjects of international law. See Anthony D'Amato, 'International Law – Content and Function: A Review,' 11 *Journal of Conflict Resolution* 504 (1967).

25 See *Discourses*, I, 3, Gilbert, I, 201.

26 Id., I, 9, Gilbert, I, 218

27 Id., I, 45, Gilbert, I, 288; id., I, 58, Gilbert, I, 315-17

that the prince's action thereby changes the law. There is no sense that whatever the prince does *is* law; quite the contrary, the prince may depart from the law and may get away with it in terms of being too powerful for anyone to enforce the law against him, but nevertheless the prince has still disobeyed the law. Machiavelli gives the example of Savonarola who got a law passed and then did not observe it; his conduct 'took influence away from him and brought him much censure.'[28]

What we have in Machiavelli, in short, is a theory of constitutional law. A constitution is a list of laws some of which restrain the people and some the government and some both. When a citizen disobeys a constitutional law, he is of course liable to punishment by the state. But what if the government disobeys a constitutional law? What if it does something it has no constitutional right to do? If the government does this, it is never punished in the same sense that a citizen may be punished. For instance, if the American Congress passes a law abridging freedom of speech, no one would ever suggest that the individual congressman who passed the law would be liable to imprisonment, nor even that the individual policemen who enforced the law would be subject to punishment. What would result is either that another branch of the government (such as the Supreme Court in the American system) would declare the law to be of no force or effect, or all parts of the government would get together and declare a 'state of national emergency' justifying the departure from the constitution. If the latter alternative is resorted to too often, or if resorted to at a time when there is no factual basis for it, the republic would weaken, people might rise up against the government, and the effective power of the government might be compromised. Thus it would appear that if a government wanted to retain its full power over the people, it would be well advised not to depart from the constitutional law except in the rare case of a true national crisis where no other alternative will keep the state together. This is precisely the advice given by Machiavelli: 'I do not think there is a thing that sets a worse example in a republic than to make a law and not keep it, and so much the more when it is not kept by him who has made it.'[29]

28 Id., I, 45, Gilbert, I, 289
29 Id., I, 45, Gilbert, I, 288

Yet in a 'serious emergency,' Machiavelli advises a republic to take refuge 'under a dictator or some such authority' to avoid ruin.[30] Except for such serious emergencies, it is better for a republic never to break her own laws to gain short-run advantages. For the example of extralegal action 'has a bad effect, because it establishes a custom of breaking laws for good purposes; later, with this example, they are broken for bad purposes.'[31]

Thus Machiavelli's concept of constitutional law is eminently realistic and indeed preferable to the various 'positivist' theories of law that came after his time. Under the positivist theory which holds that laws are sovereign commands backed by the power of the state to enforce them, constitutional law is not really 'law.' For the latter is never enforced against the government which promulgated it in the first place. But this surely is a restricted view of 'law'; it suggests that people draw a distinction between the laws they are supposed to obey and the laws that governments are supposed to obey. Yet such a distinction, Machiavelli tells us, is not drawn; to the contrary, princes set a direct example to their subjects by keeping laws.

But once we depart from the strict positivist view, a curious thing happens. Laws begin to take on a life of their own. Of course, this is simply a metaphorical statement, and yet, given the limitations of our language, it may be the most precise way of putting it. To the positivists, laws are simply commands issued by men; they derive their force from the fact that they communicate a contingent threat to the citizen (a threat that if he does not obey the command he will be punished). Governments are made up of men; they make laws; the laws do not restrain them. On the contrary, Machiavelli would impliedly subscribe to the possibility of a government of laws not of men. To him, laws may be man-made but they begin to take on a permanency that limits the action of everyone including their creator. In his *History of Florence*, Machiavelli writes a major oration for the Signore 'of most standing' which obviously embodies Machiavelli's own views. The cure for the factions which were dividing and ruining Florence in 1372, the Signore says, is a thorough change of laws: 'annul the laws that breed factions, and adopt those suitable for a

30 Id., I, 34, Gilbert, I, 269
31 Id., I, 34, Gilbert, I, 268

truly free and law-abiding government.'[32] Laws clearly can be a restraint upon the government: note the emphasis upon a 'law-abiding government.' In the *Discourses*, Machiavelli says that 'governments by princes have lasted long, republican governments have lasted long, and both of them have needed to be regulated by the laws.'[33] But why should a prince obey the laws? Machiavelli's profound answer is that by doing so the prince *increases* his own power: the mass of the people, 'for whom it is enough to live secure, are easily satisfied by the making of ordinances and laws which provide for the general security and at the same time for the prince's own power.'[34] In the security and contentment of his subjects lies the greatest power of the prince, for

> when a prince does this and when the people see that under no circumstances will he break those laws, in a short time they feel secure and contented. An example is the kingdom of France, which lives safely for no other reason than that those kings are restrained by countless laws in which is included the security of all her people.[35]

In brief, a prince in obeying the laws is not obeying someone's 'command' or even his own prior command, but rather is setting an example that increases respect for laws and thus for his own legal position of authority. This is why governments obey their own constitutions, and why the concept of 'laws' is generally applicable to situations involving deeply felt needs of stability and security and not simply the positivist situation of a citizen threatened by the force of the state to do what the state has commanded. Constitutional laws take on a life of their own because they coincide with a prince's desire for power as well as the citizen's desire for security. A prince would be 'crazy' (the choice of word indicating Machiavelli's deep conviction on this point) to do what he wants irrespective of the laws.[36]

32 *History of Florence*, III, 5, Gilbert, III, 1148
33 *Discourses*, I, 58, Gilbert, I, 317
34 Id., I, 16, Gilbert, I, 237
35 Ibid.
36 Id., I, 58, Gilbert, I, 317

International law is very much like constitutional law. Again, with the law directed at a government, it is pointless to talk in terms of the punishment of individuals or the commands of sovereigns. Rather, international law is the expression of mutually felt needs of international security, and its observance by states increases their own power internally. Machiavelli cites the example of the violation by Rome of the law of nations respecting the conduct of ambassadors.[37] The French, against whom the violation of international law was perpetrated, were 'fired with scorn and rage' and 'marched against Rome and took it, except the Capitol.' This defeat (disruption of internal power and security) came upon the Romans, Machiavelli writes, 'merely as a result of their failure' to observe the ' "law of nations." '[38] International law, like constitutional law, draws lines between permissible and impermissible conduct; it makes less difference what these lines in fact are (Machiavelli talks a lot about 'good laws' but does not spell them out) than that there be lines. For the existence of lines communicates to the governments involved the kinds of conduct that will be tolerated by others. Wars are rendered less likely if there are many international laws and they are communicated to all states. Of course wars can be started deliberately (by transgressing important international lines), but there is less room for wars starting inadvertently as a result of failure to understand what types of conduct would be considered warlike by other governments.

If law is something more than a command backed by a threat of punishment, what precisely is it? Machiavelli consciously uses the term 'justice' as synonymous with 'good and holy laws,' as well as synonymous with the idea of constitutional law in *A Provision for Infantry*.[39] The chief basis of a republic, he writes, consists of 'justice and arms.'[40] In *The Prince* he writes that 'the principal foundations of all states, the new as well as the old and the mixed, are good laws and good armies.'[41] In a sense, force and law seem to be paired opposites. But cutting into this antinomy is the notion of goodness;

---

37 Id., II, 28, Gilbert, I, 405
38 Ibid.
39 *A Provision for Infantry*, prelude, Gilbert, I, 3
40 Ibid.
41 *The Prince*, 12, Gilbert, I, 47

good laws (justice) and force work hand in hand in preserving a republic. The relation between laws and goodness finds expression in the *Discourses*: 'just as good morals, if they are to be maintained, have need of the laws, so the laws, if they are to be observed, have need of good morals.'[42] Further, in speaking of the religion introduced into Rome by Numa as among the chief reasons for Roman prosperity, Machiavelli explains that 'religion caused good laws; good laws make good fortune; and from good fortune came the happy results of the city's endeavours.'[43] By deliberately linking the concept of law with the idea of goodness – in sharp contrast to the positivist insistence on the separation of law and morals – Machiavelli suggests a normative element in law. Law is something that *ought* to be obeyed, because it is right, just, and good to do so. In this sense, law transcends its maker; it acquires an independent existence; it can serve as the foundation of something as tangible as a state. The force of arms used internationally or internally in securing obedience to good laws becomes an element that strengthens the idea of the rule of law. Machiavelli has no illusions that princes will understand this logic and will obey laws themselves and use their armies to enforce obedience by others: 'a wicked prince nobody can speak to, and the only remedy is steel.'[44] But his theory is no less compelling even if in his time it was not widely adopted. For it may be becoming most relevant to an area which Machiavelli could not have contemplated: world politics in the last half of the twentieth century. Today we are witnessing a profusion of laws on the international scene – multilateral conventions on numerous topics, vastly proliferating bilateral treaties, codification conventions under the auspices of the United Nations, and close attention to the development of customary law by the smaller states in the world. At the same time, as has been argued, the utility of force has decreased sharply. We are thus in great need of a theory of law that will explain the sense of obligation that accompanies international law. The positivist theory is no longer adequate, if it ever was. Machiavelli's writings may very well provide a starting point for the theoretical explanation of the phenomenon that is called 'international law.'

42 *Discourses*, I, 18, Gilbert, I, 241
43 Id., I, 11, Gilbert, I, 225
44 Id., I, 58, Gilbert, I, 317

Contributors

ANTHONY D'AMATO
assistant professor, Northwestern Law School

THOMAS FLANAGAN
assistant professor of political science, University of Calgary

DANTE GERMINO
professor of government and foreign affairs, University of Virginia

ALKIS KONTOS
assistant professor of political economy, University of Toronto

HARVEY MANSFIELD, JR
professor of government, Harvard University

ANTHONY PAREL
associate professor of political science, University of Calgary

JOHN PLAMENATZ
Chichele professor of social and political theory
in the University of Oxford, and Fellow
of All Souls College, Oxford

NEAL WOOD
professor of political science, York University

Acknowledgments

The editor acknowledges with thanks financial assistance from: the University of Calgary for a faculty research grant; Dr Brian G. Wilson, then Dean of the Faculty of Arts and Science, the University of Calgary, and currently vice-president (academic) of Simon Fraser University, through whose generosity a special research grant was made available; the Canada Council for a grant supporting the International Machiavelli Symposium held at the University of Calgary in October 1969 and from which this volume arose; and the Social Science Research Council of Canada for the help of a publication grant, using funds provided by the Canada Council.

Thanks also are due to R.I.K. Davidson and Jean Wilson of the University of Toronto Press Editorial Department for their assistance in preparing the manuscript for publication.